Religious Thought and Economic Society

Religious Thought and Economic Society

Four chapters of an unfinished work
by Jacob Viner

edited by Jacques Melitz
and Donald Winch

Duke University Press   Durham, North Carolina   1978

Copyright © 1978 by Duke University Press
L.C.C. no. 77-93857
I.S.B.N. 0-8223-0398-1

Printed in the United States of America

Contents

Introduction by the editors   1

Chapter One. The economic doctrines of the early Christian fathers   9

Chapter Two. The economic doctrines of the Scholastics   46

Chapter Three. Secularizing tendencies in Catholic social thought from the Renaissance to the Jansenist-Jesuit controversy   114

Chapter Four. Protestantism and the rise of capitalism   151

Appendix. Protestant casuistics   191

Index to the documentation   193
  Compiled by John A. Vickers

General index   206
  Compiled by John A. Vickers

Introduction by the editors

It is with pride and pleasure that we present four previously unpublished chapters by the late Jacob Viner. The first two deal with the economic doctrines of the Christian Fathers and the Scholastics, while the last two are each concerned with a particular aspect of the relationship between religious thought, economic ethics, and society. In view of the scholarly reputation of the author, the long delay since the manuscript was written (between 1957 and 1962), and the fact that its existence has been known to many for some time, a brief history of the manuscript seems in order.

The history began with an invitation in 1956 to contribute to an ambitious project, Religion in American Life, which was to be edited by James Ward Smith and A. Leland Jamison and published by the Princeton University Press.[1] Viner's original assignment was to write an essay of some 16,000 words on "Religion and Society" dealing with the European historical background from the point of view of an economist and intellectual historian. But Viner's view of the required textual and bibliographic coverage made it difficult for him to confine himself to these narrow limits. Thus it was eventually decided in 1959, long after the original deadline of January 1958 had passed, to convert the essay into a separate volume entitled *Religious Thought and Economic Society: The European Background*.[2] In the course of the next two years, and especially after his official retirement from Princeton University in 1960, Viner made a serious effort to complete the book, even promising delivery of a typescript of around 350 pages by August 1961. During this period he provided the Press with the following summary of the proposed contents of the book:

1. The information on which this account rests is derived from the files of the Princeton University Press and the Viner Papers, now deposited in the Seeley G. Mudd Manuscript Library of Princeton University. A good deal of the relevant information on this subject was first put together by Fritz Machlup in his article "What Was Left on Viner's Desk," *Journal of Political Economy*, LXXX, No. 2 (March/April 1972), 353–356.

2. The other volumes were two collections of essays entitled *The Shaping of American Religion* (Vol. I), and *Religious Perspectives in American Culture* (Vol. II); and *A Critical Bibliography of American Religion*, edited by Nelson R. Burr, to be the fourth in the series. These three volumes were published by the Princeton University Press in 1961.

This volume constitutes an intellectual history of the economic aspects of Christian theology from the Fathers to modern times, with particular reference to the treatment by theologians of such topics as private property, riches and poverty, commerce, and the general criteria from the point of view of Christian theology for the ethical appraisal of individual economic activity. The volume is organized as a roughly chronological series of essays, dealing in turn with: the economic doctrines of the early Christian Fathers; the economic doctrines of the Scholastics with reference to private property, usury, just price; the economic issues involved in the Jansenist-Jesuit controversies within the Catholic Church, the roles of early Protestant theology in the rise of capitalism, with special reference to the Weber-Tawney thesis of significant responsibility of Calvinist doctrine for the growth and the character of modern capitalism; the impact of the "Enlightenment" on Anglican and on Continental religio-economic doctrine; the response of nineteenth-century theology, Protestant and Catholic, to the new social problems arising out of the Industrial Revolution, and to the emergence of popular social movements hostile to the existing social structure of Europe and in large part hostile to organized religion as apologist for and supporter of the status quo. For each period, where relevant, special attention is given to the relationships of harmony or of conflict between clerical and secular socio-economic doctrine.

For the academic year 1961–62, Viner was Frank W. Taussig Research Professor at Harvard University. There he found a wealth of new primary and secondary material relevant to his theme, which he then set about using to revise completed chapters and improve others. This, together with other publishing obligations which he had accepted earlier, began to slow down his progress with the book. In September 1964 he reported to the Press as follows:

Now as to the present status of my book. I have three chapters of the six planned completely rewritten and typed them ready for the Press, but I have not reread them against my manuscript, and as my stenographer could not handle the many bibliographical references in foreign languages, I will have to do this chore before I am finally through with these chapters. They carry the Catholic side of the story up to the seventeenth century. As they are a unit in themselves and could be published as they stand, I think it would be a good idea if I turned them over for safekeeping to the Press, and perhaps also my manuscript copy so that typists' errors could be corrected from it when the occasion arose, or if something should happen to me. The fourth chapter is on Protestant Social Ethics, Reformation to the end of the seventeenth century—largely on the Weber-Tawney thesis. I have a draft of this, in varying degrees of completeness, on hand, but [it] is a hundred pages too long, and will have to be compressed and polished. I have the research completed, except for some of the recently-published material, for the two final chapters, and I have rough drafts or detailed outlines for parts of them. As I write, things always turn up that need looking into, but aside from this, and from catching up with the relevant literature of very recent publication, my research has been completed for the whole book. The last two chapters deal with (1) the "Enlightenment" in both Catholic and Protestant countries, and (2) the Industrial Revolution and Social Christian Movements. I will have a very short Epilogue giving a sort of sketch of present day developments and prospects as I see them, but basically my book will make no serious effort to carry things beyond 1914.

. . . While I plan therefore to do everything I can to bring this task to a conclusion by the end of 1965, I am sure it will involve every ounce of effort and energy I possess if I am to succeed. I am making no concessions on quality or on coverage. Beyond this, I can definitely promise only concentration on the task, and avoidance of any diversion until I have completed it.

As promised in this letter, the three early chapters were handed over to the Press for safekeeping in 1964. Since the bibliographic references in the chapters do not go beyond 1960–61, it seems clear that Viner effectively stopped work on these chapters at about that time, that is, before the letter was written.[3] He also failed to return to the tasks which he said would have to be completed before the chapters could be published. During the remaining six years of his life Viner continued to work on the fourth chapter dealing with the Weber-Tawney thesis and Protestant ethics, and to collect material for the later chapters concerned with the Enlightenment and the Industrial Revolution. But no part of the project was ever again to receive priority over his other intellectual assignments.

This failure to make further progress with the book might be attributed to a general loss of physical energy, about which Viner frequently complained in his letters during this period. Nevertheless, in

3. For example, there is an incomplete reference to a "forthcoming volume of essays in honor of Amintore Fanfani" (p. 85, n.100, below) which was not revised, even though the volume appeared in 1962.

the period between the writing of the letter to the Press and his death at the age of seventy-eight, he continued to work and publish at a pace that many younger men would have cause to envy. Thus his *Guide to John Rae's Life of Adam Smith* appeared in 1965, and he completed the Jayne Memorial Lectures, on "The Role of Providence in the Social Order" for delivery under the auspices of the American Philosophical Society at the University of Pennsylvania in 1966. He drew upon his extensive knowledge of eighteenth-century British social and economic thought in writing two related essays, "Man's Economic Status" and "Satire and Economics in the Augustan Age," which were published in 1968 and 1970 respectively.[4] He also wrote the entries on "Adam Smith" and "Mercantilist Thought" for the *International Encyclopedia of the Social Sciences* which appeared in 1968; and in his last years he was still hoping to be able to finish an essay on the history of the concept of alienation which had been commissioned by the University of Glasgow for inclusion in a volume of essays celebrating the bicentenary of the *Wealth of Nations*.

Early in 1969 Viner was diagnosed as having an abdominal aortic aneurism, which faced him with the choice of undergoing risky surgery or, in his own words, of "living the rest of my life out on a powder keg." He chose the latter course, yet attempted to live as normal a life as possible. This meant a considerable amount of reading (up to five hours a day even near the end of his life), visits to the library, note taking, and voluminous correspondence with fellow scholars around the world on the host of subjects in which he retained an active interest.

This regime, together with the evidence of other work completed during this period, inevitably raises questions about Viner's attitude towards the book on *Religious Thought and Economic Society*, and more especially towards those parts of it that are published here. Why did he not make a more determined effort after 1964 to finish a study to which he had already devoted a vast amount of time and physical as well as intellectual energy? Why did he not return to polish chapters which he considered not only to be practically finished, but as constituting a "publishable unit in themselves"? With regard to the first of these questions, Viner himself may have provided an answer when he confessed that he had seriously misjudged the size of the task he had undertaken. The only gloss on this answer we would add

---

4. The first of these appeared in *Man versus Society in 18th Century Britain*, edited by James L. Clifford, Cambridge Univ. Press, 1968. The second appeared in *The Augustan Milieu*, edited by Henry Knight Miller, Eric Rothstein, and G. S. Rousseau, Clarendon Press, 1970.

is that Viner's standards and scholarly scruples were pitched higher than most people's. He had set himself a standard of bibliographic thoroughness in the early chapters which could only be matched in the remaining chapters by investing more time and energy than he either had available or felt willing to devote to a single project in his last years. A similar answer might perhaps be given to the second question, that of his failure to polish the early chapters, at least so far as the updating of the references in these chapters is concerned. But the chief answer must be that once Viner had realized that he would not be able to do the work necessary to complete the entire project, he resigned himself to posthumous publication of the earlier chapters.

Another story attaches to the seven years that have elapsed between Viner's death in September 1970 and the publication of these chapters. Several distinguished friends and colleagues advised his widow, Frances Viner, on what should be done with the large body of letters and unpublished manuscript material left by her husband. While most of them favored publishing the more important manuscripts, including the material printed here, it was decided to send the three most polished of the chapters to two well-known medievalists for their comments. The reports by these experts contained a mixed judgment. They were impressed by the historiographic documentation and conceptual coherence of the argument, but also felt that all the chapters needed editorial attention, and that Chapters I and II in particular were flawed in some important respects—a subject to which we will return shortly. As a result of these reports, the impression prevailed among Viner's friends and close colleagues at Princeton that the work fell below Viner's superlative standards. Under the weight of this impression the impetus towards publication collapsed. It was decided to proceed with the publication of the Jayne Lectures, *The Role of Providence in the Social Order*, despite the lack of bibliographic references,[5] but the present richly annotated and more ambitious chapters were kept in storage, along with other unpublished manuscripts and letters. This remained the situation until the present editors had the case reexamined in a more favorable light and were fortunate in obtaining the permission of Viner's heirs and executors (Ellen Seiler and Arthur Viner), the encouragement of several of his friends (notably R. D. C. Black and Lionel Robbins), and the generous support of two of his friends and ex-colleagues (William Baumol and Ansley Coale).

5. See *The Role of Providence in the Social Order: An Essay in Intellectual History*, American Philosophical Society, 1972; Princeton Paperback edition, 1976.

6

Our main concern in rescuing these chapters has been to make them available to other scholars. Among other things, as former pupils of Viner, we wanted to provide a better basis for assessing the breadth and depth of Viner's interest in the relationship of religious and economic thought. There is ample testimony to this interest in the correspondence in which he engaged with many leading scholars and in the mass of bibliographic material which he assembled over the years—all of which is now housed in the Princeton University Library. But he had published very little on these matters, especially for the period covered here.[6] With the possible exception of Joseph Schumpeter, it would be hard to find an economist of equivalent standing who has taken such a broad interest in Patristic and Scholastic economic thought. Even Viner's isolation of the issues is of interest. He is certainly an expert on the way in which the canvas of economic thought over a long period should be stretched. In the light of the way in which economics has evolved in recent decades, historians of early Christianity and the Middle Ages should perhaps also be advised that they may never again see so professional an economist undertake a similar endeavor in their field.

Having said this, a number of points must be borne in mind which relate to the aforementioned flaws noted by the referees. Viner was not a Patristic or medieval scholar; he would have been the first to admit the limits of his knowledge, even though his modesty was of the well-armed variety and he clearly took pleasure from the ability to discomfort the experts which his acquaintance with the specialist literature gave him. But he entered the field as an avidly interested visitor to foreign realms rather than as someone who intended to set up permanent residence. It is only to be expected, therefore, that on many matters he contents himself with a more summary treatment than a specialist historian would provide. Some of the difficulty experienced by these specialists may stem precisely from such considerations, which probably account for a certain imbalance between the conciseness of Viner's text and the extensiveness of his bibliographic annotations. The work might have conformed to their tastes more fully if Viner had either contented himself with a simple textbook treatment of the issues or if he had confined himself, as Schumpeter did in his *History of Economic Analysis*, to a few selected aspects of Scholastic doctrine. But in such a well-documented and ambitious

6. The main published evidence of Viner's interest can be found in his review of Schumpeter's *History of Economic Analysis, American Economic Review*, XLIV (Dec. 1954), 894–910, as reprinted in Viner, *The Long View and the Short*, pp. 343–365.

enterprise, they evidently expected a fuller elaboration of the differences between individual authors and a discussion of more of the nuances in the development of certain doctrines.

It is our impression, in fact, that Viner is especially terse in the treatment which he accords to economic subjects which feature heavily in the standard secondary sources. This applies particularly to the "just price" doctrine, where he basically accepts the prevalent interpretation associated with Raymond de Roover's work. On the other hand, on the usury doctrine, where he has more to say, he develops his position more fully, though still with great brevity. Close reading will show that, on this doctrine, he steers a careful course between the narrower "natural law" conception of de Roover and Schumpeter and the broader historical view of John T. Noonan.[7] There are a number of fresh analytical observations on this question in the footnotes as well as in the text. Moreover, Viner's position is particularly discerning on various questions which have received less attention, at least from economists, such as Patristic and Scholastic views on social inequality and alms.

The most obvious criticism that can be made of Chapter II is Viner's over-reliance on the views of Thomas Aquinas. Viner was explicitly aware of the fact that Aquinas' influence was not a dominant one before the sixteenth century.[8] He also realized, no doubt, that however much Aquinas may have written on economic subjects, it was not an area which particularly excited his interest and hence where his genius was most likely to shine. Viner's decision to rely so much on Aquinas, therefore, must be put down to an unwillingness to trust to his command of the Scholastic literature rather than to a retreat behind the façade of a "representative" thinker's view.

A word or two may also be necessary to explain our reasons for including the fourth chapter on the Weber-Tawney thesis, which was left in a far less tidy state, and has needed to be pulled together on the basis of a typescript that was covered with handwritten amendments and insertions. Apart from the obvious fact that it forms an integral part of the original argument of the unfinished book, this chapter reveals a good deal about the nature of Viner's general position on the relationship between religious and economic thought, and on the im-

7. The relevant writings of Raymond de Roover are numerous, but can now be conveniently studied in the edition of his writings prepared by Julius Kirshner entitled *Business, Banking and Economic Thought*, Univ. of Chicago Press, 1974. Schumpeter's views can be found in his *History of Economic Analysis*, Oxford Univ. Press, 1954, pp. 72–107, while Noonan's position is expounded in his book, *The Scholastic Analysis of Usury*, Univ. of Chicago Press, 1957.

8. See p. 48 below. Earlier drafts make this clearer than the final text.

portant historiographic issues underlying the handling of evidence in intellectual history. For example, Viner's careful use of historical evidence to construct a case against Weber and his followers in this chapter provides an insight into the more combative side of Viner's scholarly nature, possibly reflecting the fact that in moving into the early modern period of history he is once more on home territory. Even so, there is another, less obvious, link between the fourth chapter and its predecessors, which relates to the anticlerical tenor of much of the Weber-Tawney literature. In the first three chapters Viner appears to have been partly inspired by a desire to correct the false impressions of some earlier and less friendly commentators on Catholic economic thought. Thus, the fourth chapter helps to clarify some of Viner's concerns in the first three. He approached these topics as a tolerant sceptic and humanist, interested in pointing out the biases on both sides of a highly sectarian literature. It should be added that Viner had considerable respect for the techniques and scholarly objectivity of theological argument when practiced at the highest level.

In editing these chapters for publication, we have, of course, attempted to bring them somewhere near the standard Viner himself would have required. Apart from such essential tasks as checking the typescript of Chapter IV against Viner's handwritten draft, we have filled in missing cross-references and dates, checked quotations and references (with the invaluable help of the Duke University Press), and corrected small but obvious errors. Finally, we have taken the liberty of making a substantial number of small stylistic changes in order to eliminate slight ambiguities and redundancies. All of these changes, however, involve a mere reordering of phrases and the substitution of more concise expressions.

Chapter One

The economic doctrines of the Christian Fathers[1]

The Otherworldliness of the Fathers

". . . because we do not place our hope in the present, we do not mind when men murder us, since death is inevitable anyhow";[2] "I have no concern in this life except to depart from it as speedily as possible";[3] "It is the part of a great and lofty mind to despise and trample upon mortal affairs";[4] "For as far as this life of mortals is concerned, which is spent and ended in a few days, what does it matter under whose government a dying man lives, if they who govern do not force him to impiety and iniquity."[5]

Such statements as these by the Fathers, if taken at full face value, would seem to leave no scope for a social doctrine which attaches

---

1. I have used as general sources for this chapter chiefly the following: Lujo Brentano, "Die wirtschaftlichen Lehren des christlichen Altertums," in *Der wirtschaftende Mensch in der Geschichte*, Leipzig, 1923, pp. 77–143; C. J. Cadoux, *The Early Church and the World*, Edinburgh, 1925; R. W. Carlyle and A. J. Carlyle, *A History of Mediaeval Political Theory in the West*, Vol. I (by A. J. Carlyle), *The Second Century to the Ninth*, 3rd ed., Edinburgh, 1930; F. X. Funk, "Neben Reichtum und Handel im christlichen Altertum," *Historisch-politische Blätter*, CXXX (1902), 888 ff.; Charles Guignebert, *Tertullien. Etude sur ses sentiments à l'égard de l'empire et de la société civile*, Paris, 1901; Julius Kautz, *Die geschichtliche Entwickelung der National-Oekonomik und ihrer Literatur*, Vienna, 1860, pp. 201–212; Robert von Pöhlmann, *Geschichte der sozialen Frage und des Sozialismus in der antiken Welt*, 2nd ed., Munich, 1912, II, Ch. 7; Otto Schilling, *Reichtum und Eigentum in der altkirchlichen Literatur*, Freiburg i.B., 1908; Otto Schilling, *Die Staats- und Soziallehre des hl. Augustinus*, Freiburg i.B., 1910; Ignaz Seipel, *Die wirtschaftsethischen Lehren der Kirchenvater*, Vienna, 1907; Theo Sommerlad, *Das Wirtschaftsprogramm der Kirche des Mittelalters*, Leipzig, 1903 (despite its title this study is confined to the Fathers; for its biases and over-free interpretation, see the comments in Seipel, *passim*). All of these authors work from the original texts and quote them or give references to them generously.

2. Justin Martyr, *Writings, The First Apology*, Thomas B. Falls, tr., New York, 1948, Ch. 11, p. 43.

3. Tertullian, *Apologeticus*, XLI, J. E. B. Mayor, ed., Alex Souter, tr., Cambridge, Eng., 1917, p. 121.

4. Lactantius, *The Divine Institutes*, VI, 12, in *The Ante-Nicene Fathers*, American reprint, New York, 1899, VII, 178.

5. St. Augustine, *The City of God*, V.17, Marcus Dods, tr. (1st ed., 1872), New York, 1948, I, 208.

substantial value to the temporal happiness and well-being of mankind and to make it somewhat of a puzzle why the Fathers troubled themselves as much as they did about earthly matters. The answer of some scholars is that such statements as the ones quoted above are to be interpreted as merely rhetorical, as conforming to a literary genre for sermons and homilies, or, at most, as intended to provide a special kind of theological support for appeals for generous almsgiving and for honest social behavior which really derived from moral and humanitarian concerns. Representative of this kind of interpretation is the following statement by Troeltsch:

> From the outset we can ignore all statements which ascribe private property to sin, and which describe Paradise as the home of communism; the very people who say these things urge the Church to acquiesce for the present in the social order which has been produced by sin. The only purpose served by such statements was to establish the duty of charity on a firmer basis, since charity, to some extent at least, restores the Primitive State. . . . Also the frequent exhortations to regard property as nothing, and all the talk about community of possessions which are gifts of God, like light and air, were equally only a challenge to energetic charitable activity.[6]

This statement clearly implies that the Fathers were not sincere when they minimized the importance of private property and that their sole purpose was to add to the effectiveness of their advocacy of charity to the poor. Later, Troeltsch argues against the over-stress by Kautsky on the economic motivation of the doctrines of the Fathers and insists on "the independent position of religious thought"[7]—independent presumably of economic and humanitarian considerations. These are irreconcilable interpretations, and the truth is probably somewhere in between.

That the Christian Fathers regarded this world and its goods with contempt, as a world corrupted in its nature by sin, has often been claimed, but has also often been denied, on the basis of citations from their writings which would seem to accept various kinds of temporal

---

6. Ernst Troeltsch, *The Social Teaching of the Christian Churches*, Olive Wyon, tr., London, 1931, I, 115–116. See for a somewhat similar statement Bernard Vaughan, S.J., *Socialism from the Christian Standpoint*, New York, 1912, pp. 246–247.

7. Troeltsch, I, 166.

goods as important and praiseworthy. Etienne Gilson, for instance, judges modern interpretations of the Fathers as contemptuous of temporal prosperity to be in error and largely the product of the influence of Luther, Calvin, and the Jansenists. Of St. Augustine he says that "when he characterizes as 'consolations of the miserable damned' the magnificences of this world, it is not because he gives these magnificences little weight, for they are dearer to him even than they can be to us, but because he believes that the world has known and awaits even greater ones."[8] Gilson cites in support of this interpretation several paragraphs from St. Augustine's *City of God*, of which the following passage seems most relevant to the issue:

> What wonderful—one might say stupefying—advances has human industry made in the arts of weaving and building, of agriculture and navigation! With what endless variety are designs in pottery, painting, and sculpture produced, and with what skill executed! What wonderful spectacles are exhibited in the theatres, which those who have not seen them cannot credit! How skillful the contrivances for catching, killing, or taming wild beasts! And for the injury of man, also, how many kinds of poisons, weapons, engines of destruction, have been invented. . . .[9]

St. Augustine was no admirer of spectacles or of actors, nor, presumably, of poisons, weapons, and engines of destruction. From the context in which this passage is set, Augustine's apparent praise of worldly goods seems nearer to the second than to the first of the two senses in which, according to St. Thomas Aquinas, a thing may be said to be "good": "first in the sense that it is truly good and simply perfect; secondly, by a kind of likeness, being perfect in wickedness; thus we speak of a good or a perfect thief, as the Philosopher Aristo-

---

8. *L'Esprit de la philosophie médiévale*, 2nd ed., Paris, 1944, p. 128. I have not been able to find any major criticisms of the Fathers for undue otherworldliness by early Reformers or by Jansenists. The criticism along this line which caused the most stir was made by Jean Barbeyrac, a Swiss Protestant of "enlightenment" tendencies, in the early eighteenth century. In his preface to his French translation of Samuel Pufendorf, *De Jure Naturae* in 1706, Barbeyrac charged the Fathers with a fanatic degree of disregard for the temporal values of life on this earth. Remy Ceillier, S.J., replied in *Apologie de la morale des Pères de l'église*, Paris, 1718. He claimed that Barbeyrac had exaggerated the otherworldliness of the Fathers and that in any case there was ample support in biblical texts for whatever low opinions they did express of worldly activities. In an elaborate rejoinder, *Traité de la morale des Pères*, Amsterdam, 1728, Barbeyrac reaffirmed his original position, but presented little supporting evidence as far as "economic" matters were concerned.

9. *City of God*, XXII.24, Marcus Dods, tr., II, 525.

tle observes. (Aristotle *Metaphysics*, V, text 21)."[10] Most of the passages commonly cited to show the favorable attitude of the Fathers towards worldly goods are open to a similar interpretation.

The moral character of the human person and of his actions *per se*, that is, without express reference to their objective consequences, and with "moral" understood as relating primarily to one's obligations to God, was a constant concern of the Fathers. Except incidentally, casually, and naively, the Fathers did not explore the social consequences of such action. Except as an aid to persuasion of the heathen or those of feeble faith or to defend Christianity against pagan criticism, they did not appeal to the favorable temporal consequences of specific pious or moral behavior. The Fathers were primarily theologians, preachers, moral teachers. If they were social reformers as well, they were so only or predominantly in the sense that they at times perceived and pointed out in passing that temporally beneficial social change could be an incidental or "accidental" by-product of preaching whose primary objective was religious and moral. There was, as far as I know, no early Christian "wisdom" literature linking individual piety with worldly prudence. Except as a tactical move in polemics against pagan persecutors, the Fathers rarely put any stress on the social usefulness of the Christian religion and the observance of Christian precepts.

Even if it could be shown—as perhaps it can—that at times some of the Fathers engaged in more worldly-minded discourse, it seems, therefore, nevertheless to be true that the otherworldliness manifested in the passages from the Fathers quoted above was a fundamental and dominating element in their thinking. It would be fatal to overlook this or seriously to minimize it if one wishes to understand their social doctrines. The early Christians were a minority sect, subject to persecution, recruited mainly from the more humble levels of the population, without political power or influence, and without any important role as a body or as individuals in the civil life of their communities, and therefore without immediate and obvious social responsibilities with respect to the affairs of the world at large. From the New Testament they had derived a markedly apocalyptic view of the future of this world and the belief, only slowly to weaken and disappear, that the end of the world was imminent. Nothing on this earth, therefore, was held by them to be truly important except the

---

10. *Summa Theologica*, II-II, q. 45, a. 1, English Dominican Province, tr., New York, 1947. As St. Thomas' own system of numeration of parts is clear and is followed in all editions, no page references will be given for citations of the *Summa Theologica*.

opportunity it provided or the obstacles it presented to the faithful, as individuals, to earn their own way, or to show others the path, towards personal salvation. This seems to me to be applicable to almost all of the Fathers, although as time went on, as the world persisted, and as the status of Christians in the world improved, they grew increasingly cautious and reserved with regard to the nature and time span of their apocalyptic expectations, and undue emphasis on such expectations became a mark of heresy.

Scholars differ with respect to this, but it is my impression that as the body of Christians grew in numbers, wealth, and potential political power, as persecution ceased or became intermittent and regionally limited, and finally as the State itself became Christian and the Christian Church became the privileged and to some extent the persecuting church, there was no essential change in the basic social doctrines of the Fathers. What change did occur was limited to modifications of emphasis and to the development of a position on issues which had not previously clearly presented themselves. Other apparently plausible interpretations rest substantially on selective discrimination between texts which are to be accepted literally and texts which are to be interpreted as metaphorical, or insincere, or the products of self-deception and momentary overenthusiasm.

If this interpretation is correct, the Fathers considered the only vital concern of man to be life after death. The personal path to salvation involved a disciplined and austere pattern of behavior on this earth. The Christian, however, lived in a setting of civil government and specific social institutions. Like other men he needed in some manner to acquire the necessities of earthly life. The Fathers accepted the social and political institutions of their time as facts, substantially as unchangeable facts. They commanded the faithful to obey the civil authorities except where such obedience would involve a clear breach of divine law. Where such conflict of obligations did arise, the Fathers taught passive resistance, if necessary to the point of deliberate martyrdom. On the other hand, the Fathers never expressly recommended and often strongly warned against active participation by Christians in official life, military activities, or judicial functions, largely because such occupations often involved participation in pagan rites and ceremonials. Some of them kept themselves free and advised Christians to keep themselves free from the imperial or local patriotisms of their pagan neighbors. Doctrine in these respects moderated in tone and probably in substance after the Empire had officially become Christian. But more obvious and important than this moderation in tone was the inevitable change in the day-to-day practices of lay Christians once they included in their ranks emperors, judges, tax collectors, and generals and when pagan rites were no longer associated with the performance of civil functions.

The early Christian ideal was in the political field anarchic in character and in the economic field communistic.* Within the church, especially for monks and hermits, there was some effort to approach this ideal in actual life, and this was carried further by some of the Christian heretical sects. But for the Fathers as a whole and for the bulk of non-heretical Christians, the ideal was subjected to major qualifications both in doctrine and practice in order to adjust to the practical necessities not only of social life but also of specifically religious life in a world which had undergone the Fall of man. In the political field, the qualifications were virtually without significant limits except one in particular. The sinfulness of man made coercive government necessary if chaos was to be avoided. Even when the powers of government were in heathen hands, therefore, the Christian rank-and-file were instructed by the Fathers to regard these holders of power as ordained by God; they were to be faithfully obeyed, provided they did not issue commands which called for the violation of the strictly religious obligations of Christians.

The Fathers were keenly aware that the ideal they were preaching was too exacting for the ordinary individual, and even for the exceptional one. To Hedibia, a woman asking for advice as to the path to perfection, St. Jerome conceded, with particular reference to the advice of Jesus to the rich young man to "sell all you have," that the doctrine of perfection made demands which were "difficult, hard and against nature."[11] While not in the least accepting their function as one of providing guidance to individual Christians or communities as to how temporal prosperity could be attained, they did take into account the material limitations of human capacity and make an effort to formulate Christian social doctrine in a manner that would not lead its adherents to despair of their salvation.

To achieve this end, the Fathers introduced a considerable flexibility of doctrine in the light of varying temporal circumstances and individual appetites. Thus they sanctioned what is sometimes labelled a "dual standard" of morals; but it should be remembered that by secular criteria both standards were austere and demanding, the more

---

* Editors' note: The adjective "communistic" here should be interpreted in the light of pp. 16–18 below.

11. Letter 120, J.-P. Migne ed., *Patrologiae Latinae*, Paris, XXI, col. 985: "difficile, durum est, contra naturam." This important letter, which is often wrongly cited as if directed to all Christians, does not seem to be available in an English translation. Subsequent references to it will be to a French translation, *Lettres de S. Jérôme*, Dom Guillaume Roussel, tr., Paris, 1713, where the letter is numbered 96.

exacting one being more meritorious.[12] St. Jerome expounds this doctrine in advising Hedibia that the standard of "perfection" was not a "law":

> The Lord did not make this perfection a law; he left to you the freedom to take of it (as your rule) such part as you pleased. Do you not wish to be perfect, and do you content yourself with remaining on the second level of virtue? Then abandon everything which you possess; give it to your children and your relatives [i.e., instead of to the poor]. It will not be charged against you as a crime that you confine yourself to what is less perfect, provided that you acknowledge that it is with justice that you are asked to give preference to that line of conduct which leads to perfection.[13]

St. Augustine expounds the same doctrine when he speaks of "higher perfection" as contrasted with mere obedience to commandments and when he distinguishes "counsel of perfection" from behavior acceptable from "a weaker soul, less capable of the glorious perfection."[14]

In the form of the distinction between "counsel" and "precept" this Augustinian view became a fundamental element in Catholic moral theology.[15] It made possible, and sensible, the simultaneous advocacy of the most austere behavior, while, on the other hand, tolerating a large measure of adaptation to the pressures of external conditions and the weaknesses of ordinary human beings.

The Fathers on Riches and Property

The main economic concern of the Fathers was the moral consequences and implications of the existence side by side of rich and needy poor. Their doctrines in this regard can be most conveniently examined by treating separately their views on private property and

---

12. Eberhard F. Bruck, *Kirchenväter und soziales Erbrecht*, Berlin, 1956, pp. 69–72, says that the distinction between the duties of the "perfect" and the "imperfect" was already in Stoic doctrine, and was blended with the distinction between "counsel" and "precept" by St. Ambrose. See also C. J. Cadoux, "Should We All Be Perfect?" *Hibbert Journal*, XXI (1922–23), 327–336; K. E. Kirk, *The Vision of God*, London, 1931, pp. 240–243, 254–255, 521–522.

13. *Lettres de S. Jérôme*, Paris, 1713, III, 113.

14. Letter 157 (to Hilarius), *Letters*, III, Sister Wilfrid Parsons, tr., New York, 1953, pp. 342, 347.

15. Cf. St. Thomas, *Summa Theologica*, I–II, q. 108, a. 4, and II–II, q. 185, a. 6. Cf. also Herbert Lucas, S.J., *Fra Girolamo Savonarola*, 2nd ed., London, 1906. p. 183: "No man is bound to be a saint, and heroic virtue lies outside the obligations of canonical obedience."

their views on alms, although in their own exposition these were generally not separated.

The Fathers denied that there was a natural right to private property. They maintained that in the beginnings of human society all things were held and used in common. They were influenced by the Greek and Roman myth of a primitive golden age, and at times assimilated it with the biblical myth of the Garden of Eden, perhaps in order to have a more convenient basis for social theorizing than the biblical model of a single pair living in the Garden of Eden.[16] For the gradual corruption of the original society postulated by the pagan myths, however, they substituted the Fall and original sin. Given the sinfulness of man, the Fathers conceded the necessity of some measure of private property. With the exception of Theoderetus, whom I discuss later, they never, I think, attached any religious value to private property as an institution or merit of any kind to it except in so far as there was no available substitute. They deplored the fact that under private property luxurious living and extreme poverty could exist side by side. They questioned or denied the possibility of acquiring great riches without resort to evil practices or without inheritance from persons who had resorted to them. They advised all Christians to avoid seeking riches, to avoid attaching value to them other than as reserve for almsgiving, and to beware of the propensity of the possession of riches to foster luxurious living, pride, and arrogance and distract attention from religious duties. As an ideal to keep in mind, if not to pursue actively, they pointed to the fully common use of possessions which they believed to have prevailed in the early days of mankind and among the first Christians. They did not advocate voluntary poverty, however, except as counsel for those who had a special vocation.

With the rise of socialist movements in the nineteenth century, it has become a routine phase in the discussion of the social doctrines of the Fathers to express opinions as to whether or to what extent they expounded "socialism" or "communism." Religious writers have tended either to exaggerate or to minimize the socialist character of the doctrines of the Fathers, according to their own social views. On the other hand, socialist unbelievers have found pleasure in emphasizing the socialist character of the doctrines of the Fathers and in taunting socially conservative Christians by pointing to their failure to

16. For the combination in the Patristic period of pagan "golden age" and biblical "garden of Eden" ideas, see George Boas, *Essays on Primitivism and Related Ideas in the Middle Ages*, Baltimore, 1948, pp. 15–53.

adhere to the early traditions of their faith.[17]

There was indisputably a "socialist" flavor to the treatment by the Fathers of the existence of rich proprietors and needy poor within the same community. There was, equally indisputably, an emphasis by the Fathers on the obligations of the rich to "share" with the poor and on "common use" of riches as an ideal. The Fathers, however, said nothing about production in common and often used "sharing" to mean little more than the generous giving of alms. They also refrained from advocating compulsory almsgiving either by Church rule or civil legislation. They showed no concern about economic inequality except when it involved private riches in excess of what was morally safe for the owners, or where it was a sign of lack of compassion on the part of the rich for those living in extreme poverty. Their main interest was in redistributing the general wealth and income of a community through almsgiving. Whether through lack of interest or of economic insight, they gave no attention to the possibility of finding a remedy for extreme poverty in measures or behavior which would augment community wealth and income. Above all, they refrained from recommending any action involving compulsion to relieve poverty or modify in any way the existing social structure. Any program of economic "reform" they may have entertained was restricted to advocacy of self-restraint in the pursuit of riches, just behavior in business, and generous but voluntary almsgiving to the needy poor. Their "socialism," as a program of social action, went no further than this.

Some modern writers, who wish to show that the Fathers preached a social doctrine acceptable to nineteenth-century "liberals," have cited passages in which the Fathers seem to be defending private property against a socialist type of criticism. However, with the exception of a work by Theodoretus, subsequently to be commented on, these passages are mostly contained in attacks on hereti-

17. The references in note 1 above, all discuss the alleged "socialism" of the Fathers, usually to minimize it. "Catholic Socialists" who have emphasized the socialism of the Fathers have often been men who have either broken with the Church or have been in difficulties with it; examples are: Etienne Cabet, *Le Vrai Christianisme suivant Jésus-Christ*, 2nd ed., Paris, 1847; [Charles F. Chevé], *Histoire de la communauté des biens dans l'antiquité et dans l'ère chrétienne*, Paris, 1847, especially I, 70–145; W. Hohoff, review of Otto Schilling, *Reichtum und Eigentum*, in *Archiv für die Geschichte des Sozialismus und der Arbeiterbewegungen*, I (1911), 201–202. As additional writers to those listed in note 1 above may be added, from the many available, J. J. Thonissen, *Le Socialisme depuis l'antiquité*, Louvain, 1852, I, 99–119; H. Holtzmann, *Die ersten Christen und die soziale Frage*, Frankfurt a.M., 1882; Andréas Bigelmair, "Zur Frage des Sozialismus und Kommunismus in Christentum der ersten drei Jahrhunderte," in *Festgabe Albert Ehrhard*, Bonn, 1922, pp. 73–93.

cal sects who held that according to the Gospel the rich could not be saved and that common ownership and use of property were mandatory. I will deal later with the Fathers' position with respect to the doctrines of these sects on private property.

One author who is frequently cited outside the context of the Christian heresies, however, as a critic of communism even as an ideal is Lactantius. In his case anti-communism does seem to be the tenor of the texts. In the course of his attempt to demonstrate the superiority of Christian over pagan moral doctrine, Lactantius cites as a horrible example of pagan doctrine Plato's advocacy of communism. His main attack is on community of wives, but he also argues that it would be unjust to take away one man's property to give it to another. What a man possesses through his own industry is not injurious to anyone else; in the absence of private property there is no incentive to frugality; Plato, moreover, did not see the impracticability of his proposal, since no nation had ever practiced communism (he may here have had in mind only community of wives and not community of property).[18] Elsewhere, Lactantius refers sympathetically to the account of the Saturnan age given by the poet Aratus, as reported by Cicero: "It was not even allowed to mark out or to divide the plain with a boundary: men sought all things in common." But he comments: "And this saying of the poet ought so to be taken, not as suggesting the idea that individuals at that time had no private property, but . . . as a poetical figure; that we may understand that men were so liberal, that they . . . admitted the poor to share the fruits of their labor."[19] Lactantius here rejects communism even for the Golden Age; I know of no parallel to this in the writings of other Fathers.

Theodoretus' Defense of Economic Inequality

Theodoretus, in a "Discourse on Providence" written about 435, presents an elaborate defense of the existing economic society, without any reference to its being a necessary consequence of the Fall of man. Despite his systematic citation of biblical texts, the tone and manner of his treatment of social issues in this work are distinctly naturalistic rather than early Christian. Indeed, it anticipates to a remarkable degree the apologetics for the social *status quo* prevalent, for instance, in eighteenth-century Anglican sermons. Socrates and other philosophers, he writes, knew about virtue. "Divine law [i.e.,

---

18. *The Divine Institutes*, III. 21–22, and *The Epitome of the Divine Institutes*, XXXVIII, in *The Ante-Nicene Fathers*, New York, 1899, VII, 92–93, 236–237.
19. *The Divine Institutes*, V.6, in *The Ante-Nicene Fathers*, VII, 140–141.

Revelation] did not bring new enlightenment, and only recalled the laws of nature.'' God had given different functions to different men, each according to his nature, and had so arranged things that each was serviceable to the community. If riches were equally distributed, no one would be willing to do humble tasks for others. Either each would do everything needed for himself, or mankind would lack necessaries. But without specialization of occupations, there would be lack of skill. Inequality, therefore, is a mode of social organization which yields to the poor as to the rich a more agreeable life, since it is the mode by which all satisfy their needs by mutually supplying each other with what is lacking to them.[20]

The service which the rich render to the poor is that of providing a market for their products.[21] Theodoretus admits that most of the rich live unjustly, but claims that the existence of some rich people who managed their riches with justice and honesty, who had not exploited the sufferings of the poor to increase their own wealth, and who had given the needy poor a share of their opulence, sufficed to limit condemnation to the unjust rich.[22] I interpret this to mean that existing inequities were due to personal rather than institutional shortcomings.

Theodoretus proceeds to apply similar reasoning to the relations of masters and slaves. The servant has advantages over the master. The latter has to occupy himself with the needs of his family, to pay taxes, to find a market for the surplus of his products and a source of supply for what he lacks. He is subject to crop failures; if, on the contrary, the harvest is abundant, he faces the problem of finding buyers. The slave, on the other hand, eats heartily, sleeps well, and has no responsibilities. Many masters work as hard as or even harder than their slaves, if worry is included as work. If there are faultless servants who have to endure unjust masters, then: ''We can see that God, master of the universe, in response to the excessive malice of men, often leaves loose the reins of his government, and permits mankind to toss itself about as it wishes.''[23]

---

20. Theodoret de Cyr, *Discours sur la providence*, Yvan Azéma, ed. and tr., Paris, 1954, pp. 212–219 of the Sixth Discourse.

21. Etienne Chastel, in his *Etudes historiques sur l'influence de la charité*, Paris, 1953, p. 216 n., quotes Theodoretus as saying at this point that the rich also provide the poor with the raw materials they work on and lend to the poor. But I cannot find corresponding passages in Azéma's translation.

22. *Discours sur la providence*, pp. 219–220.

23. *Ibid.*, the Seventh Discourse, especially pp. 237–244. Theodoretus here refers to Zech. XI.9–10. I presume that he is referring particularly to the text: ''For before those days [when the temple was built] there was no hire for men, nor any hire for beasts, neither was there any peace to him that went out or came in, because of the adversary; for I set all men every one against his neighbor.''

Theodoretus later argues at length that virtue brings its own rewards of a material kind on this earth, but concedes that a full appraisal of the wisdom of Providence requires that account should also be taken of the rewards and punishments of another life.[24]

This seems to me a substantially different approach to the question of rich versus poor than that of the other Fathers. As in the case of many seventeenth- and eighteenth-century writers who argued on closely similar lines, Theodoretus seems to be providing both a theological apologetic for the social *status quo* and an argument for the operation of a benevolent Providence, by appealing to the attractive features of an essentially harmonious, non-socialist economic society which is the creation of Providence. I know of no other instance until many centuries later of a similar use of an optimistic picture of the existing *social* (as distinguished from the physical) structure of the world.

The Fathers on Alms

The Fathers, apart from insisting that the rich should abstain from methods of acquiring wealth which involved the impoverishment of others, proposed no remedy for poverty except almsgiving to the needy poor. What they proposed has been characterized as "almsgiving on a grand scale, and as an obligatory act of justice, not of pity or self-complacent benevolence."[25] But moving appeals to pity were also made, and the "justice" invoked was moral, not legal; it implied a moral obligation to "charity." The Fathers did not assert that any of the poor as such had specific rights or claims against any particular rich as such. The obligation of the rich to give alms was a specifically religious one; it was "precept," because expressly enjoined by the Scriptures. Almsgiving was recommended to the rich, however, not only as a religious duty but, within limits, as sin-redeeming. It was a means of "building up treasure in Heaven," and, when carried far enough, a remedy against the moral dangers of the possessing of great riches and luxurious living. Those who had more than was immediately required for their own needs were obliged to give to the poor some of the excess. But the Fathers insisted that alms were meritorious only when freely given; and they expressly rejected any suggestion that the Church should establish a formula for the proper scale of almsgiving, such as the tithes of the Old Testament, even if

24. *Ibid.*, the Ninth Discourse, pp. 281–293.
25. Arthur O. Lovejoy, "The Communism of St. Ambrose," *Essays in the History of Ideas*, Baltimore, 1948, p. 304.

the formula was only to be used for guidance. The amount of almsgiving was expressly left to individual conscience.

It was not the function of almsgiving to eliminate poverty, only to relieve extreme distress. The existence of poor and rich was in accordance with the wishes of God, so that each could provide the other with the opportunity for the exercise of the virtues appropriate to them, charity for the rich, patience and humility for the poor.[26] The Fathers thought that more alms should be given than was actually the case, and some of them at least thought that if all gave what they should, there would be sufficient to relieve the needy poor. However, the amount of almsgiving that most of the fathers hoped for, or at least undertook to plead for strongly, was not enough to bring about anything resembling a levelling of possessions or consumption. One exception, though, was St. Basil. In one of his sermons, he says that he who obeys the command to love one's neighbor as one's self should treat him as he treats himself, and therefore should not reserve a larger portion of his estate for himself. To the question, how could one subsist if one gave away all possessions, St. Basil replied that it was not for him to justify the Lord's commands, but so wise a legislator could not have commanded impossible things.[27] Elsewhere, St. Basil cites with apparent approval the advice a bishop had given him with respect to charity: "the rule ought to be that everyone should limit his possession to one garment." But he is reporting this advice to another cleric, and therefore may not have had the ordinary laic in mind.[28]

All the Fathers condemned luxurious living. Their main concern seems to have been not only that excess resources should be available for almsgiving, but also that the life of the Christian should be different from the life of the pagan; and that the temptation to licentious living and pride, and the distraction from religious observances resulting from free spending, should be avoided. Some of the Fathers, however, also condemned frugality unless what was consequently unspent was given as alms. Lactantius held that parsimony, to be

26. See Alexandre Guillaume, *Jeûne et charité dans l'église latine*, Paris, 1954, especially p. 126.

27. *Sermons de S. Basil le Grand*, Paris, 1691, Sermon II (on Matthew XIX), pp. 19, 24. This is the most comprehensive collection of St. Basil's homilies that I have found in a modern language translation.

28. Letter 150 (to Amphilochius), in *A Select Library of Nicene and Post-Nicene Fathers*, 2nd series, New York, 1895, VIII, 208. See Stanislas Giet, *Les Idées et l'action sociales de Saint Basile*, Paris, 1941, for a comprehensive account and appraisal of St. Basil's social ideas, and Yves Courtonne, *Saint Basile, homélies sur la richesse*, Paris, 1935, for the historical setting of his charity sermons.

meritorious, must be accompanied by generous giving of alms.[29] St. Basil declared that after one had dissipated much of one's riches in foolish expenditures, one should not hide the remainder in the ground: "It was the extreme of folly to dig to the center of the earth for gold, and then to rebury in the ground what had been extracted from it."[30] St. Asterius, to whose sermons on charity St. Basil was much indebted, portrayed the avaricious man as one who spared himself no pains and no exercise of his ingenuity to amass wealth, but refrained from disposing of any of it. To heap up wealth without enjoyment was more evil than spending it.[31]

A number of the Fathers rejected as an adequate motive for accumulation the desire to provide for children or for old age, or the leaving of money to charity at the time of death. Charity, said St. Basil, should not be put off to old age:

One does not trade after the market is closed; he is not crowned who does not enter the lists until after the combat has ceased. Sudden death may interfere with one's plans. If one accumulates for the sake of children they may use their inheritance for debauchery and libertinage. One should prefer one's soul to one's children. One should first look after meriting Heaven, and after that one may work to leave enough for one's children to subsist. The children who do not succeed to the estate of their fathers can acquire wealth by their own industry but if you abandon the care of your soul, who will have pity on you?[32]

St. Cyprian even maintained that the greater number of children a man had, the greater should be the amount of alms he should give, since the greater would be the number of sins [of the children?] to be atoned for and the number of souls to be saved.[33] Salvian treated testamentary bequests to family or friends as a form of selfishness and urged that estates should be given to the Church at death, or

29. *Divine Institutes*, VI.17, in *The Ante-Nicene Fathers*, VII, 182.

30. *Sermons de S. Basil le Grand* (on Matthew XIX), p. 23. Cf. St. Ambrose, *De Nabuthae*, Martin R. P. McGuire, tr. and ed., Washington, D.C., 1927, p. 55. "You dig up gold from the veins (of) metal and again hide it away. How many lives you bury in that gold!"

31. *Les Sermons de Saint Astère*, appended with separate pagination to *Sermons de S. Basile le Grand*, Paris, 1691, Sermon II (on Luke 16.2), p. 38.

32. *Sermons de S. Basile le Grand* (On Matthew XIX), pp. 34–35; see also *ibid.*, Sermon XVIII (on good works), p. 257.

33. *The Genuine Works of Saint Cyprian*, Nath. Marshall, ed. and tr., London, 1717, § 15, p. 208. See also *ibid.*, pp. 199–213, and "Of Good Works and Alms" (*De Opere et Eleemosynis*), §§ 14–20.

preferably earlier.[34] No Father seems to have recognized the possibility that income or property in excess of current need might help the poor more if used productively to provide them with cheap necessaries or with remunerative employment than if distributed as alms. St. John Chrysostom is reported, however, to have declared that it was a genuinely spiritual and incomparable work to fulfill the duties of one's occupation diligently, and thus to be able to accumulate savings with which to help the needy.[35] This would constitute an approach, at least, to a formulation of the doctrine of the "calling," whose origin modern writers, as we shall see later, have often attributed to the Protestant Reformation, and especially to the Calvinists.

Protestant writers were later to charge that it was Catholic doctrine and practice for alms to be given to all who asked for them without discrimination between the deserving and the undeserving. As far as the later Church is concerned, this charge will be dealt with in the following chapter. As far as the Fathers are concerned, there is little to support the charge, and considerable evidence to rebut it.

The *Didache* ("The Teaching of the Twelve Apostles"), which is usually dated no later than the first century, urges giving without reserve or qualification, but it also says: "However, in this regard there is also a word of Scripture: Let your alms sweat in your hands until you find out to whom to give."[36] Guignebert comments that as far as he knows this passage is unique in the first centuries, and he cites St. Justin, Tertullian, and Clement of Alexandria as opposing discrimination between seekers for alms, lest a mistake be made and a deserving man be refused.[37] In the fourth century, St. John Chrysostom advised against attempts to distinguish carefully between the deserving and the undeserving, though he acknowledged that this advice would anger his hearers; he justified himself on the grounds that "if we investigate the lives of men too carefully, we shall never have pity on anyone."[38]

Guignebert, however, himself presents some evidence that the Fathers did not, as a rule, advocate wholly undiscriminating almsgiving. Additional evidence to the same effect is readily available. St.

---

34. *Ad Ecclesiam (The Four Books of Timothy to the Church)*, in *The Writings of Salvian the Presbyter*, J. F. O'Sullivan tr., New York, 1947, especially pp. 320 ff.

35. See Georg Kopp, *Die Stellung des hl. Johannes Chrysostomus zum weltlichen Leben*, Münster, 1905, p. 35.

36. *The Didache (Teaching of the Twelve Apostles)*, 1, James A. Kleist, S.J., ed. and tr., Westminster, Md., 1948, p. 16.

37. Charles Guignebert, *Tertullien*, pp. 342–343.

38. *Sermon on Alms*, Margaret Sherwood, tr., New York School of Philanthropy, *Studies in Social Work*, No. 10, Feb. 1917, pp. 20 ff. [at p. 24].

Augustine, commenting on Matthew V.39–42, "Give to everyone who asks," says that it should not be read as "Give him everything he asks." What was meant, he said, was that "you are to give in accordance with propriety and justice," and this may upon occasion mean that the seeker for alms should be given "correction" rather than alms.[39] St. Jerome advised a priest:

> Your possessions are no longer your own but a stewardship is entrusted to you. . . . be careful for your part not rashly to squander what is Christ's. Do not, that is, by an error of judgment give the property of the poor to those who are not poor, lest, as a wise man (Cicero) has told us, charity prove the death of charity.[40]

Franz Ehrle, S.J., in a monograph which aims to refute the charge that the Catholic Church regularly advocated indiscriminate almsgiving, concedes that the Church may have occasionally encouraged such practice or engaged in it itself, but denies that it ever did so as a general rule or principle. He presents a substantial amount of evidence showing that the Fathers advised giving preference to the pious over the sinners and to the unfortunate over the lazy and dishonest beggars.[41]

In the Middle Ages and later, Christian doctrine with respect to alms generally maintained that "needs" varied with social status, and that in ordinary circumstances the rich had no obligation to give alms to an extent which would encroach on what was required to meet the conventional standard of living of their class. I have not found any expression of this idea by a Father, though St. Jerome came close to it.[42]

The general impression to be gained from the writings of the Fathers is that they thought the needy and deserving poor were great in number. Stray passages of a contrary tendency can, however, be

---

39. *Commentary on the Lord's Sermon on the Mount*, D. J. Kavanaugh, O.S.A., tr., New York, 1951, p. 94.

40. Letter 58, to Paulinus, *Letters and Select Works*, in *A Select Library*, reprint, Grand Rapids, 1954, p. 122. Cf. also Letter to Hedibia, *Lettres de S. Jerôme*, III, 108, containing the advice that alms be given only to the "true" poor. In *Lettres*, p. 517, however, St. Jerome is cited from an unspecified source as saying: "When one restricts one's alms to persons known to be in distress, and does not give undiscriminatingly to all who ask, one often abandons him who best deserves to receive aid." There is no reason to suppose that St. Jerome, or any other Father, wanted alms bestowed on the undeserving, but they sometimes chose in favor of undiscriminating charity rather than accept the risk of refusing a deserving claimant.

41. *Beiträge zur Geschichte und Reform der Armenpflege, Stimmen aus Maria-Laach*, Erganzungshefte, No. 17, 1881, pp. 11–12, 15–16.

42. See Otto Schilling, *Reichtum und Eigentum*, p. 152.

found. Clement of Alexandria asserted that the deserving poor were rarely without bread and that this could occur only where there were no just men, presumably among those better off.[43] "No one is destitute when it comes to the necessities of life, nor does any man need to look far for these."[44] This would suggest that he had no misgivings as to the adequacy of the resources of the rich to take care of the urgent needs of the poor.

I have found nothing in the secondary accounts of the writings of the Fathers, or in such reading of them as I have done, to indicate that they demanded or even approved of almsgiving for the purpose of raising the living standards of the "poor" who were not in urgent need. Their writings indicate that relief should be limited to the bare minima of food, shelter, and clothing, plus medical and other care for the aged, the sick, and the infirm, and provision of marriage dowries for girls. In principle, they called for whatever amount of almsgiving would be necessary to relieve or prevent urgent need, but it is not clear that in practice they asked for or expected almsgiving to occur on a "heroic" level except in times of special emergency.

One would not expect to find the Fathers dealing with charity in statistical terms. One of the Fathers, St. John Chrysostom, did deal with it, however, in a surprisingly modern-sounding way. Speaking in Antioch, he estimated that there were 100,000 Christians there, among whom the rich were sufficiently numerous to be able to give adequate relief to the needy.[45] Speaking in Constantinople, he presented estimates of the amount of money which would be available for alms if all Christians of the city disposed of their substantial properties, and of the number of poor (not all of whom, however, were in need), and reached the conclusion that the needs of the poor could thus be met. In order to obtain economies in consumption, he proposed that the poor, while continuing their external occupations, should be gathered into special houses and fed at common tables. Were the experiment to succeed, he suggested, all gentiles would be attracted to Christianity. "If God grant life, I trust that we shall soon bring you over to this way of life."[46]

St. John Chrysostom urged rural proprietors to build churches on

43. *Christ the Educator (Paedagogus)*, Bk. III, Ch. 7, No. 40, Simon P. Wood, tr., New York, 1954, p. 232.

44. *Ibid.*, Bk. II, Ch. 1, No. 14, p. 106.

45. Homily 85, on Matthew 27.10, *The Homilies . . . on the Gospel of St. Matthew*, Part III, in *A Library of the Fathers of the Catholic Church*, London, 1893, p. 1124. For a general account of Chrysostom's social doctrines, see Aimé Puech, *St. Jean Chrysostome et les moeurs de son temps*, Paris, 1891, pp. 46–92.

46. Homily 11, *The Homilies on the Acts of the Apostles*, Part I, in *A Library of the Fathers*, Oxford, 1851, pp. 161–163.

their estates for the primary purpose of saving souls. He argued that it was not a valid objection that the proprietors could not afford it. The influence of the churches on their tenants, and of the presence of priests among the tenants, would make them better, more productive, more docile workers. Thus the landlords would receive temporal rewards for their good deeds, as well as spiritual ones.[47]

The Fathers and Slavery

Slavery was, in the time of the Fathers, as it was to continue to be until the nineteenth century, a respectable private-property institution. If a few brief expressions of disapproval be disregarded, the Fathers accepted it as such; and it would be difficult to show from their writings that they were more hostile to slavery than to private property in general. The early Church itself acquired slaves as soon as it acquired property. In order to protect its assets, it imposed restrictions on the right of subordinate Church officials to free Church-owned slaves. Furthermore, it never engaged in, nor advocated, a mass enfranchisement of slaves; and some of the Fathers themselves owned slaves. The Church, however, did treat the liberation of Christian slaves as a merit, especially when the owners were pagans, and the Church freed such slaves as it ordained as priests:

> Christian teachers [in the early days of the Church] following the example of St. Paul, implicitly accept slavery as not in itself incompatible with the Christian law. . . . This estimate of slavery continued to prevail until it became fixed in the systemized ethical teaching of the schools; and so it remained without any conspicuous modification until the end of the eighteenth century.[48]

> There is no evidence that either Christian or pagan enemy [of Christianity] in the first three centuries saw Christianity as a threat to the institution of slavery.[49]

> Slavery, then, in the judgment of the Fathers, is a legitimate and useful institution.[50]

The early Christian leaders, however much they deplored the essential doctrine of enslavement, accepted its practice *in toto* as

47. Homily 18, *ibid.*, pp. 260–265.
48. James J. Fox, "Slavery," *Catholic Encyclopaedia*, New York, 1912, XIV, 40.
49. E. C. Colwell, "Popular Reactions Against Christianity in the Roman Empire," in J. T. McNeill et al., eds., *Environmental Factors in Christian History*, Chicago, 1939, p. 66 n. 39.
50. A. J. Carlyle, in R. W. Carlyle and A. J. Carlyle, *A History of Mediaeval Political Theory in the West*, 3rd ed., Edinburgh, 1930, I, 123.

a part of the divine dispensation working in society as God had established it for His own ends . . . the early Church fathers . . . failed to reject the fundamental moral concepts of the system itself.[51]

Some pagan philosophers, both Greek and Roman, with the notable exceptions of Plato and Aristotle, condemned slavery in principle as inhumane, or as contrary to natural law, but carried on no crusade against it. The Fathers, while not condemning it as an institution, pressed for such practices by masters as would have made Christian slavery a much less inhumane institution, according to modern standards, than pagan slavery is said to have been or than modern negro slavery was.

Such defense of slavery as can be found in the writings of the Fathers rested primarily on the proposition that slavery was a punishment for sin and to some extent a remedy for it.[52] This was a novel argument for slavery, unavailable to the pagan Greeks and Romans. It did not mean, however, that the Fathers had adopted and provided a religious support of the Aristotelian view that slaves were by nature an inferior species of man, from whom the dignity of human personality could justly be withheld. On the contrary, the Fathers insisted that slavery was a merely material condition not affecting the spiritual quality of the slave. Many slaves, they said, were better men than their masters. Before God all men were equal. The only real slavery was the slavery to sin and subjection to the evil passions; the virtuous slave had more true freedom than the sinful master. Of itself, slavery in the objective sense was morally neutral; it was good or bad according to the disposition of the souls submitted to this trial. Aristotle and Plato excepted, this was a more favorable view of the ethical

51. William L. Westermann, "The Slave Systems of Greek and Roman Antiquity," *Memoirs of the American Philosophical Society*, XL (1955), 128. See also, to the same effect, pp. 130, 154 ff. For similar accounts of the position of the Fathers with respect to slavery, see Patrice Larroque, *De l'esclavage chez les nations chrétiennes*, 2nd ed., Paris, 1864; Franz Overbeck, *Studien zur Geschichte der alten Kirche*, Schloss-Chemnitz, 1875, I. Heft, pp. 158–230; Friedrich Schaub, "Studien zur Geschichte der Sklaverei im Frühmittelalter," *Abhandlungen zur mittleren und neueren Geschichte*, Heft 44, Berlin, 1913, pp. 29–71; Ettore Cicotti, *Il tramonto della schiavitù nel mondo antico*, new ed., Udine, 1940, Introduction, pp. 45–98 (a Marxian interpretation); Charles Verlinden, *L'Esclavage dans l'Europe médiévale*, Vol. I, Brugge, 1955, pp. 25–56.

52. For St. Augustine, see *City of God*, XIX.15, Marcus Dods, tr., II, 323–335; *Expositions on the Book of Psalms*, C.7, in *A Select Library*, New York, 1888, VIII, 489; Sister Margaret Mary, "Slavery in the Writings of St. Augustine," *Classical Journal*, XLIV (1954), 363–368.

quality of slavery as an institution than prevailed in the writings of the pagan philosophers.

According to St. Augustine the mission of the Church was not to free the slaves, but to make good servants out of bad servants. "How much do the rich owe to Christ, who orders their house for them."[53] According to Lactantius, slavery would persist even into the millennium, when some of the living would be allowed to survive to become slaves of the resurrected, "as victory for God, that they may be the occasion of triumph to the righteous, and may be subjected to perpetual slavery."[54] St. Basil, in apparently his only substantial treatment of slavery, begins with a denial that any man is a slave by nature, but continues with what seems to be an unqualified acceptance of slavery, as being in accord with worldly practice or in the interest of the slaves themselves in cases where they are by nature inferior to their masters:

> . . . among men no one is a slave by nature. For men are either brought under a yoke of slavery by conquest, as when prisoners are taken in war; or they are enslaved on account of poverty, as the Egyptians were oppressed by Pharaoh, or, by a wise and mysterious dispensation, the worst children are by their fathers' order condemned to serve the wiser and the better; and this any righteous enquirer into the circumstances would declare to be not a sentence of condemnation but a benefit. For it is more profitable that the man who, through lack of intelligence, has no natural principle of rule within himself, should become the chattel of another, to the end that, being guided by the reason of his master, he may be like a chariot with a charioteer, or a boat with a steersman seated at the tiller.[55]

When in the late eighteenth and nineteenth centuries slavery first became an affront to the conscience of any considerable section of mankind, the absence of an active crusade against the institution by the Fathers and the early and later Catholic Church became something of an embarrassment to pious Christians, and especially Catholics. They were unwilling to take refuge in the position that even in the case of the Church it was not fair to judge the doctrines of one age by the—possibly transitory—moral standards of a later age.

53. *Expositions on the Book of Psalms*, CXXV.7, in *A Select Library*, VIII, 602.
54. *Divine Institutes*, VII, 24, in *The Ante-Nicene Fathers*, New York, 1890, VII, 219.
55. *On the Spirit* (*De spiritu sancto*), XX.51, in *A Select Library*, 2nd series, New York, 1895, VIII, 32. I know of nothing like this in the writings of other Fathers.

There sprung up an extensive literature, sometimes critical of the Church's record, but more often trying to reconcile it with nineteenth-century anti-slavery doctrines.[56]

One line of defense was to claim that the Fathers did expressly condemn slavery in their writings. But apart from the evidence presented to demonstrate that the Fathers approved of the freeing of individual slaves by individual Christian masters as meritorious acts, and the citation of a few stray passages from the writings of the Fathers expressing some criticism of slavery,[57] this argument seems to me, as it has to others, to be without substantial historical support.[58]

Another and more common line of argument was that the Fathers, while hostile to slavery, deliberately and wisely decided that it was so deeply imbedded in the civilization of their time that to attack it openly would result in social disturbance and danger to the Church. They decided that the sudden abolition of slavery would result in economic chaos, and that the slaves themselves would not benefit from freedom until the spread of Christianity among both masters and slaves had prepared them morally for life in a free society. It was therefore the policy of the Fathers and the Church to moralize the institution as long as it persisted, and to prepare the way, by their religious and moral teaching, for its gradual and peaceful obsolescence.[59]

56. The works I have found most useful for the information they provide, or the point of view they reflect, follow: Paul Allard, *Les Esclaves chrétiens*, 5th ed., Paris, 1914; Edouard Biot, *De l'abolition de l'esclavage ancien en Occident*, Paris, 1840; E. J. Jonkers, "De l'influence du christianisme sur la législation relative à l'esclavage dans l'antiquité," *Mnemosyne: Bibliotheca Philologica Batava*, 3rd series, I (1934), 241–280; Alphons Steinmann, *Sklavenlos und alte Kirche, apologetische Tagesfragen*, Herausgegeben vom Volksverein für das katholische Deutschland, 4th ed., M. Gladbach, 1922; Franz Vollman, *Über das Verhältnis der späteren Stoa zur Sklaverei im römischen Reiche*, Stadamkof (Regensburg), 1890; Henri A. Wallon, *Histoire de l'esclavage dans l'antiquité*, 2nd ed., Paris, 1879, Vol. I; J. B. Mullinger, "Slavery," in Sir William Smith, ed., *Dictionary of Christian Antiquities*, London, 1880, II, 1902–1910; J. Dutilleul, "Esclavage," in A. Vacant, ed., *Dictionnaire de théologie catholique*, Paris, V (1913), Part I, cols. 457–520; and the works cited in notes 1 and 51 above.

57. A short list of references to such passages is given by Julius Kautz, *Die Entwickelung der National-Oekonomik und ihrer Literatur*, Vienna, 1860, p. 211. Those I have been able to check fail utterly to support his interpretation of these passages as clear indicators of the unworthy and unchristian character of slavery in the minds of the Fathers.

58. In a letter of 1878 to W. R. Brownlow, who had claimed that the Fathers had vigorously opposed slavery, Cardinal Newman stated that on the basis of the historical evidence he found it difficult to accept that either the Apostles or the Fathers regarded slavery as "a first-class evil." (W. R. Brownlow, *Lectures on Slavery and Serfdom in Europe*, London, 1892, Introduction, p. xvii.)

59. This is the position of most of the writers cited in note 56 above. It is also the

The Attitude of the Fathers
Towards Economic Prosperity

It was the inevitable and emphatic position of the Fathers that individual Christians must subordinate their temporal to their spiritual objectives, and especially must so discipline and govern their hopes and ambitions with respect to temporal goods that they did not interfere with preparation for the life after death. The Fathers, nevertheless, did not reject as impermissible for Christians a limited measure of enjoyment of the commodities and activities of this world for their own sake. God had created all the things of this earth, and He had done so in order that his creature, man, should enjoy them. "It is possible," said Clement of Alexandria, "to be a listener to Divine wisdom, and at the same time to live one's life as a citizen, and a man is not prevented from conducting worldly affairs decorously in conformity with God."[60] It was meritorious for the aspirant to perfection to retire to the desert or the convent, to practice renunciation and abstain from the pleasures of human friendship and of family and civil life, but it was not required of the ordinary Christian. The Fathers clearly did not regard it as their function to guide man to temporal prosperity. But the question still remains whether all or any of the Fathers believed that—or cared whether—Christianity was on the whole favorable to such prosperity.

Often cited in support of the position that the Fathers believed that Christianity was favorable to the prosperity of Rome, and were glad of it, is a famous passage of Tertullian, in which he denies that the Christians were unprofitable members of the Roman community or abstained from the social life of the world. His only concession was that Christians avoided excessive or evil use of the goods of this world, did not buy idolatrous commodities, and did not make contributions to the pagan temples.[61] Any testimony of this sort by Tertullian is especially significant, since he was one of the most rigorous of the Fathers and was eventually to break with the Church to become an adherent of the ascetic Montanist sect. But this passage of

position taken by Pope Leo XIII, in his letter, *In Plurimis*, to the Bishops of Brazil, May 5, 1888, of which an English translation is given in W. R. Brownlow, *Lectures on Slavery and Serfdom in Europe*, Introduction, pp. xxvii–xlvii, and in Joseph Husslein, S.J., *Social Wellsprings: Fourteen Epochal Documents by Pope Leo XIII*, Milwaukee, 1940, pp. 94–112.

60. *Paedagogus*, III, xi, 78, as cited by C. J. Cadoux, *The Early Church and the World*, p. 395. Other translations of this passage vary somewhat from Cadoux's version. See, for example, *Christ the Educator*, S. P. Wood, tr., New York, 1954, pp. 258–259.

61. *Apologeticus*, XLII, J. E. B. Mayor, ed., Cambridge, Eng., 1917, pp. 121–125.

Tertullian's was part of a defense of the Christians against pagan criticism during a period of persecution. For the purposes of this defense he described how Christians actually behaved, without necessarily approving of their behavior from a religious point of view. Among the specific claims he made on behalf of the Christians was that "we also sail with you and serve in the army." But in other works he urged Christians not to engage in overseas trade and not to enter the army. There is much in his other writings which suggests that he would have been happier if the pagan charges that the Christians did not participate in the social life of the Empire had been more fully justified by the facts.[62]

In reply to the charge against the Christians that the anger of the gods against them had brought unusual calamities to the world, including economic ones, Arnobius of Sicca (ca. 300 A.D.) argued in effect that the course of temporal affairs had a naturalistic explanation, or was to be explained by the broader cosmic purposes of God, and was neither related to the religious behavior of men nor to divine objectives with respect to the temporal prosperity of mankind. In the course of history since the advent of Christianity, periods of abundance had alternated with periods of scarcity, and Christians and pagans had been affected alike, as also had regions with or without Christian residents. Implicit in his whole argument is the doctrine that Christianity has no tendency either to promote or to impair temporal prosperity.[63]

In no case that I know of did any of the Fathers approve, propose, or condemn any law or activity of an economic character solely or predominantly on the basis of its consequences for temporal prosperity.[64] When the Fathers praised labor, they no doubt were aware of its contribution to economic productivity. But what they emphasized was its value in promoting moral discipline, its merit in

---

62. As evidence, see (though keeping in mind that the authors may be exaggerating Tertullian's anti-social position) Guignebert, *Tertullien*, pp. 145–147, 156–157, and Louis Rougier, *Celse ou le conflit de la civilisation antique et du christianisme primitif*, Paris, 1925, p. 196. Rougier reports Tertullian (although without a specific reference) as saying: "For us Christians, nothing is as foreign as the republic. . . . One must live, it is said, for one's country, for the empire, for one's own family? No one is born for others since one dies for one's self alone."

63. *The Case Against the Pagans (Adversus Gentes)*, George E. McCracken, tr. and ed., Westminster, Md., 1949, I, 64–73.

64. Perhaps an exception should be made, however, for the view of Tertullian, in reply to the pagan charge of the lawlessness of the Christians, to the effect that the pagans were themselves lacking in needed civic discipline, for they had abolished sumptuary laws, "the necessary and most appropriate elements of their rule of life." *Apologeticus*, VI, Alex Souter, tr., pp. 21–22.

agreeing with the express command of the Scriptures, and its importance as a protection against the moral hazards of idleness. When they condemned usury, wholesale trade, foreign trade, or luxury, they may have had some adverse economic consequences of these phenomena in mind, but the injustice or moral hazards associated with them was their predominant concern. I have found very few instances where a Father has given assurance to the worthy of temporal awards for meritorious behavior. As one instance, though, St. Basil, speaking to artisans who were listening to his sermon when they could be at work, told them not to worry. "The time which you lent to God is not lost: He will return it to you with large interest. Whatever difficulties may trouble you the Lord will disperse them. To those who have preferred spiritual welfare, He will give health of body, keenness of mind, success in business, and unbroken prosperity."[65]

If exception is made for Tertullian's condemnation of the repeal of sumptuary legislation (see n.64), I have found only two instances where Fathers appraised the mode of operation of Roman government on grounds that were at least partly economic in character.

Lactantius, criticizing Diocletian as a persecuting emperor, presents a sweeping arraignment of his tyranny, his maladministration of government, his extravagance, his burdensome taxation, and his insatiable avarice. As part of his indictment of Diocletian, Lactantius condemns his famous price-fixing ordinance:

> He also, when by various extortions he had made all things exceedingly dear, attempted by an ordinance to limit their prices. Then much blood was shed for the veriest of trifles [Lactantius is referring here to the imposition of capital punishment for violations of the ordinance]; men were afraid to expose aught to sale, and the scarcity became more excessive and grievous than ever, until, in the end, the ordinance, after having proved destructive to multitudes, was from mere necessity abrogated.[66]

Lactantius, however, does praise the public services of some of the emperors in this work, and in another work he agrees with Cicero that in order of merit the philosophers are to be ranked below "those men employed in civil affairs, who govern the state, who found new

---

65. *The Hexaemeron*, Homily III, in *A Select Library*, 2nd series, New York, 1895, VIII, 65.

66. *Of the Manner in Which the Persecutors Died (De mort. pers.)*, ca. 314 A.D., in *The Ante-Nicene Fathers*, New York, 1890, VII, 303. The price-fixing ordinance of 301 A.D. is here in question.

cities or maintain with equity those already founded, who preserve the safety and liberty of the citizens either by good laws or wholesome counsels, or by weighty judgments."[67]

Salvian, writing in the fifth century from the comparative safety of Gaul when Rome had fallen to the barbarians, criticizes the corruption and tyranny of the imperial officials with as much sharpness as Lactantius.[68]

The doctrines of the Fathers with respect to celibacy and population are somewhat ambiguous in their bearing on the Fathers' concern for temporal prosperity. If they had preached that celibacy was mandatory for all Christians, or even that celibacy was counsel which *all* Christians should follow, this would have implied that they were content either to have the world come to an early end or that it should be peopled wholly by pagans. St. Augustine is reported to have expressed such views.[69]

But in all the exhortations to chastity by the Fathers that I have seen it is made clear that chastity is a counsel of perfection, and only a precept for those who have vowed themselves to it. Even St. Jerome, often singled out later as the most fanatic exponent of chastity, treated marriage not as something evil, but as a second-best to virginity. "Wedded women may congratulate themselves that they come next to virgins. 'Be fruitful,' God says, 'and multiply, and replenish the earth.' He who desires to replenish the earth may increase and multiply if he will."[70] Posing the hypothetical question, if all were virgins, what would become of the human race, St. Jerome replied: "Have no fear that all will become virgins; virginity is a hard matter, the rarer because it is the more difficult." Thus he made it clear, I think, that he had no expectation or wish that all would follow the counsel of celibacy.[71]

To meet the objection that the call to chastity in the New Testament conflicted with the command in Genesis to be fruitful and multiply, a number of the Fathers, including St. Jerome, made use of an argument which clearly implies that considerations of temporal prosperity are entitled to some weight. They maintained that in the Old

---

67. *Divine Institutes*, III.16, in *The Ante-Nicene Fathers*, VII, 85.

68. *On the Government of God (De gubernatione Dei)*, Eva M. Sanford, tr., New York, 1930, pp. 138–146.

69. See D. S. Bailey, *The Man-Woman Relation in Christian Thought*, London, 1959, p. 43, where references are given to *De Nupt. et Concup.* I and *De Bono Conj.* X and XIII, *Analyse raisonnée de Bayle*, London, 1770, VIII, 158. (This is a re-arrangement of Bayle's *Dictionnaire* without references to texts.)

70. Letter XXIII, 19 (to Eustochium), *The Principal Works of St. Jerome*, in *A Select Library*, 2nd series, Vol. VI, reprint, Grand Rapids, 1954, p. 29.

71. *Against Jovinianus*, I.36, *ibid.*, p. 373.

Testament times the world was empty, but now it is full of people and there is no longer any need for concern lest population diminish. As St. Jerome put it:

> The old law had a different ideal of blessedness, . . . But in those days the world was still unpeopled. . . . But gradually the crop grew up and then the reaper was sent forth with his sickle [i.e. of virgin life].[72]

> The field is sown that it may be reaped. The world is already full, and the population is too large for the soil. Every day we are being cut down by war, snatched away by disease, swallowed up by shipwreck, although we go to law with one another about the fences of our property.[73]

A similar statement by Tertullian, although not made with reference to celibacy, is of interest for its markedly Malthusian flavor:

> . . . everywhere are houses, and inhabitants, and settled government, and civilised life. What most frequently meets our view (and occasions complaint), is our teeming population. Our numbers are burdensome to the world, which can hardly support us from its natural elements; our wants grow more and more keen, and our complaints more bitter in all mouths, whilst Nature fails in affording us her usual sustenance. In very deed, pestilence, and famine, and wars, and earthquakes have to be regarded as a remedy for nations, as the means of pruning the luxuriance of the human race.[74]

The Fathers on Commerce*

There were no comprehensive or sustained discussions by the Fathers of commerce, and what comments they made were invariably incidental to other matters, especially the exposition of the required,

---

72. Letter XXII.21 (to Eustochium), *ibid.*, p. 30.

73. *The Perpetual Virginity of Blessed Mary*, 23, *ibid.*, p. 345.

74. *De Anima: A Treatise on the Soul*, XXX, in *The Ante-Nicene Fathers*: American reprint, Vol. III, New York, 1899, p. 210. References to additional statements by the Fathers that the world was overcrowded are given in E. Chastel, *Etudes historiques sur l'influence de la Charité*, Paris, 1853, pp. 103–104, and United Nations, *The Determinants and Consequences of Population Trends*, New York, 1953, Ch. 3, reprinted in Joseph J. Spengler and O. D. Duncan, *Population Theory and Policy*, Glencoe, Ill., 1956, p. 7.

* Editors' note: This section may profitably be read in conjunction with Jacob Viner's second Jayne Lecture as published in *The Role of Providence in the Social Order: An Essay in Intellectual History*, American Philosophical Society, Vol. 90, Philadelphia, 1972.

desired, or permitted behavior for Christians. The Fathers were in-
heritors of a long-standing classical Greek and Roman tradition that
was hostile to commerce as being associated with fraud and avarice,
catering to luxury, and a potential source of moral corruption and
deterioration of manners by virtue of the contacts involved with bar-
barian merchants and customs. The Greek and Roman philosophers
and poets often showed no interest in the possible economic benefits
to be derived from trade, and sometimes questioned or belittled the
effects of trade on material well-being. The Fathers not only expressed similar views but reinforced them by expressly religious considerations.

There was extremely meager material in either the Old or New
Testament which, except by inference, provided any basis for an appraisal of the significance of trade either for salvation or for temporal
welfare. Trade was treated in biblical texts as being peculiarly associated with avarice, riches, and luxury. Here the pagan and biblical
traditions had much in common. The chasing of the money-
changers from the temple was sometimes interpreted as a condemnation of the activity itself, rather than the pursuit of it at an inappro-
priate place and time. Another biblical passage often invoked was
Psalm LXXI.15 (in the Latin numbering Psalm LXX.15X). Its meaning is apparently obscure in all extant versions: in the Septuagint
version which the Latin Fathers commonly used it reads: "quia non
cognovi negotiationem, introibo in potentias Domini." St. Augustine
somewhat reluctantly accepted this assertion as an outright condemnation of trading for Christians. He was aware, however, that in some
versions "learning" (or "letters") was substituted for "trading" (i.e.,
negotiatio), and he presented, without adverse comment, a putative
reply by a trader to the effect that if any fault attached to the trader, it
was not for trading in itself. Thus if the trader turned to a craft, such
as shoemaking, he would still have an opportunity for lying—for example, about the time when the shoes would be done—and for fraud
in the quality of the sewing.[75]

The Greek and Roman pagan writers saw no economic or moral
justification for the derivation of income by a merchant from purely
middleman activities, that is, from resale activities involving no
further processing of the goods. This belief that the middleman's gain

---

75. *Expositions on the Book of Psalms*, in *A Select Library*, Vol. VIII, New York,
1888, pp. 320–321. For later use of the Septuagint version as a basis for the association of trade with sin, see Otto Schilling, *Die Staats- und Soziallehre des hl.
Augustinus*, p. 252 (Cassiodorus in the sixth century), and G. G. Coulton, *Five Centuries of Religion*, Cambridge, Eng., 1936, III, 669–670 (Peter of Blois in the twelfth
century).

per se was economically and morally illegitimate was shared by at least some of the Fathers. St. Jerome gave it a precise formulation and a wide application: "It is not without reason that the Gospel calls the riches of this earth 'unjust riches,' for they have no other source than the injustice of men, and no one can possess them except by the loss and the ruin of others."[76]

As support for a sweeping moral condemnation of commercial gain or profit, St. Jerome's proposition continued to be expressed occasionally throughout the Middle Ages and later. With the rise of nation-states, exponents of mercantilism applied the proposition to the aggregate trade relations between countries and made it a key argument for national restrictions on foreign trade.

More prevalent in the writings of the Fathers than the outright condemnation of gainful trade as inherently sinful, however, was the recognition that trade was permissible and even useful if conducted honestly and for legitimate ends. This recognition, though, was accompanied by the warning that as ordinarily carried on, trade presented almost irresistible temptations to fraud, lying, avarice, luxury, and other sins. Here also, biblical texts, often of doubtful relevance, were freely cited. Certainly relevant enough, however, were some verses in Ecclesiasticus:

> A merchant shall hardly keep himself from doing wrong
> And a huckster shall not be freed from sin . . .
> As a nail sticketh fast between the joinings of the stones,
> So doth sin stick close between the buying and selling.[77]

The attitude of either the pagan philosophers or the Fathers cannot be properly described, however, as universally and unqualifiedly hostile to or suspicious of trade. The pagan writers were of two minds in their treatment of the "sea," which was for them a symbol of contact, including commercial contact, with other peoples. While some were averse to all contact with the sea,[78] others eulogized it as serving to unify peoples and as facilitating a commerce which enabled societies

---

76. *Lettres de S. Jérôme* (Letter to Hedibia), p. 110. In the original version, the last part of this passage was to become a stereotype: "nisi alter perdiderit, alter non potest invenire" (J.-P. Migne, ed., *Patrologiae Latinae*, XXII, col. 985). St. Augustine's version reads: "Si unus non perdit, alter non acquirit," *Ad fratres Eremo*, Sermon 32, *Patrologiae Latinae*, XL, col. 1345.

77. This is the King James Version, Chs. 26–27. Ecclesiasticus is not included in the Protestant Old Testament canon. It was frequently cited by the Fathers.

78. Cf. Marcus Wheeler, "Self-Sufficiency and the Greek City," *Journal of the History of Ideas*, XVI (1955), 416–420; M. L. Clarke, *The Roman Mind*, London, 1956, pp. 101, 161.

to meet each other's deficiencies in the necessities of life.[79] Especially important for present purposes is a statement by Libanius, a pagan teacher or rhetorician of Antioch in the fourth century, whose pupils included St. Basil and St. John Chrysostom and who was apparently the first writer to give a religious turn to praise of commerce and the sea by arguing that a providential design underlay the fact that different regions were differently provided with needed goods, thereby providing motives for commerce and mutual contact:

> God did not bestow all products upon all parts of the earth, but distributed His gifts over different regions, to the end that man might cultivate a social relationship because one would have need of the help of another. And so He called commerce into being, that all men might be able to have common enjoyment of the fruits of earth, no matter where produced.[80]

There is an echo of Libanius in a passage of St. Basil's Commentary on Genesis where, in discussing the text "and God saw that it was good" (Gen. I.10), he eulogizes the sea as good in the eyes of God because it facilitates the mutual exchange of necessities between peoples and thus operates as a factor unifying mankind.[81] Also plausibly deriving from Libanius is a similar eulogy of the sea by Theodoretus stressing the lower costs and lesser difficulties of transport by water as a reason for the special benefit of overseas commerce to mankind. The differences in natural endowment between different regions is also explained as a part of a providential design to ensure that peoples would not lack incentives to maintain friendly contacts with each other.[82]

According to Otto Schilling, this doctrine had wide currency among the Fathers, but apart from a citation of St. Basil's text and an undocumented reference to St. Augustine, he presents no supporting evidence. While inclined to emphasize—in my judgment to overemphasize—the possibilities of fitting the economic doctrines of the Fathers into a pattern with substantial resemblance to moderate nineteenth-century economic liberalism, Schilling acknowledges the ambivalent

79. See J. Denis, *Histoire des théories et des idées morales dans l'antiquité*, Paris, 1856, II, 437–438.

80. The passage originally appeared in Libanius, *Orationes* III, but this speech has apparently never been translated into a modern language. Modern citations of the passage invariably derive from Grotius. The text as given above is taken from Grotius, *War and Peace*, II.II.13.5, F. W. Kelsey, tr., Oxford, 1925, p. 200.

81. *The Hexaemeron*, Homily 4, in *A Select Library*, 2nd series, Vol. VIII, New York, 1895, § 7, p. 75. Georg Kopp, *op. cit.*, p. 40, gives a translation of a similar text of St. John Chrysostom.

82. *Discours sur la Providence*, Azéma tr., pp. 129–130 of the Second Discourse.

character of the attitudes of the Fathers towards commerce:

> If one takes a general view of the patristic doctrine on trade, its twofold character must strike one, on the one hand, the impartial, wide-ranging manner in which the Church Fathers esteem the social contribution of trade in binding peoples together and by its manifold equalization of needs through reciprocal giving and receiving brings them into organic union, and, on the other hand, the mistrust with which they look upon the actual trade of their time and the motivation of those who were engaged in it.[83]

In a form that remained surprisingly close to Libanius' formulation, the doctrine continued to have some currency in the Middle Ages.[84] After its exposition by Jean Bodin in several of his works published toward the end of the sixteenth century, and similarly by Grotius early in the seventeenth century, it became somewhat of a stereotype, constantly repeated in the discussions of commerce by theological and lay writers alike.[85] The doctrine was freely invoked in favor of free trade in England in the nineteenth century, and occasionally reappears in the twentieth century.

The Fathers and the Property Doctrines of the Heretics

The Church of Rome had begun to encounter heretical sects by the end of the second century, and the Fathers carried on a vigorous polemic against them. The major issues between orthodoxy and heresy were of a purely theological or ecclesiastical character and are therefore not relevant here. There was, however, a social aspect to

83. *Die christlichen Soziallehren*, Cologne, 1926, pp. 82–83.

84. I cite from the dozen or so medieval statements of the doctrine. A. Lecoy de la Marche. *La Chaire française au moyen âge*, Paris, 1886, p. 410 (Humbert de Romans in the thirteenth century); Carl Ilgner, *Die volkswirtschaftlichen Anschauungen Antonius von Florenz*, Paderborn, 1904, p. 48; John Laures, S.J., *The Political Economy of Juan de Mariana*, New York, 1928, p. 96. For additional references, see Alexander Rüstow, *Das Versagen des Wirtschaftsliberalismus*, 2nd ed., n.p., 1950, pp. 121–122.

85. Ernst Oberfohren, in *Die Idee der Universalökonomie in der französischen wirtschaftswissenschaftlichen Literatur bis auf Turgot*, Jena, 1915, and in journal articles, traces the history of the doctrine in France from Bodin to the Physiocrats. After Bodin and Grotius had presented the doctrine, it was a commonplace of both secular and theological literature. Except by Grotius, however, no reference was made to the early history of the doctrine, and Oberfohren himself, for some obscure reason, has insisted on Bodin's origination of the doctrine. The doctrine was usually invoked to support the freeing of foreign trade, at least partially, from official restraints, but it was often so manipulated as to become an argument for some particular types of trade restriction. As recently as 1932 the doctrine was presented without change in substance from Libanius' version at a French Catholic conference on social questions. See *Semaines sociales de France*, 24th session, Lyon, 1932, p. 68 n.

the doctrines of many of the heretics, the Ebionites, the Manichaean Gnostics, the Carpocratians of Alexandria, the Montanists, the Apostolics, the Pelagians, the Donatists, and others. The sects were in part to be explained as protest movements against what they regarded as a departure of the Church of Rome and its members from the full rigor of social doctrine and practice preached in the Gospel and practiced by the first Christians. The sects gave a decidedly communist slant to their interpretation of the Gospel; and in many cases there was a chiliastic underpinning to their social doctrines.[86]

The heretical sects seem to have found their recruits largely among the lower social levels of the population. It is a familiar interpretation of the origins of religious sects with radical economic tendencies to say that they are a rebellion of the "disinherited" against the existing class structure of society, and that the religious framework in which their social views are presented is a superstructure or rationalization for what is fundamentally a social protest generated by economic pressures rather than religious beliefs. It would be a mistake, no doubt, to deny any element of truth to this theory, but the generality of its application seems highly doubtful. In the case of the Donatists in particular, it seems to have been genuine religious convictions rather than economic pressures which first led to the foundation of the movement; it was not because they were "disinherited" that they became schismatics, but because they were persecuted as schismatics and social radicals that they became "disinherited."

In modern times, the radical social doctrines of the early Christian heretics have attracted the attention of scholars, especially socialist historians, who have often had little or no interest in the theological doctrines of the sects *per se* and have tended to give an economic interpretation of their social doctrines.[87] Similarly, the Fathers' criticisms of the social doctrines of the heretics have often been abstracted from their religious framework and treated as defenses of the social *status quo* against radical critics. Conservatively inclined scholars

---

86. On the historical and logical associations between chiliasm and social radicalism, see the recent study by Norman Cohn, *The Pursuit of the Millennium*, Fair Lawn, N.J., 1957. Martin Werner interprets early orthodox Christianity as marked by a "catastrophic" degeneration of social doctrine from a "world-despising" one to accommodation to the social status quo, as the result of the gradual weakening of its "eschatological sense of imminence" (*The Formation of Christian Dogma*, J. F. Brandon, tr., London, 1957, pp. 300–302).

87. See M. Beer, *The General History of Socialism and Social Struggles*, new ed., New York, 1957, Vol. I, and Georg Adler, *Geschichte des Sozialismus und Kommunismus von Plato bis zur Gegenwart*, Leipzig, 1920, pp. 69–76, and the bibliography (by P. Lippert) on p. 271.

have praised the Fathers for these criticisms, while writers with socialist views have attacked them on this score. The writings of the Fathers have thus been interpreted both as socialist in tone and as defenses of the existing social order.

An early example of praise of the Fathers by a conservative for social criticism of the economic views of the heretics (with particular reference to the Apostolici) is provided by Joseph Bingham, an eighteenth-century Anglican ecclesiastical historian:

> . . . [a sect] . . . called themselves Apostolici . . . and Apotactici, from a shew of renouncing the world more than other men. St. Austin says, they arrogantly assumed these names, because they would not receive into their communion any who were married, or kept the possession of any thing in property to themselves; and that they allowed no hope of salvation to such as used either of those things which they renounced. . . .
>
> So that this was a general sort of invasion, of the rights and properties of mankind, robbing them of everything in an unusual and extraordinary way, not by any open violence, or secret stealth, but by turning religion into an art, and inducing men to rob themselves of every thing under pretence of piety and greater heights of devotion. The factors and agents in this cause seem not to have had any design to enrich themselves, but to make all men poor, and bring them to a level, and lay all things common: which was such a scandalous representation of the Christian religion in the eyes of the heathen, that the Fathers thought they could not be too severe upon it, however it was coloured over with the varnish and disguise of holiness, pretending a great contempt of the world, and a divine and heavenly temper.[88]

A contrasting example, characteristic of the interpretation of the social doctrines of the later Fathers by many writers of leftist tendencies, is the statement by Roy Pascal: "From the third century . . . the Church abandoned these [earlier] communistic ideals, and entered fully into the system of property, becoming both a great land-owner and the moral sanction of the existing system of ownership and of government."[89] Whatever element of truth there may be in this, however, the available texts make it possible to account logically for the position of the Fathers with respect to the social doctrines of the heretical sects on the basis of purely theological considerations.

---

88. *Origines Ecclesiasticae: or, The Antiquities of the Christian Church*, London, 1722, Bk. IX, p. 288; Bk. VII, p. 499.

89. "Communism in the Middle Ages and Reformation," in Lewis, Polanyi, and Kitchin, eds., *Christianity and the Social Revolution*, New York, 1936, p. 123.

On questions of social attitude, the Fathers were more accommodating to the world than the heretical sects, but on such theological issues as the doctrine of grace, which were without obvious social implications, they were more rigorous. The sects treated as mandatory, as "precept," in the economic field what the Fathers and the official Church treated as ideal, as "counsel of perfection." On the evidence known to me, however, this difference of doctrine would not have led the Fathers to condemn the sects if the latter had not attempted to make acceptance of their doctrine a condition of Church membership or a ground for schism from the Catholic Church. The Fathers particularly objected to the heretics' twin postulates of the impossibility for a rich man to attain salvation and the ineligibility for church membership of those who refused to renounce private possessions. Among the Fathers, the chief critics of the social doctrines of the heretics were Clement of Alexandria and Augustine. Their relevant writings provide no basis for maintaining that they carried their criticism of the social doctrines of the heretics (if the issue of marriage versus celibacy is not regarded as a "social" issue) further than was necessary to reject these two key postulates.[90]

Clement of Alexandria, who has been given the title "The Consoler of the Rich," denied the claim of the heretics (the Carpocratians in particular) that no rich man had any chance of salvation, and he found no moral advantage in poverty unless voluntarily incurred. He interpreted Jesus' advice to the rich young man as metaphorical, not as precept. Otherwise, he was in many respects one of the most austere Patristic moralists and can be cited as representative of their rigorism and "socialism" more readily than as an accommodator to the world.[91]

St. Augustine wrote extensively against the Manichaeans, the Donatists, and the Pelagians, even though criticism of their social

90. With one exception, the social doctrines of the heretics have been accessible to me only through the accounts of the Fathers. The exception is an anonymous Latin treatise, *Tractatus de Divitiis*, written early in the third century. It is extremely radical in tone, especially in its insistence that no rich have just claims to their wealth, and that the rich are the cause of the poverty of the poor. This writing has claims, I should think, to be the earliest known socialist tract. For present purposes its most significant aspect is its treatment as precept of passages in the New Testament which the Fathers as a rule treated as counsel of perfection. The tract was first published in a printed version in Rome in 1571. It has never been translated. The only modern text is in C. P. Caspari, *Briefe, Abhandlungen und Predigten*, Christiania (Oslo), 1890, pp. 25–67. Accounts of its contents are in Caspari, *ibid.*, pp. 256–268; and Pöhlmann, *Geschichte der sozialen Frage*, II, 642–643.

91. See "The Rich Man's Salvation" (*Quis Dives Salvatur*), in G. W. Butterworth, ed. and tr., *Clement of Alexandria*, London, 1919, pp. 265–367; and *Christ the Educator (Paedagogus)*, Simon P. Wood, tr., New York, 1954.

doctrines was a minor element in his writings.[92] In dealing with the Pelagians, the chief concern of St. Augustine is to refute the doctrine that "a rich man who continues to live rich cannot enter the kingdom of heaven unless he sells all he has, and that it cannot do him any good to keep the commandments while keeping his riches."[93] St. Augustine argues that the New Testament passages cited in support of renunciation of all possessions are either "counsel of perfection" or refer to special situations where a believer is "faced with the alternative of not having [possessions] unless he gave up Christ." Alternatively, they are to be interpreted metaphorically. He says that there are members of the Church "who even think that the Christian religion ought to help them to increase their riches and multiply earthly delights." These he rejects as not true Christians, but he excludes from this class "the rich Christians who, although they possess riches, are not possessed by them, because they have renounced the world in truth and from their heart, and who put no hope in such possessions." He advises that the critics "in their sermons, encourage man to higher things without condemning lower [permitted?] ones." He claims to have personally attempted to follow the higher counsel (presumably by renouncing riches) and urges others to follow it. "Yet, we follow it while holding to sound doctrine; we are not so presumptuous as to judge those who do not follow us [in this higher line of conduct?] . . . lest by such statements we be found accusers of the Holy Scriptures instead of expounders of them."[94] All that St. Augustine is rejecting here is the treatment of a counsel of perfection as a precept. Elsewhere in his discussion of the Apostolici, St. Augustine makes it even clearer that it is not communism which is heretical but insistence on it as a condition of Church membership and as a requirement for salvation:

> The Apostolici have given themselves that name, with great arrogance, because they refuse to admit into their membership people who make use of marriage and those who possess private

92. The most useful secondary works dealing with St. Augustine's attitude toward the social doctrines of the heretics are Otto Schilling, *Die Staats- und Soziallehre des hl. Augustinus*, 1910, and Bernard Roland-Gosselin, *La Morale de Saint Augustin*, Paris, 1925, pp. 168–218. St. Augustine deals with the property doctrines of the Apostolici in his *De Haeresibus*, and those of the Manichaeans in *Contra Faustum Manichaeum*. He deals with the economic doctrines of the Pelagians in Letter 157 (to Hilarius), *Letters*, III, Sister Wilfrid Parsons, tr., New York, 1953, pp. 319–354; and of the Donatists in Letter 93 (to Vincent), *Letters*, II, New York, 1953, pp. 56–106; and Letter 185 (to Boniface), *Letters*, IV, New York, 1955, pp. 141–189.

93. This is the Pelagian doctrine as presented for comment to St. Augustine by his correspondent, Hilarius, Letter 156, *Letters*, III, 318.

94. Letter 157, *Letters*, III, 348–352.

property. The Catholic Church has very many monks and clerics who live this type of life. But the Apostolici are heretics because, separating themselves from the Church, they think that they who make use of the things from which they themselves abstain have no hope for salvation.[95]

The doctrine held by St. Augustine seems to have been precisely the official doctrine of the Church at that time. The Council of Gangra, held at an unknown date in the fourth century, condemned various propositions attributed to the Apostolics (or Eustatheans) which are without social implication, including their major proposition that the rich who did not abandon all their possessions could have no hope of salvation. The Council maintained that those who have aspirations to perfection can seek their realization by voluntarily adopting the monastic or clerical life, but that renunciation of the goods of this earth was not required of the simple faithful Christians; they need only give alms. The Church did not despise riches if managed by their owners with justice and benevolence.[96] Later councils repeated the same doctrine, and it was incorporated in the Theodosian Code.[97]

The polemics of St. Augustine against the Donatists were in a different setting. The Donatists, having seceded from the Church of Rome, were suffering severe persecution by the State, acting on behalf of the Church. St. Augustine originally opposed persecution, but was converted to it by its success, in one instance at least, in bringing the dissidents back to the Church. One of the measures of persecution was large-scale seizure of the property of the schismatic churches. In reply to complaints against this action by spokesmen for the Donatists, St. Augustine not only asserted that if the persecution was successful in bringing them back to the Catholic Church it would prove a benefit instead of an injury to them, but gave two answers in defense of the property seizures, each of which was in later times to prove somewhat embarrassing for the Church. St. Augustine maintained that there were only two valid titles to property: first, by virtue of divine law, and second, by virtue of human law. On neither count, he said, did the Donatists have a valid claim. They had no title on the

---

95. *The De Haeresibus*, Ch. 40, L. G. Muller, ed. and tr., Washington, D.C., 1956, pp. 79–81. St. Thomas Aquinas, *Summa Theologica*, II–II, q. 66, a. 2, echoes this passage in his comment on the Apostolics.

96. K. J. von Hefele, *Histoire des conciles d'après les documents originaux* (tr. from the German), Paris, 1907, I, Part II, 1043.

97. *The Theodosian Code*, V.5, Laws 7, 8, Clyde Pharr, tr. and ed., Princeton, 1952, p. 452.

basis of divine law, because as schismatics from the true Church they came under the words of Proverbs XIII.22, "The wealth of the sinner is laid up for the righteous," and of Wisdom X.20, "Therefore the righteous spoiled the ungodly." They had no title under human law, because under such law everything depended on the power and decrees of the kings of the earth, and their property had been expropriated under the authority of valid imperial legislation.[98] The doctrine that the dominion over all things belongs to the righteous was later to be expounded in denying the property rights of heretics and infidels; but it was a weapon later to be used against the Catholic Church itself. St. Augustine's doctrine of an absolute power over property by government was in sharp conflict with the doctrine of the natural rights of individuals to property which the Church later adopted as its official position in the nineteenth century.

It has been claimed that Imperial Rome and the Church were moved to persecute the Donatists because they were social revolutionaries, and not because of their specifically religious doctrines. In his book on the Donatists, W. H. C. Frend puts exclusive stress on social doctrine and describes the struggle between the Church and the Donatists as one between a church deeply entangled in the social evils and inequalities of Imperial Rome, enjoying and profiting from them itself, and a people imbued with a sense of social justice, for whom "evangelical poverty was enjoined on clergy and people alike." The issues between the Church and the Donatists "were not those of 'truth' versus 'heresy,' but involved two opposed attitudes to society, attitudes which have persisted throughout the history of the Christian Church down to the present day."[99] St. Augustine is described as sharing fully in the socially conservative, landowner approach to the controversy. He himself was a "pluralist," in the sense of a holder of more than one remunerative office in the Church.[100] "The ideal of Augustine and his friends was not the safeguarding of the city-state or even the active farming of a villa, but *otium liberale* (*Confessions*, VI.14)—the mere enjoyment of the fruits of a great rural domain. This entailed the maintenance for their own benefit of a system which Optatus of Thamugadi and other Donatist clergy were attempting to overthrow."[101] This account of the relationship of St. Augustine to

---

98. Letter 93, *Letters*, II, 59–60; Letter 185, *Letters*, IV, especially 175–176; *Letters on Tractates on the Gospel According to St. John*, VI.25, in *The Works of Aurelius Augustine*, Vol. X, Edinburgh, 1873, pp. 90–91.
99. *The Donatist Church*, Oxford, 1952, pp. 331–332.
100. *Ibid.*, pp. 328–329.
101. *Ibid.*, p. 235.

the Donatist controversy raises issues which mere intellectual history has no means of resolving.[102] But in the same way that the Pelagian controversy, which revolved around points of strictly theological and ecclesiastical doctrine, provides a logically sufficient explanation of St. Augustine's declared position, so in the Donatist controversy the issue of schism in the Church provides a logically sufficient basis for St. Augustine's stand without the need to invoke social bias or defense of private vested interests.

102. Hans-Joachim Diesner, *Studien zur Gesellschaftslehre und sozialen Haltung Augustins*, Halle, 1954, argues very much as does Frend that St. Augustine was unduly influenced by his association with the Roman upper classes. Gerhart B. Ladner, in *The Idea of Reform: Its Impact on Christian Thought and Action in the Age of the Fathers*, Cambridge, Mass., 1959, pp. 463–467, rejects Frend's argument.

Chapter Two

The economic doctrines of the Scholastics

Introduction

In this chapter I will deal with the economic doctrines of the Scholastics, interpreting the term Scholastic broadly to cover all Catholic moral theologians and canonists who wrote in the central tradition of the Church from the late Middle Ages to the end of the sixteenth century.

The Catholic Church from its beginning had claimed to be a divinely appointed and inspired guardian, teacher, and enforcer of the moral law for members of the Church. As Europe was converted to Christianity and later as the fall of the Roman Empire led to a strengthening of the position of the Church relative to the civil authorities, the Church developed elastic claims to exercise a measure of temporal authority in all matters having a moral aspect. At the height of its power and prestige, it had at its command a wide range of means for obtaining compliance with its moral teaching. These means fell roughly into five categories: (1) the influence of its preaching and counselling on princes and the general public; (2) the wide participation of clerics, as rulers, magistrates, and officials, in civil government; (3) the exercise of political sovereignty in papal states, in ecclesiastical principalities, and on estates in which church organizations were the feudal landlords; (4) the exercise of judicial authority by ecclesiastical courts over a wide range of transactions of economic significance: transactions among clerics and between clerics and laics, tithes, marriage rites and contracts and property disputes between husband and wife, certification of legitimacy of offspring, the adjudication of disputes arising out of promises made under oath, suits in which widows and orphans were parties, transactions in which usury was present or suspected; and many other types of transactions varying with time and place;[1] (5) the spiritual penalties which the Church could impose.

---

1. For specific illustrations of the wide range of activities over which the ecclesiastical courts exercised legal jurisdiction either alone or in partnership (or rivalry) with civil courts, see Sir Frederick Pollock and F. W. Maitland, *The History of English Law Before the Time of Edward I*, 2nd ed., Cambridge, Eng., 1899, I, 124–131; Oliver Martin, "L'Assemblée de Vincennes de 1329 et ses conséquences," *Travaux Juridiques et Economiques de l'Université de Rennes*, 1909, 1st supplement, pp. 14–50,

Members of the Church were in some periods and countries required to make confession at least once a year. To be given access to the sacraments, they were sometimes required to present a ticket signed by the confessor to whom they had been assigned. To receive absolution before death, they could be required to make restitution, or to instruct their heirs to make restitution, for offenses such as usury committed during their lifetime. If they failed to receive absolution before death, they could be denied burial in a sanctified burial place. The most formidable sanction in the Church's arsenal was excommunication, which could be decreed against individuals, governments, or even towns and their inhabitants, and could mean not only the stigma of public condemnation and exclusion from the sacraments but also subjection to social and economic boycott[2] and sanction of confiscation of the offender's property by the civil authorities.[3] For a time, excommunication was used by the Papacy to serve all kinds of purposes.[4] It was, for instance, used in routine fashion as a penalty for non-payment of debts.[5]

379–392; J. L. Cate, "The English Mission of Eustace of Flay (1200–1201)," *Etudes d'histoire dédiées à la mémoire de Henri Pirenne*, Brussels, 1937, pp. 67–87; R. Boutruche, "Aux origines d'une crise nobiliaire," *Annales d'Histoire Sociale*, I (1939), 161–177; R. Aubenas, "L'Ordinatio pro Anima en Languedoc au XVe–XVIe siècles," *Revue d'Histoire de l'Eglise de France*, XXIX (1943), 257–262; Lucien Febvre, *Le Problème de l'incroyance au XVIe siècle*, Paris, 1947, pp. 375–378; Armando Sapori, *Le Marchand italien au moyen âge*, Paris, 1952, Introduction, pp. xx–xxi.

    A corresponding blend of ecclesiastical, civil, and feudal law and administration, and of law and religious and moral counsel survived into eighteenth-century France. For evidence, see R.-A. de la Palmelle, *Résolutions des plus importantes questions de la coutume et du barreau, et de plusieurs cas de conscience touchants les droits et devoirs réciproques des seigneurs et des vassaux, des patrons et des curés*, 3rd ed., Rouen, 1746. The author was priest, feudal seigneur, and lawyer. The book was a manual addressed to parish priests, confessors, seigneurs and vassals, and lawyers.

    2. See M.-L. Boutteville, *La Morale de l'Eglise et la morale naturelle*, Paris, 1886, p. 378, for decrees of various Church Councils calling for complete boycott of excommunicated persons.

    3. Louis the Good refused to confiscate the goods of some of his subjects who had failed to come to terms with the Church on some disputed matters unless it was proved to him that they were in the wrong. The bishops rejected this condition, as giving the king jurisdiction over ecclesiastical proceedings. Jean Sire de Joinville, *The History of St. Louis*, Joan Evans, tr., London, 1938, pp. 18–19.

    4. For the interdict by Pope Paul II in 1471, renewed in 1507 by Pope Julius II, against all cities who bought alum originating in Mohammedan territories, see Charles Singer, *The Earliest Chemical Industry*, London, 1948, pp. 139–164; J. A. Goris, *Etude sur les colonies marchandes méridionales . . . à Anvers de 1488 à 1567*, Louvain, 1925, pp. 205–207; Jakob Strieder, *Studien zur Geschichte der kapitalistischen Organisationsformen*, 2nd ed., Munich, 1925, pp. 168–183. The papal monopoly over alum mined in its own territory, which the interdict was intended to protect, was not a purely commercial enterprise. It was in part a measure of economic warfare against the Turks and a means of financing the holy war against them.

    5. See Roger Aubenas and Robert Richard, *L'Eglise et la Renaissance*

The moral doctrines of the Church were thus not merely a matter of preaching and moral influence but were of direct and practical consequence as effective social discipline in a period of almost universal faith. These doctrines were derived from revelation, as presented in the Scriptures and interpreted by the Church, from church tradition, and from "reason," both intuitive and discursive, as embodied in "natural reason" or "natural law," including as such, at least from St. Thomas on, some Aristotelian metaphysics. The doctrines were immutable in principle, but the Church's knowledge of them could develop under divine inspiration, and both the growth in understanding by the Church and changes in social conditions could bring changes in the mode and substance of the application of the doctrines to concrete cases. It was the function of the "doctors" of the Church, by study of the Scriptures and church tradition, and by the application of trained and disciplined thought to specific problems, to clarify and otherwise improve the formulation of what in principle was eternal and unchangeable truth. From the thirteenth century on, after the discovery of Aristotle in the western world, and especially after the absorption of Aristotelian teaching by Albert the Great and St. Thomas Aquinas, Christian moral theology became a tremendous synthesis of biblical teaching, church tradition, Greek philosophy, Roman and canon law, and the wisdom and insights of the Scholastics themselves. It took some time for the influence of St. Thomas to become powerful and authoritative, but by at least the sixteenth century it was dominant. From the seventeenth century on, other influences, from within the Church and from outside, contested with it for supremacy, but it remained powerful, at least among theologians. Not until modern times, however, did it reach its peak of authority within the Church. In 1879, Pope Leo XIII proclaimed the authoritative status of St. Thomas as a guide to doctrine; the new (1917) Codex of Canon Law prescribes that professors of philosophy and theology in seminaries, etc., shall teach "according to the arguments, doctrine, and principles of St. Thomas which they are inviolately to hold."[6] In the account which follows of the Scholastic treat-

---

(1499–1517), Paris, 1951, pp. 325–326; Lucien Febvre, "L'Application du Concile de Trente et l'excommunication pour dettes en Franche-Comté," Revue Historique, CIII (1910), 224–227; CIV (1910), 1–39; W. K. Gotwald, Ecclesiastical Censure at the End of the Fifteenth Century, Baltimore, 1927. See K. J. von Hefele, Histoire des Conciles, H. Leclercq, tr., Paris, 1916, VII², 884, for an acknowledgment by the Council of Basel, 1435, that excommunication had been resorted to so immoderately as to have caused many scandals.

6. The encyclical letter of Leo XIII of August 4, 1879, establishing the authoritative status of St. Thomas, and the relevant canons of the New Code of Canon Law

ment, I will rely heavily on the writings of St. Thomas, and will deal only occasionally and meagerly with the divergences of doctrine within the ranks of the Scholastics.

Until the Renaissance, the Church had a near-monopoly of learning. The interest of the Church in economic matters, aside from its interest in conducting its own substantial material affairs, was confined practically exclusively to their actual or supposed religious and moral aspects. The study of economic process out of scientific interest or with a view to the discovery of means of promoting temporal prosperity did not come within the range of interest or duty of the Scholastics. The late Scholastics did in fact make contributions of value to economic theory and to the understanding of economic process, but this was mainly a fortuitous by-product of their examination of various types of economic transactions to determine whether they were morally licit or not. Not until the seventeenth century or even later was there a substantial and challenging secular literature of economic analysis which could compete with, substitute for, or influence the economic content of Scholastic moral theology. By the time an influential secular body of economic analysis had developed, with methods and tools of its own, and with substantial or complete separation from theological considerations, formal Catholic moral theology had in its economic aspects largely become frozen into its medieval shell and, aside from the one issue of usury, maintained a secluded existence in the seminaries and the confessional, with little influence on or responsiveness to the new tides of secular social thought. This situation was reinforced by the avoidance of the vernacular by the Church, its adherence to ancient terminology often ill-adapted to dealing with new phenomena and new ideas, and its reliance on Scholastic modes of argument and exposition of doctrine which "humanists," even those who remained general believers, found distasteful on aesthetic as well as on logical grounds.

The late Scholastics developed an elaborate system of detailed casuistics which endeavored to deal with the complexities of place, time, and circumstance, but its application to concrete cases must have strained the capacity of a large proportion of the clergy, narrowly educated and often semi-literate as, according to much contemporary evidence, many of them were. It is often said that Scholas-

---

are given in English translation in the American edition of the English Dominican translation of his *Summa Theologica*, I, vii–xvi. The reverence with which St. Thomas' texts are sometimes dealt with is manifested in the comment of Vincent McNabb, O.P., *The Catholic Church and Philosophy*, New York, 1927. p. 51: ". . . almost seven hundred years of criticism have not discovered one word used wrongly [by St. Thomas] or one argument that was disqualified as mere reasoning."

tic doctrine reflects the social and economic structure of the late Middle Ages. If so, the reflection was a pale one; in St. Thomas' writings there is meager evidence that he lived in an era when feudalism was dominant in the rural areas and the gild system in the towns.[7] In any case, by the seventeenth century the Middle Ages were over, intellectually and politically, as well as in economic thought and economic institutions.

The Scholastics, it needs always to be remembered, were not, even when discussing economic matters, trying to be economists before their time, but were providing religious and ethical guidance for individual behavior. They recognized in some measure that virtue had social implications, but in the main they confined their discussion of these implications to repeated emphasis on the priority of the common good over the individual and to scattered and occasional insights on almsgiving and questions of commutative justice arising from transactions between individuals in the ordinary course of their worldly life. They said almost nothing about the impact of individual behavior on social institutions, or the impact of social institutions on individual behavior, or the possibilities of deliberate or spontaneous remoulding of existing institutions.

The Doctrines of the "Common Good" and the "Scale of Values"

The medieval moral theologians could have found the maxim that the "common good," or the "public good," had priority over the good of the individual in Cicero or Seneca, and later in the Latin translations of Aristotle. They made repeated appeals to it, St. Thomas, perhaps, most of all.[8] Aristotle's statement of the doctrine is as follows:

> . . . the good of man. And grant that this is the same to the community, yet surely that of the latter is plainly greater and more perfect to discover and preserve; for to do this even for a single individual were a matter of contentment; but to do it for a

---

7. Cf. Alfred O'Rahilly, *Aquinas versus Marx*, Oxford, 1948, p. 14: "Nowhere in his voluminous writings does St. Thomas mention the gilds"; Werner Stark, *The Contained Economy*, The Aquinas Society of London, *Aquinas Paper* No. 26, London, 1956, p. 11: "St. Thomas virtually ignores the existence of the feudal system . . . ."

8. A modern scholar has collected 163 texts involving the concept of the supremacy of the common good from the writings of St. Thomas. Th. Eschmann, O.P., "A Thomistic Glossary on the Principle of the Preeminence of a Common Good," *Medieval Studies*, V (1943), 123–165.

whole nation, and for communities generally, were more noble and godlike.[9]

The Scholastics presented the maxim as a self-evident one, presumably as a proposition of natural law. It survives to this day as a central element in Catholic formal moral theology. What it meant in medieval times, or what it means when invoked today in a moral treatise, is, however, far from self-evident. A distinguished medievalist has characterized the doctrine as expounded by the medieval moral theologians as "one difficult to survey and hard to grasp." A professor at the University of Louvain, reacting against the uncritical acceptance of whatever St. Thomas happened to say, has claimed that in a single passage of St. Thomas he has found four meanings of "common good" that are so diverse as to raise the question whether the term does not engender more confusion than enlightenment.[10]

One possible meaning of the maxim is that where a good of a given kind, such as health, of equal *per capita* intensity, is available either to a particular individual or to the rest of the community except him, the latter alternative should be chosen. Where only these alternatives need to be considered, this seems too trite a meaning to explain the popularity of the maxim. If other considerations need to be recognized, the maxim does not have obvious general application.

Another conceivable meaning or application of the maxim is that the good of a whole state or society has priority over the good of its members even in the aggregate. Medieval writers were fond of the organic metaphor and especially of analogies of societies with the human body, and it was an easy step for them to move from the priority of a living body over its limbs or eyes or ears to the priority of a society over its members. When the issue was sharpened, they would concede that the analogy was imperfect. They did insist, however, that there were "common goods," such as the order, peace, and dignity of a society, which were neither a simple summation of nor a substitute for the particular goods of individual members of that society.[11] Aside from questions of Church versus State, the "prince" or ruler was commonly accepted as the divinely ordained custodian

9. *Nicomachean Ethics*, I.2, 1094b, D. B. Chase's translation, in the Everyman edition.
10. Dom Odon Lottin, as quoted by Th. Eschmann, "A Thomistic Glossary," p. 123; Jacques Leclercq, *La Philosophie morale de Saint Thomas devant la pensée contemporaine*, Louvain, 1955, p. 310.
11. See Ewart Lewis, "Organic Theories in Medieval Political Thought," *American Political Science Review*, XXXII (1938), 849–876; Th. Eschmann, "Bonum commune melius est quam bonum unius," *Medieval Studies*, VI (1944), 63.

and judge of the common good; but on social matters where the personal morals or interests of the prince were or could be involved, as in questions of coinage or taxation, it was often recognized that princes might be tyrants or scoundrels. Georges de Lagarde cites a medieval writer, Godefroid de Fontaines, who complained that St. Thomas invoked the principle of the common good too freely with respect to the actions of public authorities. Princes were always ready to appeal to the principle to justify their exactions, and the violation by princes of the interests of particular individuals itself constituted a violation of the common good.[12]

A. P. Verpaalen, S.C.J., suggests that the fact that St. Thomas lived in the reign of Louis the Good, a time when consciousness of tension between the individual and the state would not arise, explained his readiness as a rule to accept the will of the prince as the expression of common good. He criticizes modern writers who, living in an age of tension between individual and State, unlike St. Thomas, anachronistically appeal to St. Thomas' version of the "common good" doctrine in support of "individualist," "personalist," or "solidarist" proposals—of which St. Thomas had no prevision—as the solutions to present-day problems.[13]

A contemporary critic of Dante's exaltation of the State as against the Church, Guido Vernanus, denied that there was such a thing as a "common good" specifically distinguishable from the good of individuals. The end of society, he maintained, was nothing but a compound of the ends of individuals. The force which attracts particular individuals to each other is the same as the force which operates within a whole community of individuals and is analogous to the way in which gravity works in the physical universe.[14]

Some modern interpretations of St. Thomas' doctrine of the "common good" divorce it entirely from such realistic issues. Their exponents find in his concept of the "common good" reference only to a transcendental or spiritual good which is "common" strictly in the sense that all mankind has an opportunity to share in it, whatever form of social organization is adopted. They thus manage to engage in subtle analysis of the doctrine without making any reference to gov-

---

12. *La Naissance de l'esprit laïque au déclin du moyen âge*, IV, Saint-Paul-Trois-Chateaux and Paris, 1934, p. 201.

13. "Der Begriff des Gemeinwohls bei Thomas von Aquin," *Sammlung Politeia*, VI, Hamburg, 1954.

14. *De Reprobatione Dantes Monarchiae*, Jano, ed., Florence, 1906. See Georges de Lagarde, "Individualisme et corporatisme au moyen âge," in *L'Organisation corporative du moyen âge à la fin de l'ancien régime*, Louvain University, *Recueil de Travaux . . . d'Histoire et de Philologie*, 2nd series, fascicule 44, 1937, Part I, p. 34.

ernment or economic welfare.[15]

St. Thomas made it abundantly clear that he regarded everything related to the life of man as subordinated to the one final end of beatitude. He found it possible, nevertheless, to operate to some extent on lower levels of ends, and he often used the term "common good" to refer to these lower ends, meaning thereby such matters as peace, order, subsistence, and material welfare in general. In the following passage, indeed, he seems to use the term "common good" as if it were relevant only to these lower values, to the exclusion of purely spiritual values!

> . . . law . . . is ordained to the common good, wherefore there is no virtue whose acts cannot be prescribed by the law. Nevertheless human law does not prescribe concerning all the acts of every virtue; but only in regard to those that are ordainable to the common good;—either immediately, as when certain things are done directly for the common good,—or mediately, as when a lawgiver prescribes certain things pertaining to good order, whereby the citizens are directed in the upholding of the common good of justice and peace.[16]

The doctrine of the priority of the common good over individual good is really a phase of a more wide-reaching doctrine, that of the scale of values, and is subordinate to that wider doctrine. Common good and the good of the individual are values on *one* scale of values, but there are other scales of value. As St. Thomas put it:

> The good of the universe is greater than the particular good of one, if we consider both in the same genus. But the good of grace in one is greater than the good of nature in the whole universe.[17]

---

15. C. H. Miron, *The Problem of Altruism in the Philosophy of St. Thomas*, Washington, D.C., 1939, p. 56, translates Thomas' term *felicitatem communem* as "common happiness" and makes "happiness" synonymous with "beatitude." Louis Lachance, in *Le Concept de droit selon Aristote et St. Thomas*, Montreal, 1933, Ch. 2, "Droit et bien commun," makes no reference to any economic or other temporal constituents of the "common good." Jacques Maritain, in "Humanisme de Saint Thomas Aquin," *Medieval Studies*, III (1941), 183, says that for St. Thomas "common good" has for its "principal" value the accession of human persons to immanent and immaterial riches, and that "his theocentric humanism was too great for his time." Th. Eschmann, "Bonum commune," p. 62, says that the personal "perfection of the saint is the intrinsic constituent of the common good."

16. *Summa Theologica*, I–II, q. 96, a. 3.

17. *Ibid.*, q. 113, a. 9, ad 2. Richard Egenter, "Gemeinnutz vor Eigennutz," *Scholastik*, IX (1934), 89, reports Remigius of Florence (d. 1319), a student of St. Thomas', as rejecting the "goods in the same genus" qualification to the common good doctrine.

Here the scale of values which ranks the common good higher than the good of an individual is treated as subordinate to another scale of values, that which relates to grace and nature. But I cannot find that St. Thomas has given clear-cut answers anywhere to the question of the order of priority as between the different kinds of scales of value, or as to how this order is to be ascertained either by the theologian or by the ordinary individual faced with the need to make moral and religious decisions. Jacques Maritain, commenting on the passage from St. Thomas which I have just quoted, says that it rests on the distinction between the "individual" (who must always yield to the common good?) and the "person," and adds: "Unfortunately a right understanding of it [this distinction] is difficult to achieve and requires an exercise of metaphysical insight to which the contemporary mind is hardly accustomed."[18] But as best I can discover the attempt to distinguish formally between the "person" and the "individual" is a quite recent development confined to Catholic philosophers.

The history of the doctrine of the scale of values has not to my knowledge been explored as yet, despite the fact that it has been a staple element in moral philosophizing from ancient times to the present day. I enter here into a tricky field without benefit of an urgently needed guiding hand. According to the "scale of values" doctrine, values have inherent ordinal ranking within their class in terms of their "degree" or "intensity." The one aspect of interest here is how the doctrine could be applied to concrete ethical issues, involving a choice between a high-degree value of a low-ranking class and a low-degree value of a high-ranking class. I will ignore the easy and probably rare cases where the lowest relevant degree of the value which ranks high by class has inherent priority over the highest relevant degree of the value which ranks lower by class—though it is with such cases (or alleged cases) that the relevant literature largely concerns itself.

The issue used to trouble economists and was often discussed by them in terms of the diamond-water "paradox." In some sense it seemed obvious that water ranked higher, but in the market-place a diamond would be ranked higher than any ordinary quantity of water. With the development of the "utility theory" of economic value, and especially with the development of the theory of diminishing utility of successive units of a good at a given moment of time, economists

18. "The Person and the Common Good," *Review of Politics*, VIII (1946), 419. See also Bishop Andrew Beck, "The Common Good in Law and Legislation," in Richard O'Sullivan, ed., *The King's Good Servant*, Oxford, 1948, p. 79.

learned that for their purposes there was normally nothing to be gained by seeking to rank diamonds and water in a value scale. All that was needed, and perhaps all that was meaningful, was to compare increments (of specified size) of diamonds (of a specified kind) with increments (of a specified size) of water, in a specified time and place and with reference to specified persons or groups of persons.[19]

St. Augustine presented a scale of values of "creatures," in "the order of nature," in which creatures with life ranked higher than those without it; sentient creatures were above those without sensation; and among sentient creatures the intelligent were above those without intelligence. But in another ranking, according to "utility" to man, the order changes:

> Who, for example, would not rather have bread in his house than mice, gold than fleas? But there is little to wonder at in this, seeing that even when valued by men themselves (whose nature is certainly of the highest dignity) more is often given for a horse than for a slave, for a jewel than for a maid. . . . But of such consequence in rational natures is the weight, so to speak, of will and of love, that though in the order of nature angels rank above men, yet, by the scale of justice, good men are of greater value than bad angels.[20]

St. Augustine seems here to be dealing simultaneously with three different scales of value, relating to order of nature, utility, and justice, each involving its own criterion for ranking. He does not explain what principles should determine which scale to apply to a particular case. However, when not dealing with a concrete case, theologians frequently present a single scale of values, without discussing whether

19. See my comments on this issue in "Bentham and J. S. Mill: the Utilitarian Background," *American Economic Review*, XXXIX (1949), 377–378, reprinted in my *The Long View and the Short*, Glencoe, Ill., 1958, pp. 326–327. See also J. M. Clark, "Aims of Economic Life as Seen by Economists," in A. Dudley Ward, ed., *Goals of Economic Life*, New York, 1953, p. 27: "[Economists] do not arrange generic values in an order of priority (e.g. health is, or is not, more important than freedom) and they would consider such a scale misleading. . . . [Their] policy decisions deal with marginal increments; and, at some point, every generic class of values has to be limited in the interest of others."

James Bonar, both a moral philosopher and an economist, represents an interesting transition phase in the history of economic value theory when the ranking of different goods by their genus was retained (although this ranking plays no detectable part in Bonar's description of the choice process), and yet it was recognized that increments of different kinds of goods must be compared. See his "The Austrian Economists and Their View of Value," *Quarterly Journal of Economics*, III (1888/89), 1–31.

20. *City of God*, XI.16, Dods tr., I, 456.

there could be cases of conflict with another relevant scale, where their single scale does not have absolute priority. I present three such statements, all from high sources:

> If anyone saith, that the marriage state is to be placed above the state of virginity, or of celibacy, and that it is not better and more blessed to remain in virginity, or in celibacy, than to be united in matrimony, let him be anathema.[21]
>
> The Church . . . regards this world, and all that is in it, as a mere shadow, as dust and ashes, compared with the value of one single soul. . . . She holds that it were better for sun and moon to drop from heaven, for the earth to fail, and for all the many millions who are upon it to die of starvation in extremest agony, so far as temporal affliction goes, than that one soul, I will not say should be lost, but should commit one single venial sin, should tell one wilful untruth, though it harmed no one, or steal one poor farthing without excuse. She considers the action of this world and the action of the soul simply incommensurate, viewed in their respective spheres; she would rather save the soul of one single wild bandit of Calabria, or whining beggar of Palermo, than draw a hundred lines of railroad through the length of Italy, or carry out a sanitary reform in its fullest details, in every city of Sicily, except so far as these natural works tended to some spiritual good beyond them.[22]
>
> The fatherland must be loved, from which we receive the enjoyment of mortal life; but we must love the Church more to whom we owe the love of the soul which will last forever, because it is right to hold the blessings of the spirit above the blessings of the body, and the duties toward God as much more sacred than those toward men.[23]

A moral theologian's unqualified statement of the priority of a particular scale of values does not necessarily mean, however, that he will not introduce qualifications when dealing with actual cases involving conflict between different scales of value. St. Thomas, for example, after stating that spiritual alms are, for a number of reasons, of superior merit to corporeal or material alms, says there are

---

21. *Canons and Decrees of the Council of Trent*, Session XXIV, Canon X, James Waterworth, tr., London, 1848, p. 195.

22. John Henry Newman, *Lectures on Certain Difficulties Felt by Anglicans in Submitting to the Catholic Church*, new ed., Dublin, 1857, p. 190.

23. Leo XIII, Encyclical *Sapientiae Christianae*, Jan. 10, 1890, in Henry Denzinger, *The Sources of Catholic Dogma (Enchiridion Symbolorum)*, St. Louis, 1936, pp. 481–482.

circumstances in which this does not hold: "for instance, a man in hunger is to be fed rather than instructed, and as the Philosopher observes . . . for a needy man money is better than philosophy, although the latter is better simply."[24] On the question "whether it is better to pray than to spin," medieval moralists did not always give an unqualified affirmative answer.

Modern theologians who expound the scale-of-values doctrine handle the problem of conflict between different scales of values in several different ways. Some simply ignore the problem. Others deny the possibility of its existence. When a French theologian, Guy de Broglie, asserted that it was both logically conceivable and practically observable that Christian morality and the welfare criteria of sound "political science" sometimes came into conflict with one another, he was answered by the view that spiritual good is itself an essential ingredient of the humanly good, and therefore disharmony could not exist between spiritual good and what was politically or socially or individually good.[25]

Another way of dealing with the problem of a plurality of scales of value is to treat only one of the scales as having ethical significance, while ascribing to the others ontological, economic, sentimental, or some other kind of significance.[26] But this leaves open the question of which scale is significant for decision-making in cases of imperfect harmony between the scales. A partial solution is to present each scale on a *ceteris paribus* basis. But this has the defect of offering no help in the numerous cases where other things that deserve consideration are not equal. St. Thomas, in effect, frequently varies his answer to ethical problems depending on which scales of value compete against one another. As one example, to the question "whether one

24. *Summa Theologica*, II–II, q. 32, a. 3. Elsewhere, St. Thomas says that "though for each individual it is better to abstain from what is needful for the community, and to occupy himself with better things, it is not good that all so abstain." *Summa Contra Gentiles*, Book III, Chs. 96–97, English Dominican Fathers, tr., London, 1928, III, Part II, p. 154. This leaves an opening for an incremental approach, as in economic value theory.

25. De Broglie presented his argument in a series of articles in *Recherches de Science Religieuse*, Vols. XVIII to XXV, 1928 to 1935. The reply was by Joseph Vialatoux, in *Questions disputées, morale et politique*, Paris, 1931, which I have not been able to consult. A report of Vialatoux's argument is to be found in J. J. Tonneau, O.P., "Morale et politique," *Bulletin Thomiste*, IV (1935), 463–472. Suzanne Michel, in *La Notion thomiste du bien commun—quelques-unes de ses applications juridiques*, Nancy, 1931, p. 200, also dismisses de Broglie's problem by asserting the impossibility of conflict between a spiritual and a temporal "common good" when both are "properly conceived."

26. This is the position that A. P. Verpaalen, *Der Begriff des Gemeinwohls*, p. 55, attributes to St. Thomas and accepts for himself, if I understand him correctly.

ought to give alms to those rather who are more closely united to us,'' he first answers affirmatively, but immediately proceeds to qualify his answer, leaving the solution to ''discretion'' or human prudence:

Nevertheless in this matter we must employ discretion, according to the various degrees of connection, holiness and utility. For we ought to give alms to one who is much holier and in greater want, and to one who is more useful to the common weal, rather than to one who is more closely united to us. . . .[27]

I have been able to find only a few instances where the usefulness of reasoning involving ranking of values of different classes of goods on a single scale is questioned. The earliest, and yet to my mind the most penetrating, was by Theophrastus (died ca. 287 B.C.) in his Essay on Friendship, as reported by Aulus Gellius in the second century A.D. In the following passage, Theophrastus is considering the question how far one is justified in helping a friend by means which in themselves are improper:

I cannot say whether there is here anything to which one should give absolute priority, and whether one of two objects being compared, taken in whatever proportion, should always prevail over the other. Thus, one cannot say absolutely that gold is more precious than brass; any quantity whatsoever of gold need not always be preferred to any other quantity of brass, but the evaluation must also consider volume and weight. . . . The appreciation of more and less in these sorts of things and in general the examination of these questions of conduct depend on many and diverse external considerations; let considerations of persons, of causes, of the time, of a crowd of circumstances which the current maxims cannot embrace, determine and regulate our duty, and sometimes give us, sometimes withhold from us, the authority to act.[28]

Henry of Ghent, in 1256, recognized clearly the difficulties presented by conflicts of values of different classes and degrees, but offered no formal solution. He accepted as a general principle the primacy of the common good over the individual good, but held that this principle was subordinate to the primacy of spiritual over tem-

27. *Summa Theologica*, II–II, q. 32, a. 9.
28. *Les Nuits attiques d'Aule-Gelle*, in *Pétrone, Apulée, Aule-Gelle. Œuvres complètes*, M. Nisard, ed. and tr., Paris, 1842, p. 433. [Aulus Gellius, I, Ch. 3, §§ 26–28.] See also Raymond Thamin, *Un Problème moral dans l'antiquité: étude sur la casuistique stoicienne*, Paris, 1884, pp. 326–327.

poral good, and made more limited qualifications in cases of conflict between an individual and a common spiritual good, or where there was extreme difference in "need" for the goods involved.[29]

Jeremy Taylor accepted the proposition that spiritual things are "better" than temporal, but did not find it an adequate guide to action:

> But when a temporal necessity and a spiritual advantage are compared, the advantage, in the nature of the thing, is overbalanced by the degree of necessity, and the greatness of the end; and it is better to sell the chalices of the Church and minister religion in glass or wood, than to suffer a man to starve at the foot of the altar.[30]

Systematic and elaborate formulation of scale-of-value doctrine is in modern times apparently more common in non-Catholic treatises on ethics than in the Catholic moral theology literature, although appeal to the doctrine as an effective instrument in deciding moral issues continues to be standard Catholic procedure. In the non-Catholic, as in the Catholic, literature the value ranking of different classes of goods is generally assumed, without argument, to be objectively given, essentially as a religious or moral datum. In fact the non-Catholic literature—more than the earlier and modern Catholic literature—generally ignores, or fails to discuss, the problem of conflict between low-ranking goods on a higher-ranking scale and high-ranking goods on a lower-ranking scale.[31]

In this respect, R. B. Perry's *General Theory of Value* contrasts with the rest of the literature in its emphasis on problematic features: the subjective (or psychological) aspects; the simultaneous existence for each valuing individual of a plurality of subjective "orders of preference" as between classes of goods or "objects" (all of them

29. *Quodibet*, IX, q. 19, as reported by Georges de Lagarde, *La Naissance*, II, 2nd ed., Louvain, 1958, pp. 174–180, and *ibid.*, 1st ed., III, Saint-Paul-Trois-Chateaux and Paris, 1942, pp. 246–248, 256.

30. "The Rule of Conscience," *Works*, Richard Heber, ed., London, 1828, XIII, 506.

31. For modern moral philosophizing explicitly resting on "scale of value" doctrine, but in my opinion offering no help in resolving ethical problems where a high-degree value of a low-ranking class clashes with a low-degree value of a high-ranking class, see James Martineau, *Types of Ethical Theory*, 2nd ed., Oxford, 1886, II, 325–331; W. R. Sorley, *Moral Values and the Idea of God*, 2nd ed., Cambridge, Eng., 1921, pp. 40–52; W. D. Ross, *The Right and the Good*, Oxford, 1930, Ch. 6, "Degrees of Goodness," especially pp. 149–154; R. G. Collingwood, *An Essay on Philosophical Method*, Oxford, 1933, Ch. 3, "The Scale of Forms," pp. 54–91; W. G. De Burgh, *From Morality to Religion*, London, 1938, pp. 256–257.

accepted as relevant for moral decisions); the possibility and even prevalence of conflicts between various "orders of preference"; the absence of comparability in a measurement or quasi-measurement sense between the different "orders of preference"; and the actual or potential non-existence of any formal or logical method of resolving a conflict between different orders of preference. But because Perry, unlike the moral theologians, refuses to fall back on external authority or dogma, it seems to me that he is even less successful than they have been in presenting a logical case, or discovering a practical function, for the concept of hierarchical ordering of preferences by *classes* of objects or goods. Although he pays more attention than other writers on this topic to economic value theory, he does not explore the possibility that value decisions are ordinarily made in life by exercising preferences between particular increments of goods regardless of their "class."[32]

John Laird rejects Perry's denial of the possibility of comparing values belonging to different orders of preference:

> Different values *have* to be compared if it is necessary to choose between them, and if any rational justification for the choice can be given. . . . If a man cannot write a study when his children are imitating fog-horns within earshot, he *has*, at certain times, to choose between the enjoyment of family-affection and the sedulous pursuit of knowledge.[33]

I venture two comments on Laird's critique of Perry. First, since a key element in Perry's argument is that a "rational" criterion for value decisions is unavailable (if a "rational" criterion is taken to mean one demonstrable by reasoning), Laird meets the issue only by dogmatic assertion. Second, the problem of dealing with a momentary interference with the pursuit of knowledge by a child's tooting of a horn can surely be resolved without invoking the choice between scholarship *in general* and family affection *in general*.

The most extreme manifestation of confidence in the potentialities of scale-of-value reasoning as a source of moral guidance that I have encountered is by Johannes Haessle, in a book on the labor doctrines of Catholicism. Haessle presents a quasi-geometrical, quasi-algebraic diagram, in which the "true order of values" (die wahre Güterordnung) of Catholicism is contrasted with the order of values of "false" or "pseudo" capitalism. In the "true" order, "perfect blessedness"

32. *General Theory of Value*, New York, 1926, especially pp. 616–617, 626–627, 633–639, 669–674.

33. *The Idea of Value*, Cambridge, Eng., 1929, pp. 357–358; the italics are Laird's.

is at the top, "imperfect blessedness" at an intermediate range, and material goods at the bottom; in the order of values of pseudo-capitalism, the ranking is exactly reversed.[34]

The General Attitude of the Scholastics
Towards Temporal Prosperity

In the formal exposition of medieval moral theology, the primacy of "spiritual" over "temporal" goods was always emphasized, and attachment to individual riches was treated as a danger to morals and even as sin. Voluntary poverty, however, was not recommended or even approved, except for the few who sought and had an aptitude for perfection. There was complete tolerance of those rich who, while giving alms generously to the poor, attempted within reason to maintain their social status and lived according to the customary standards of expenditure of their class. The economic welfare of the community was ordinarily included as an important part of the "common good" which it was a duty—especially for rulers—to serve. But the Scholastics did not regard it as part of their function, and probably were not emotionally disposed, to furnish advice as to how the temporal prosperity of communities could be promoted. Roger Bacon is an exception; writing in the thirteenth century, he ascribed to Christian wisdom the functions both of guiding the Church for supernatural ends and guiding the Christian republic to temporal welfare. He made clear enough what he meant by temporal welfare: "What individuals and peoples required to conserve their health, to prolong their life . . . , to acquire the goods of fortune, virtue, judgment, peace, justice, and to triumph magnificently over all that was an obstacle to this."[35] But Roger Bacon often took an original line, and his orthodoxy was questioned by contemporaries, including members of his own order. Another exception is Giovanni Botero, who, in an economic treatise first published in 1589, claimed that religion, or at least ecclesiastical establishments, caused commerce to flourish and cities to prosper.[36] But as far as I have been able to discover, it was from Protestant-Catholic polemics that there first emerged a literature of any consequence emphasizing the benefits of religion to the material interests of mankind.

---

34. *Das Arbeitsethos der Kirche nach Thomas von Aquin and Leo XIII*, Freiburg i.B., 1923. The diagram constitutes a two-page unpaginated appendix to the book.

35. *Compendium studii philosophiae*, J. S. Brewer, ed., London, 1859, p. 393, as cited by Etienne Gilson, *Les Métamorphoses de la cité de Dieu*, Louvain, 1952, p. 81.

36. *Greatness of Cities*, Robert Pearson, tr., London, 1956, pp. 247–250.

Scholastic doctrine is commonly characterized as having condemned as sinful, or at the least as having strongly disapproved, striving on the part of individuals to raise their social status, to rise in the world, to accumulate wealth for themselves or their children. But very few citations of texts clearly and strongly supporting this interpretation are presented in the secondary literature. The most frequently cited text, and by far the most pertinent, is a statement by Henry of Langenstein, a fourteenth-century theologian:

He who has enough to satisfy his wants, and nevertheless labors to acquire riches, either in order to obtain a higher social position, or that subsequently he may have enough to live without labor, or that his sons may become men of wealth and importance—all such are incited by a damnable avarice, sensuality, or pride.[37]

St. Thomas is commonly interpreted as holding that it is unlawful for a man to strive to raise his social status. Most often cited in support is the following passage:

Covetousness may signify immoderation about external things in two ways. First, so as to regard immediately the acquisition and keeping of such things, when, to wit, a man acquires or keeps them more than is due. In this way it is a sin directly against one's neighbour, since one man cannot overabound in external riches, without another man lacking them, for temporal goods cannot be possessed by many at the same time.[38]

Here St. Thomas is apparently following St. Jerome's dictum that one man's gain must be another man's loss. In his discussion of accumulation, saving, avarice, and covetousness, as is generally the case in Scholastic discussion, there is no express recognition, and much that seems to imply denial, of the possibility that the most socially beneficial use that some individuals can make of their abilities and wealth is to engage in productive enterprise and to reinvest their

37. *Tractatus bipartitus*, I, xii, as translated by R. H. Tawney, *Religion and the Rise of Capitalism*, New York, 1926, p. 36, from a secondary source. (The Latin text is given in Manuel Rocha, *Travail et salaire à travers la scolastique*, Paris, 1933, p. 46.) But Victor Brants, in *L'Economie politique au moyen-âge*, Louvain, 1895, p. 42, quotes Henry of Langenstein as taking a seemingly more moderate view in another work (*De Contractibus*, 1a pars, q. 12): "The good worker, wishing to please God, should not think only of his advancement or profit, but should also think of his neighbours' and of the common utility."

38. *Summa Theologica*, II–II, q. 118, a. 1.

earnings, thereby involving indefinite accumulation as a by-product, or as a means, regardless of whether or not also as an end.

St. Thomas commends "liberality" and "magnificence" as good uses of wealth, the former applying to the moderately wealthy and the latter to men of great wealth. These meritorious uses of wealth clearly include expenditure for display in proportion to one's wealth, on gifts to others, and, in the case of "magnificence," for "great deeds," which could, among other possibilities, take the form of large-scale expenditure on things of use or ornament to the city.[39] His praise of "magnificence" derives directly from Aristotle, for whom it represented the expenditure suitable in form and proportion to the aristocrat of great wealth, including expenditure for display "upon any occasion of peculiar interest to the state or the upper classes."[40] Pope Pius XI, in his encyclical, *Quadragesimo Anno*, 1931, was the first to interpret St. Thomas' concept of "magnificence" as including large-scale productive investment:

> The investment of rather large incomes so that opportunities for gainful employment may abound, provided that this work is applied to the production of truly useful products, we gather from a study of the principles of the Angelic Doctor, is to be considered a noble deed of magnificent virtue, and especially suited to the needs of the time.[41]

On this passage, Oswald von Nell-Breuning, S.J., has commented:

> Pius XI revives it [i.e., *magnificentia*] not in its feudal form, but rather modernized throughout. The *magnificentia* of Pius XI is a genuinely capitalistic virtue, indeed, the Pope makes it the virtue of the entrepreneur, not in the sense that all present-day employers practice this virtue, but meaning that it is the virtue proper of the capitalistic employer.[42]

Another writer, Sister Francis A. Richey, although objecting to Nell-Breuning's characterization of St. Thomas' treatment of magnificence as "feudal" in form, agrees with his appraisal of Pius XI's formulation:

39. *Ibid.*, q. 134, a. 2 and a. 3.

40. *The Nicomachean Ethics*, II.vii, J. E. C. Welldon, tr., London, 1908, pp. 107–108; and IV. iii.

41. As translated in Denzinger, *The Sources of Catholic Dogma* [*Enchiridion Symbolorum*], No. 2257, p. 600.

42. *Reorganization of Social Economy: The Social Encyclical Developed and Explained*. Translated from the original German by Bernard W. Dempsey, S.J., (1936), 3rd printing, St. Louis, Mo., 1939, p. 115.

It is a legitimate, indeed a well-nigh inevitable development or modern adaption of Saint Thomas' *magnificentia*; for, it will be remembered, the highest expression of that virtue involves large scale and appropriate service of the common weal. It is, as we have pointed out, adjustable to time and place and circumstance and civic need.[43]

Sister Richey claims also that it is a mistake to interpret St. Thomas as being unqualifiedly hostile to striving to better one's social status in the world. According to her, what St. Thomas condemned, aside, of course, from striving out of unlawful motives, was living above one's status, or discontent with one's status when it is suitable to one's capacities. She cites various texts in support, interpreting them somewhat freely; the most persuasive is a passage in St. Thomas' discussion of "pusillanimity," a quality which he defines elsewhere as "a deficiency in pursuing great things":

Pusillanimity makes a man fall short of what is proportionate to his power, by refusing to tend to that which is commensurate thereto. Wherefore as presumption is a sin, so is pusillanimity. Hence it is that the servant who buried in the earth the money he had received from his master, and did not trade with it through fainthearted fear, was punished by his master (Matth. XXV; Luke XIX).[44]

Amintore Fanfani interprets Pius XI's position in *Quadragesimo Anno* as being further from "the formal letter of Thomism" than from the position of St. Bernardino of Siena, who "prefers a man to enrich himself in order to profit his neighbor by new enterprises, rather than to sit idle for fear of growing too rich."[45] In line with

---

43. Sister Francis A. Richey, *Character Control of Wealth According to Saint Thomas Aquinas*, Washington, D.C., 1940, pp. 113–114. Alexander Pope, *Epistle to Burlington* (1731), lines 197–202, gave praise to devotion to "public works" as an aristocratic activity, even if the works are privately owned and profitably operated. In English eighteenth-century usage, "public works" would include such things as bridges, roads, harbors, and docks. Earl R. Wasserman, *Pope's Epistle to Bathurst*, Baltimore, 1960, p. 37, interprets these lines as dealing with "magnificence" in the Aristotelian sense, and comments: "Magnificence necessarily remained a purely worldly virtue that could not be assimilated into a theological virtue."

44. *Summa Theologica*, II–II, q. 133, a. 1; Sister Richey, *Character Control*, pp. 97 ff.

45. *Catholicism, Protestantism and Capitalism*, New York, 1935, p. 130. See also, for more detail, Fanfani, *Le origini dello spirito capitalistico in Italia*, Milan, 1933, pp. 106–119. In general, St. Bernardino was fairly "rigorous," and I am not convinced from my attempt to read his texts in context that he was not merely expressing a preference, as the lesser of two evils, of striving in business over torpor or sloth.

Sister Richey's interpretation, this would suggest that St. Bernardino was perhaps following St. Thomas' statement regarding "pusillanimity."

Modern scholars who have made a special search have apparently found only one passage in the writings of prominent medieval moral theologians in which clear and unambiguous sanction is given to men striving to raise their social status, and even this is subject to important qualifications as to ultimate motives, etc. The passage appears in the *Commentary* on Saint Thomas' *Summa* by Cardinal Cajetan (1468–1524). Cajetan discusses there the passage (II–II, q. 118, a. 1) from St. Thomas' *Summa* quoted above,[46] which he interprets as condemning the ambition to rise above one's existing status. He qualifies this view by pointing out that everyone is permitted to wish for himself and his family full participation in the human felicity to which all men are eligible, and to strive to deliver them from the necessity of manual and commercial labor. Those who have special aptitudes may lawfully obtain for themselves the means to use their capacities to the full; they may maintain a corresponding status, provided they do not do so from pride or in an effort to raise themselves without limit.[47]

There is an apparent scarcity of statements comparable to that by Cajetan, for over a century at least, and a lack of evidence to show that Cajetan's statement attracted much attention before it was rediscovered in the nineteenth century. Nevertheless, some modern commentators attach historical importance to it as marking a lasting modification of Catholic social doctrine: "The rigidity of Thomism has been tempered by Gaetano's interpretation, by which a man endowed with exceptional qualities may lawfully seek the wealth that will procure him a status comparable with his qualities."[48]

The only additional material on this subject of any consequence that I can adduce from Scholastic sources is provided by later moral theologians who were subsequently to be charged with being laxists.

See, for instance, *Le prediche volgari di San Bernardino da Siena*, Luciano Banchi, ed., Siena, 1888, III, 204.

46. See p. 62, above.

47. *Comment. ad S. Thom.* III, 397, as cited by Victor Brants, *L'Economie politique au moyen-âge*, p. 41. Brants was apparently the first modern writer to call attention to this passage. Wilhelm Weber, *Wirtschaftsethik am Vorabend des Liberalismus*, Münster Westfalen, 1959, p. 95, cited Luis Molina as going beyond Cajetan in mentioning, apparently without express disapproval or ethical reservation, the possibility of a merchant raising his social status by the accumulation of wealth. He gives a reference to Molina, *De Justitia et Jure*, Tr. II, d. 339, n. 4.

48. Fanfani, *Catholicism, Protestantism and Capitalism*, p. 132. See also Friedrich Engel-Janôsi, "Soziale Probleme der Renaissance," *Beihefte zur Vierteljahrschrift für Sozial- und Wirtschaftsgeschichte*, IV (1924), 21.

A supporter of Vasquez reports him as having stated, in his discussion of the limitations to the principle of giving to the poor from one's "superfluity," that "the laics have the right to reserve from their patrimony the means of raising their status or that of their family, and what they so reserve is not to be regarded as superfluity."[49] In a 1593 manuscript which remained unpublished until 1912, L. Lessius presented the same argument when examining the definition of "superfluity."[50]

Even if, before the sixteenth century, the Scholastics were hostile towards striving for enrichment, and especially towards striving to rise above one's social status by birth, it should not be taken for granted that the businessmen of the time, in the Italian cities of the Renaissance and elsewhere, accepted as binding doctrine that it was wrong to endeavor to rise above one's accustomed status. Lecoy de la Marche may have exaggerated when he said of the thirteenth-century townsmen: "Every townsman dreamt, as today, for his son opulence or distinction; the immobility of social ranks was no longer so rigorous." But the story he tells, of an ex-peddler of meat who mounted in gold and silver the simple platter he had once used, as an emblem of his rise from poverty to great wealth, indicates what was then possible.[51]

The remainder of the chapter will mainly deal with the application by the Scholastics of their general doctrines relating to economic activity to such concrete issues as property, almsgiving, just price, usury, and coinage.[52] Treatment of the so-called laxist-rigorist con-

49. See [Gabriel Daniel], *Réponse aux Lettres provinciales . . . ou entretiens de Cléandre et d'Eudoxe*, Cologne, 1696, pp. 223–234.

50. Victor Brants, "Un fragment inédit de L. Lessius, *De Eleemosyna* (1593)," *Analectes pour servir à l'Histoire Ecclésiastique de la Belgique*, XXXVIII (1912), 65–75, especially pp. 65–68, and *idem*, "L'économie politique et sociale dans les écrits de L. Lessius (1554–1623)," *Revue d'Histoire Ecclesiastique*, XIII (1912), 80. The "rigorists" were later sharply to criticize the "laxist" definitions of "superfluity."

51. *La Chaire française au moyen âge*, 2nd ed., Paris, 1886, pp. 404–405. See also Lujo Brentano, *Die Anfänge des modernen Kapitalismus*, Munich, 1916, p. 187, and, for the attitudes of the Renaissance merchants, see Ch. 3, pp. 123–27, below.

52. Notable among the scholarly general accounts of the economic doctrines of the Scholastics are Wilhelm Endemann, *Die nationalökonomische Grundsätze der kanonische Lehre*, Jena, 1863; *idem*, *Studien in der romanischen-kanonistischen Wirtschafts- und Rechtslehre*, 2 vols., Berlin, 1874, 1883; Charles Jourdain, "Mémoire sur les commencements de l'économie politique dans les écoles du moyen âge," *Mémoires de l'Institut National de France*, XXVIII (Paris, 1874), Part I, pp. 1–51; Victor Brants, *L'Economie sociale au moyen-âge*, Louvain, 1881; *idem, L'Economie politique au moyen-âge*, Louvain, 1895; W. J. Ashley, *An Introduction to English Economic History and Theory*, Vol. I, Part II, *The End of the Middle Ages*, London, 1893, Ch. 6. "The Canonist Doctrine," pp. 377–488; Edmund Schreiber, *Die volks-*

troversy will be given in the next chapter. For lack of competence, I do not attempt to deal with the thesis propounded by some modern students of Scholastic economic doctrine that there was a systematic difference between "realists" and "nominalists," with the former tending to "statism" and "socialism" while the latter prepared the way for the doctrines of "economic freedom" and "individualism" that prevailed in the eighteenth century and beyond.[53]

Property

In medieval moral theology, the institution of private property was accepted without question as lawful under existing circumstances, but there was no unanimity of opinion as to the origin of the institution. The Christian Fathers had maintained that under the original or pre-lapsarian law of nature all property was held in common, and that the Fall of man had made private property a necessary institution, both as a restraint on the cupidity of man and as a means of lessening dispute and disorder. St. Augustine had gone further than this in his polemics with the Donatists in declaring that under human law all property rights derived only from civil law. St. Thomas maintained a closer link between private property and natural law than either the Fathers had done, or his pre-nineteenth-century successors were to do. Community of property, he said, had been ascribed to natural law not because natural law dictates that all things should be held in common, but because positive law first established private property. "Hence the ownership of possessions is not contrary to the natural law, but an

wirtschaftlichen Anschauungen der Scholastik seit Thomas v. Aquin, Jena, 1913; Giuseppe Salvioli, "L'economia medievale e le dottrine economiche nella scolastica pretomista," *Società Reale di Napoli, Atti . . . di Scienze Morali e Politiche*, XLVIII (1923), 95–135; Charles Turgeon, "L'économie chrétienne du moyen âge," and succeeding articles, *Travaux juridiques et économiques de l'Université de Rennes*, XIII (1934), 8–94, XIV (1935), 36–78; XV (1936), 5–51; XVI (1937), 5–34.

53. See Charles Secrétan, *La Philosophie de la liberté: l'histoire*, 3rd ed., Paris, 1879, pp. 54–57; Karl Pribram, *Die Enstehung der individualistischen Sozialphilosophie*, Leipzig, 1912, pp. 1–18; P. Honigsheim, "Die sozialogische Bedeutung der nominalistischen Philosophie," *Errinerungsgabe für Max Weber*, Munich, 1923, especially pp. 199–205. Meyrick H. Carré, *Realists and Nominalists*, London, 1946, does not deal with the economic aspects of the doctrines of the two schools. Georges de Lagarde is sceptical of the possibility of drawing distinctions between the two schools, *La Naissance*, 1st ed., III, 394. But in the course of various volumes of his work he cites statements of nominalists, especially Duns Scotus and Ockham, which seem to me to distinguish nominalists from the main line of Scholastic doctrine with respect to economic issues. Bernard Landry, *Duns Scotus*, Paris, 1922, pp. 258–261, also reports some unusual economic doctrine in Duns Scotus' writings, and Wilhelm Weber, *Wirtschaftsethik am Vorabend des Liberalismus*, pp. 45–55 and *passim*, finds evidence of the influence of a modified nominalism (leading to some beginnings of "economic liberalism") on the "Molinists" or "laxists" of late Scholasticism.

addition thereto devised by human reason."[54] St. Thomas interprets the statement of St. Ambrose that a man should hold things, "not as his own, but as common" as applying only to use and not to ownership.[55] Furthermore, he does not seem to mean much more by "common use" than the obligation of the rich to give alms to the poor out of their "superabundance." It is the "law of nations" (*jus gentium*), derived from the natural law, which validates private property. But the specific rules governing the holding of property belong to the civil law, on the basis of which each state decides what is best for itself.[56]

St. Thomas adopts from Aristotle the distinction between "commutative justice," which is concerned with transactions between pairs of persons, and "distributive justice," which is concerned with the relations of the community to its members. Following Aristotle closely, he states that commutative justice follows the principle of arithmetical proportion, i.e., equality, whereas distributive justice follows the principle of geometrical proportion, i.e., proportionality to the status of the individual in the community:

> Consequently in distributive justice a person receives all the more of the common goods, according as he holds a more prominent position in the community. This prominence in an aristocratic community is gauged according to virtue, in an oligarchy according to wealth, in a democracy according to liberty, and in various ways according to various forms of community.[57]

This is the only statement by St. Thomas that I have been able to find which has direct bearing on the question of the appropriate or ideal distribution of wealth in a community. Even this statement, which belongs to a discussion of "commutative justice" and is confined to "common goods," should not necessarily be interpreted as an expression of St. Thomas' views with respect to the general distribution of private property or income. In any case, it reveals no preferences as between different possible systems of distribution of wealth.[58]

---

54. *Summa Theologica*, II–II, q. 66, a. 2, ad 1. He refers to another passage (II–II, q. 57, a. 2, ad 2), where he had explained: "The human will can, by common agreement, make a thing to be just provided it be not, of itself, contrary to natural justice and it is in such matters that positive right [positive law] has its place."

55. *Ibid*. q. 66, a. 2, ad 3.

56. See *ibid*., I–II, q. 95, a. 4, where private property is not specifically referred to, but presumably is included under "just buyings and sellings, and the like."

57. *Ibid*., II–II, q. 61, a. 2.

58. Modern Catholic moral theologians frequently give a broader meaning to "dis-

Ockham went further than St. Thomas in providing a basis in natural law for private property: after the Fall the power of the individual to appropriate property became a right as absolute as a moral precept, a right of which no one could lawfully be deprived without his consent; when a positive-law right to private property was introduced later, the right still rested on natural law.[59] For the most part, however, the medieval moral theologians seem to have adhered without modification to the position of the early Fathers that private property was introduced by civil law, and was the result of, and made necessary by, sin. Henry of Ghent defended Platonic communism against such Aristotelian criticisms as that of St. Thomas, appealing to the priority of the common good over the individual good.[60] Luca de Penna, a fourteenth-century civil lawyer, denied that the existing order of private property accorded with the idea of natural law embodied in the law of nations, or that it was based on natural justice. The concepts of *meum* and *tuum*, he asserted, arose not out of justice, but out of mortal sin (*iniquitate mortalium*).[61] John Colet and Erasmus rejected formulations of the law of nature, or other systems of law, which presented a moral justification of private property:

> . . . the corrupt law called the *law of nature* . . . the same as that law of nations . . . a law which brought in ideas of *meum* and *tuum*—of property, that is to say, and deprivation; ideas clean contrary to a good and unsophisticated nature; for that would have a community in all things . . . . Thus the law of human nature was one great iniquity; a perverted reason and design; a mother of sin and of all base and hurtful action; and the wages thereof of everlasting death.[62]

You have riches, be aware that you are a steward, not a master, and give careful attention to how you use them for the common good. Are you of the opinion that only to the monk is property forbidden and poverty commanded? You are in error:

---

tributive justice," so that it covers government action intended to reduce inequalities in the existing social structure. Similarly, they term commutative and distributive justice as "social justice" or some equivalent. See the interesting discussion in Alfred O'Rahilly, *Aquinas versus Marx*, Oxford, 1948, Ch. 2, "The Kinds of Justice."

59. See Georges de Lagarde, *La Naissance*, 1st ed., VI, 1946, 177 ff.; Heinrich Rommen, "The Church and Human Rights," in Waldemar Gurian and M. A. Fitzsimmons, eds., *The Catholic Church in World Affairs*, Notre Dame, Ind., 1954, pp. 134–135.

60. Georges de Lagarde, *La Naissance*, 1st ed., III, 155, 262.

61. See Walter Ullman, *The Medieval Idea of Law as Represented by Lucas de Penna*, London, 1946, p. 47.

62. "Exposition of St. Paul's Epistle to the Romans," in *Joannis Coleti Opuscula Quaedam Theologica*, J. H. Lupton, ed. and tr., London, 1876, pp. 134–135.

both hold for all Christians. The [civil] law punishes you if you steal another's property; it does not, however, punish you if you withhold your own property from your needy brother. Christ, however, will punish both.[63]

Whereas John Colet and Erasmus rejected natural law when it was invoked to support private property, Bishop Stephen Gardiner of Winchester, around 1535, rejected it when it was invoked in the interest of equalitarianism by John Rastell, a Protestant. Rastell had attacked the levying of tithes on the poor for the maintenance of curates, who, he held, should be supported by the rich. Gardiner replied as follows:

Mr. Rastell, what you mean by the law of nature, of man, and of God, I cannot tell, but of this I am sure, that the vilest parts in the creation of nature take most labours and pains. And contrarily, the chiefest members which are set next to the noble blood labour least.[64]

In the next century Blaise Pascal was to write that "law"—with the law of property obviously included—had originated in usurpation, and had become reasonable only with the passage of time. "We must make it [be] regarded as authoritative, eternal, and conceal its origin, if we do not wish that [private property] should soon come to an end."[65]

These references to sceptical attitudes at the end of the Middle Ages towards the doctrine of a natural-law foundation of the institution of private property indicate that St. Thomas' use of even a quasi natural-law justification of private property was by no means universally accepted. It seemed to some, therefore, that Pope Leo XIII broke sharply with traditional doctrine when he went beyond St. Thomas in his campaign against nineteenth-century socialist doctrine,

---

63. Erasmus, *Handbüchlein des christlichen Streiters* (*Enchiridion Milit. Christ.*, Canon 6), Hubert Schiel, tr., Freiburg i. B., 1952, p. 149.

64. Manuscript in Public Record Office, London (State Papers Domestic, of Henry VIII, 6.9. no. 19, folios 120 ff., pp. 239–240).

65. *Pensées*, 294, Modern Library ed., New York, 1941, p. 102. St. Ambrose had said that "nature . . . created common right, usurpation (*usurpatio*) made private right (*De Officiis Ministrorum*, 1.28), and this was often repeated later. F. Desjacques, "Les Saints Pères et les origines du droit de propriété," *Etudes Religieuses Philosophiques Historiques et Littéraires*, 26th year, 6th series, II (1878), 366, claims that the Latin word *usurpare* was only rarely used to mean "to usurp" and that its ordinary meaning was "to employ, to take for one's use"; it is a mistake, he says, to conclude from the use by some jurist, or by St. Ambrose, of some such phrase as *usurpatio jus fecit privatum* that he attributes to usurpation—in the modern, pejorative, meaning of the word—the origin of private property.

by proclaiming as an integral part of natural law the right of private property. Leo XIII, however, may have conceived "natural law" as including the "law of nations" or *jus gentium*, which some medieval theologians regarded as a kind of "natural law," or an evolution from "natural law," and not a category of law sharply distinct from it. An influential moral theologian, St. Alphonse Liguori (1696–1787), has been ascribed the role of so completely identifying *jus gentium* with *jus naturale* that *jus gentium*—in its medieval sense of a body of law intermediate between natural and civil law—was completely dropped from Catholic expositions of natural law.[66]

Leo XIII's important text is the encyclical *Rerum Novarum*, of May 15, 1891, but in his encyclical *Quod Apostolici Muneris* of December 28, 1878, he had already written of "the right of property, sanctioned by the law of nature," and had condemned socialists who publicly proclaim the "monstrous views" that there should be held in common "all that has been individually acquired by title of lawful inheritance, through intellectual or manual labor, or economy in living"; "the Church . . . enjoins that the right of property and of its disposal, derived from nature, should in the case of every individual remain intact and inviolate."[67]

In the *Rerum Novarum*, Leo XIII presented the doctrine that the right of private property was prior to government and rested on natural law, in terms which, in their stress on labor as constituting the original title to property, resembled closely, both in substance and wording, those used by John Locke in his *Civil Government* treatise of 1690:

Here, again, we have further proof that private ownership is in accordance with the law of nature. Truly, that which is required for the preservation of life, and for life's well-being, is produced in great abundance from the soil, but not until man has brought it into cultivation and expended upon it his solicitude and skill. Now, when man thus turns the activity of his mind and the strength of his body towards procuring the fruits of nature, by such act he makes his own that portion of nature's field which he cultivates—that portion on which he leaves, as it were, the impress of his individuality; and it cannot but be just that he should possess that portion as his very own, and have a right to hold it without any one being justified in violating that right.[68]

---

66. Wilhelm Weber, *Wirtschaftsethik am Vorabend des Liberalismus*, pp. 88–89.
67. *The Great Encyclical Letters of Pope Leo XIII*, New York, 1908, pp. 23, 30.
68. *Ibid.*, pp. 212–213.

John Locke wrote:

> Though the earth and all inferior creatures be common to all
> men, yet every man has a "property" in his own "person." . . .
> The "labor" of his body and the "work" of his hands, we may
> say, are properly his. Whatsoever, then, he removes out of the
> state that Nature hath provided and left it in, he hath mixed his
> labor with it, and joined to it something that is his own, and
> thereby makes it his property.[69]

There is no reason to suppose that Leo XIII was directly influenced by a personal knowledge of Locke's work, which in so far as it was known, generally met, and continues to meet, with a hostile reception in Catholic circles. It has been claimed, however, that a Lockean influence could have been (or was) exercised on the Pope indirectly through an Italian Jesuit theologian and social theorist, Luigi Taparelli d'Azeglio (1793–1862), with whom he had intellectual associations.[70]

Taparelli d'Azeglio does argue that there is a natural right to property, and that it arises in part out of the right of a man to the product of his labor. But he makes occupation the origin of the right, with the labor title only coming after.[71] While there are resemblances of doctrine between Taparelli and Locke, the two are not especially close except in their stress on labor. If indebted to Locke at all, Taparelli was probably influenced by him indirectly through Lacordaire, whom he cites in other connections, and who, like Leo XIII, comes close also to Locke's wording, as the following will show:

> When you have mixed your [sweat] with the land, and you have
> thus made it fertile, it belongs to you, for it has become a portion
> of yourself, an extension of your own body; it has become your
> flesh and your blood, and it is just that domain over it should rest
> with you, in order that dominion over yourself should rest with
> you.[72]

69. *Two Treatises of Civil Government* [1690], Book II, § 27, Everyman ed., p. 130, where, however, the section is wrongly numbered 26.

70. L. de Sousberghe, S.J., "Propriété de 'droit naturel,' " *Nouvelle Revue Théologique*, LXXII (1950), 580–607; Cyrill K. von Krasinski, O.S.B., "Über die Krisis des modernen Sondereigentumsbegriffes," *Freiburger Zeitschrift für Philosophie und Theologie*, I (1954), 64–87.

71. *Essai théorique de droit naturel, basé sur les faits* [1st Italian ed., 1844–45], 3rd ed., Tournai, 1883, I, 161 ff.

72. H-D. Lacordaire, *Conférences de Notre-Dame de Paris*, Vol. II [1844–1845], in *Œuvres*, Paris, 1871–1872, III, 296.

Wilhelm Weber questions the indebtedness of Leo XIII to Locke or to Taparelli—as it is argued by de Sousberghe—on the ground that modern Catholic handbooks of moral theology attribute the doctrine of a natural right to property to De Lugo. Since De Lugo preceded Locke, it is unnecessary to invoke Locke as a source. Weber seems to be overlooking, however, de Sousberghe's valid point that it was the attribution of the origin of property rights to labor, rather than to natural law, which was specially "Lockean."[73] Locke, I would add, had forerunners on this point, but they were English Protestants, and no one so far seems to have discovered a Catholic who presented the labor origin of the right to property before Locke, unless De Lugo qualifies.[74]

Charity

All the medieval moral theologians stressed the duty of almsgiving, although usually as a duty of "charity" not of "justice." This duty, however, had limits which it would be wrong to exceed when encroachment on other obligations was involved. Since the religious "merit" of alms for the donor depended on its voluntary character, the Church in the main limited itself to moral suasion, and carefully avoided prescribing precise formulae as to how much should be given. Once more, a detailed account will be given only of St. Thomas' discussion, in the belief that this is reasonably representative of late medieval teaching as a whole.

St. Thomas says that almsgiving is a matter of precept, but that the precept requires alms to be given only out of "surplus," or "superfluity." Alms also need to be given only to those in extreme need. To give beyond these limits is a matter of counsel, not precept. "Surplus" is explained as what the donor does not need for the time being, "as far as he can judge with probability," or "according as

73. *Wirtschaftsethik am Vorabend des Liberalismus*, pp. 88–90. The first edition of De Lugo's *De Justitia* was in 1642.

74. For additional discussions of the relation of the property doctrine in *Rerum Novarum* to the traditional doctrine of the Church, see an important series of articles by Auguste Onclaix, who had a part in the translation of Taparelli d'Azeglio's book into French, in *Revue Catholique des Institutions et du Droit*, 2nd series, Vols. XII and XIII; Lujo Bretano, "Zur Genealogie der Angriffe auf das Privateigentum," *Archiv für Sozialwissenschaft*, XIX (1904), 251–271; L. Garriguet, *Manuel de sociologie et d'économie sociale*, Paris, 1924, pp. 137 ff.; Canon Tiberghien, "Comment intégrer dans l'économie moderne les conceptions chrétiennes sur la propriété, le prêt à intérêt, le juste prix?" *Semaines Sociales de France*, 23rd session, Mulhouse, 1931, p. 176; W. J. Macdonald, *The Social Value of Property*, Washington, D.C., 1939, p. 158.

things probably and generally occur."[75] What a man "needs," St. Thomas explains, is what a man must have if he is to live "in keeping with his social station as regards either himself or those of whom he has charge." To go further in almsgiving would be "inordinate," for "no man ought to live unbecomingly." To give as alms what is needed "if one's life or the life of those under our charge would thereby be endangered," is "altogether wrong." But to give alms from what is not thus needed, provided enough is left "for the decencies of life in keeping with his own position," while neither precept nor counsel, is "good." He cites three cases of almsgiving to an extent that would encroach on the needs of one's status as being nevertheless commendable: (1) when a man enters a religious order; (2) when what a man deprives himself of, while required for the decencies of life, can be easily recovered; (3) "in presence of extreme indigence of an individual, or great need on the part of the common weal."[76]

The care with which St. Thomas formulates the maximum permissible as well as the minimum obligatory in alms, reverses the appeal for heroic charity and represents a change in tone, if not in formal doctrine, when compared with the position of the early Fathers. One writer at least in the Patristic period upheld the view that only an excess over needs constituted resources from which almsgiving was obligatory; but he defined "needs" much more narrowly than St. Thomas. To quote the relevant passage from a sermon often included in the works of St. Augustine but which modern scholars attribute to a somewhat later writer, St. Caesarius: "The part of your income as an official or landowner which God bestows on you in excess of what is needed for a simple and reasonable mode of life is not given to you as a true property, but as a deposit for which you are accountable to the poor." What it is permissible to retain for oneself is further restricted to "sufficient nourishment and a simple wardrobe, avoiding in everything the expenditure and the luxury which corrupt."[77]

75. *Summa Theologica*, II–II, q. 32, a. 5, and ad 3. In dealing with the charitable activities of the Church itself, St. Thomas elsewhere interprets Matt. VI. 34, "Be . . . not solicitous for the morrow" in effect as meaning "be not unduly solicitous." For he recommends that the Church, unless facing a pressing need for helping the poor, should use its surplus "in buying property, or [lay] it by for some future use connected with the Church or the needs of the poor" (*ibid.*, q. 185, a. 7). This would apply also, I presume, to individual almsgiving. If so, it could lead to a justification of reinvestment of savings from current income.

76. *Ibid.*, q. 32, a. 6. In *ibid.*, a. 10, St. Thomas says that "abundant giving" is praiseworthy; "nevertheless the conditions must be observed which were laid down when we spoke of giving alms out of one's necessary goods."

77. *De Dilectione Parentum et Dedicinis*, available in French translation in St. Au-

According to St. Thomas, alms should not be given to enable the recipient to have an easy life, or be in excess of the latter's need. In appraising need, consideration should be given to such things as age and weakness, and whether the recipient has fallen from riches to indigence through no fault of his own, "and having been more delicately nurtured, needs finer food and clothing."[78]

St. Thomas deals with lay begging only incidentally, as part of his discussion of begging by clerics, but he apparently applies substantially similar principles to both. Begging is permissible if other means of support are unavailable, or if the purpose is a useful one rather than to allow the beggar to live in idleness. "On the other hand, he lives not idly who in any way lives usefully." He apparently approves, and in any case does not expressly disapprove, of the civil legislation "which imposes a penalty on able-bodied mendicants who beg from motives neither of utility nor of necessity."[79]

St. Thomas does not deal with the practical administration of relief of the poor. He does not discuss remedial aid as contrasted with mere relief of immediate need; or the possible deleterious effects of alms on economic incentives; or whether the benefit to the poor from alms is as great as the potential benefit to them of the donors' productive investment of their "surplus." He accepts the economic and social *status quo*, as ameliorated by alms to the very poor, without express or implied criticism.

Beginning in the fourteenth (or fifteenth) century the decay of the feudal system, the prevalence of war, and other factors led to more widespread (or perhaps more conspicuous) poverty and to extensive vagabondage and systematic begging. These facts, together with widespread charges of inefficiency and laxity in the administration by the Church of its poor funds, occasionally led to the introduction of public administration of poor relief as a substitute for, or in rivalry with, the poor relief administered by Church agencies. This situation gave rise to public controversy over the principles of poor relief in which, for the first time, laics took a prominent part. In the sixteenth century, the Protestant Reformers, and especially Luther, severely criticized the almsgiving doctrines and practices of the Catholic Church, and in Protestant countries—though not only there—the civil authorities undertook much of the responsibility for poor relief. For

---

gustine, *Œuvres complètes*, Paris, 1873, Vol. XX, Appendice, ser. 4, Sermon 276, p. 523. The friendly treatment of tithes is part of the evidence which leads modern scholars to date it later than St. Augustine's time.

78. *Summa Theologica*, II–II, q. 32, a. 10, and ad 3.

79. *Ibid.*, q. 187, a. 5, and ad 2.

over a century—and again in the nineteenth century—actual and alleged differences between Catholic and Protestant doctrines and practice in the field of charity constituted a subject of polemical debate. Protestants criticized Catholic charity on many grounds: for its alleged emphasis on the sin-redeeming quality of alms and the benefits to the donor instead of the needs of the recipients; for making no distinction between "deserving" and "undeserving" poor, thereby helping to demoralize and pauperize the poor and to check economic progress; and for making a public ceremonial of the distribution of trifling alms, to the glorification of the Church and the humiliation and demoralization of the poor. Catholics retorted that the Protestant denial of the "merit" of almsgiving for salvation eliminated one of the strongest motives to generous giving; that the dissolution of the monasteries and the diversion and dissipation of their resources to non-charitable uses had deprived the poor of their greatest source of relief; that the substitution of compulsory or "legal" charity for voluntary poor relief was damaging to the essential spirit of charity; and that in general Protestant charity was lacking in warmth and inadequate in extent. Because much of the literature on the history of charity has been written in a polemical spirit, as a by-product of Catholic-Protestant controversy, or, in more recent years, in the service of "leftist" bias, historical objectivity and unprejudiced selection and interpretation of the facts are too often sadly lacking in this literature.

The approaches to poverty and its relief have varied; the following have been employed at various times and in differing combinations: (1) the ascetic idealization of the state of poverty, voluntary or involuntary, as in some sense "blessed"; (2) the recognition of a religious obligation to relieve extreme poverty, as a command of God and as "good works" which are soul-saving and sin-redeeming for the giver; (3) the acceptance of a humanitarian obligation to relieve the pain and misery of the poor; (4) the desirability for the temporal welfare of the community and/or the long-run benefit to the poor themselves of methods of poor relief that would eradicate begging and voluntary idleness and promote the will and ability of the poor to attain self-support; (5) the expediency of aid to the poor to forestall unrest and civil disturbance; (6) the balanced consideration of the relative merits of spontaneous versus organized or compulsory almsgiving, and of church versus civil authority in the administration of funds available for poor relief; (7) the belief that the poor were ordained to be so by God, or were poor as divine punishment for their sins, and that it would therefore be both an interference with Providence and wasted effort to attempt to eliminate poverty on a large scale; and finally, (8) the belief that it was necessary for the comfort and prosperity of the upper classes that the poor should on the whole remain poor. I will confine myself at this point to two issues which first attained prominence in the sixteenth century and were emphasized in Catholic versus Protestant polemics both then and later: the question whether there should be systematic discrimination between the deserving and the undeserving poor, and the question of the relative merits of ecclesiastical versus civil administration of poor relief, involving the issue of organized versus spontaneous and individual efforts to relieve the poor, and the issue of compulsory versus voluntary aid to the poor.

In the literature of the Weber-Tawney thesis on the role of Protestantism as a promoter of modern capitalism—a thesis which I deal with in considerable detail in a subsequent chapter—a humane and warm-hearted medieval Catholic doctrine of charity was contrasted with a harsh attitude to the indigent poor in Protestant doctrine and practice. Not surprisingly, some Catholic writers have welcomed this praise of the Catholic moral tradition coming from non-Catholic sources. Before the appearance of the Weber-Tawney thesis, however, some Catholic scholars were concerned to free the Catholic record from the charge of irresponsibility, sentimentality, and failure to distinguish between deserving and undeserving poor. In recent years, other Catholic scholars, writing as objective historians, have presented abundant evidence of the lack of any clear-cut difference between Protestant and Catholic practice with respect to treatment of the indigent poor.[80]

---

80. The most comprehensive histories of attitudes and practices with respect to poor relief, whose usefulness is somewhat impaired by strong bias and unobjective selection of material, are the works of two Catholic writers, Georg Ratzinger, *Geschichte der kirklichen Armenpflege*, Freiburg i.B., 1884, and Léon Lallemand, *Histoire de la charité*, 4 vols., Paris, 1902–1912. On the Protestant side, Gerhard Uhlhorn, *Christian Charity in the Ancient Church*, tr. from the German, New York, 1883, suffers from an extreme anti-Catholic bias. Noteworthy for their historical solidity and objectivity are the more special studies of Berrat Saint-Prix, "Recherches sur le paupérisme en France au XVIe siècle," *Mémoires de l'Académie Royale des Sciences Morales et Politiques de l'Institut de France*, IV (1844), 513–538; Franz Ehrle, S.J., *Beiträge zur Geschichte und Reform der Armenpflege, Ergänzungshefte zu den Stimmen aus Maria-Laach*, No. 17, Freiburg i.B., 1881; Brian Tierney, *Medieval Poor Law*, Berkeley, 1959. Some representative items in the early English polemics on the Protestant side are: John Stockwood, *A Very Fruitful Sermon Preached at Paules Crosse*, London, 1578/9; Andrew Willett, *Synopsis Papismi, That Is, a General View of Papistry*, London, 1592; [James Harrington], *Some Reflexions upon a Treatise Called Pietas Romana et Parisensis*, Oxford, 1688; Thomas Tenison, *A Sermon Concerning Discretion in Giving Alms*, 2nd ed., 1688. W. K. Jordan, *Philanthropy in England, 1480–1660*, London, 1959, is valuable for historical background and bibliography, and especially for the comparison of pre-Reformation and

Some of the Catholic saints and mystics of the Middle Ages no doubt preached and practiced undiscriminating charity. It may well be that there is no close parallel to this, or to papal scattering of coins and other similar church practices on special occasions, in Protestantism. But it seems a valid generalization that any such major differences as did exist between Catholicism and Protestantism with respect to charity and the treatment of the poor can be more plausibly explained in terms of differences in time and circumstance than in terms of differences in fundamental doctrine.

On the question of discrimination between the deserving and undeserving, we have seen that the Christian Fathers advocated some discrimination.[81] The issue became a pressing one from the fourteenth century on, when the dissolution of feudalism and other factors, which were accentuated in Protestant countries by the dissolution of the monasteries, gave rise to conspicuous increases in the extent of begging, pauperism, and vagabondage. From at least 1350 on, ordinances were issued in France and other countries against mendicity; habitual beggars were pilloried, marked on the forehead with a red-hot iron, and so on.[82] From early in the sixteenth century, heavy penalties were imposed on able-bodied beggars in the Papal States.[83] The English record of harshness in dealing with the able-bodied vagrant or beggar both before and after the Reformation is too familiar to need documentation here. What calls for notice is that harshness did not begin with the Reformation, since parallel practice was present at some times and in some parts of Catholic Europe after the Reformation.

In the first half of the sixteenth century, important innovations in the methods of dealing with pauperism were made in a number of towns, beginning apparently in some German Lutheran towns, especially Nuremberg, in 1522, but also in Ypres (possibly influenced by the German experiments) in 1525.[84] The innovations were an in-

---

post-Reformation attitudes; H. R. Trevor-Roper, *Historical Essays*, London, 1957, pp. 128–129, provides some additional bibliographical references. On the English Catholic side, note Robert Parsons, *A Memorial of the Reformation of England*, 1596, and [John Gother] *Good Advice to the Public*, London, 1687, an ironic reply to Tenison's anti-Catholic treatise.

81. See Ch. 1, pp. 23–25 above.

82. See Léon Lallemand, *Histoire de la charité*, III, 342–352, IV, 175–181, 187–189, 197–199; Berrat Saint-Prix, "Recherches sur le paupérisme," *op. cit.* n.80, pp. 517–521.

83. Léon Lallemand, *Histoire de la charité à Rome*, Paris, 1878, pp. 71–90; Jean Dulameau, *Vie économique et sociale de Rome dans la seconde moitié du XVIe siècle*, Paris, 1959, I, 404, 411.

84. See J. Nolf, *La Réforme de la bienfaisance publique à Ypres, au XVIe siécle*,

creased role of the State in poor relief activities; the introduction of workshops and other means of providing employment, even on a compulsory basis in the case of the voluntarily idle; and the use of state funds for poor relief on a systematic and continuing basis.

In 1526, Juan-Luis Vives, a Spanish Catholic humanist, submitted a memoir to the senate of the town of Bruges which contained, perhaps for the first time, a systematic discussion of the problem of pauperism and the merits of the alternative institutional arrangements available or conceivable for dealing with it. Vives criticized in sharp and unfriendly terms the quality of administration of the poor-relief activities of the Catholic Church. He recommended that the civic authorities should take over all administrative responsibility, rigorously suppress lay mendicity, provide organized and assured relief for the needy, provide work facilities for the able-bodied indigent, and provide education for the children of the poor—all of this to be financed not from taxes but from voluntary gifts. He explained his objectives as follows:

> We are not to chase away the poor, but to rescue them from their abject state, to restore to them their quality of manhood and thus render them worthy of alms. We will not suppress poverty, but relieve it. If, as is impossible, we could abolish the poverty of monetary resources [i.e., unemployment of the able-bodied?], there would always remain the poor in strength, health or mind who would need help. But it is those who are poor in resources whom we are to assist, whether in special institutions or in their miserable dwellings.[85]

In 1531 an edict of Charles V provided for a large measure of centralization of poor-relief administration in the Spanish Low Countries under joint civil and ecclesiastical jurisdiction. A Bruges poor-relief project of 1562, somewhat along the lines of Vives' memoir of

University of Ghent, *Recueil des travaux publiées par la faculté de Philosophie et Lettres*, 45e fascicule, Ghent (Gand), 1915.

85. Cited from Vives, in M. Bataillon, "J. L. Vives, réformateur de la bienfaisance," *Bibliothèque d'Humanisme et Renaissance*, XIV (1952), 141–158, at p. 156. See also P. Bonenfant, "Les origines et le caractère de la réforme de la bienfaisance publique aux Pays-Bas sous le règne de Charles Quint," *Revue Belge de Philosophie et d'Histoire*, V (1926), 887–904, VI (1927), 207–230. A Spanish translator of Vives' memoir commented that it was Vives' aim "that the workshops should not lack hands and that the poor should not lack workshops." See M. Bataillon, *op. cit.*, p. 148. "Concerning the Relief of the Poor," New York School of Philanthropy, *Studies in Social Work*, No. 11, Feb. 1917, is an English translation of a portion of Vives' memoir by Margaret Sherwood.

1526, was both attacked and defended by theologians.[86] In France, England, and Holland, the sixteenth century was marked by a shift of responsibility for poor relief from the church to local government agencies, and by legislation to suppress and penalize vagabondage and begging as a social evil.[87]

Modern commentators have tried to find a sharply divergent trend in these sixteenth-century events, with the Protestant countries moving more rapidly and drastically than the Catholic countries towards transfer of administration of poor relief from ecclesiastical to civic agencies, and towards harsher and more vindictive measures against the able-bodied poor. The evidence does seem to show that in the Catholic countries ecclesiastics took a prominent part in scrutinizing and proposing amendments to the new measures. They insisted on maintaining the permission to beg, for example, where adequate provision for relief by other means was not guaranteed. By contrast, in Protestant countries the churches had lost their traditional functions and authority with respect to organized charitable activities and played little or no part in the framing of the new measures. Except for one unique feature of English poor-law legislation (the establishment of legal rights for the poor who met certain qualifications to claim relief from public funds derived from special local poor relief taxes), the following verdict by Brian Tierney on England seems to apply to western and northern Europe as a whole, whether Catholic or Protestant:

> From the reception of Gratian's *Decretum* in the mid-twelfth century to the final codification of the Elizabethan poor law in 1601, a single developing tradition without any sudden break or reversal of policy can be traced. Even the substitution of secular coercion for ecclesiastical coercion was a gradual business; the process began in the fourteenth century and was not quite complete by the end of Elizabeth's reign. . . . The most important new element in Tudor poor law, apart from the changes in administrative machinery, lay in its attempts to develop a constructive approach to the problem of the able-bodied unemployed from 1536

86. See Ehrle, *Beiträge*, pp. 52–55; and Canon de Ram "Opinions des théologiens de Louvain sur la répression administrative de la mendicité, en 1562 et 1565," *Bulletins de l'Académie Royale des Sciences, des Lettres et des Beaux Arts de Belgique*, XXII (1855), 256–277.

87. For France, as an additional reference see J. Besse, "Hospitaliers," in *Dictionnaire de théologie catholique*, VII, 193; for England, see W. J. Ashley, *Economic History of England*, London, 1893, Vol. I, Part II, pp. 305–376; for Holland, see Christine Ligtenberg, *De Armezog te Leiden tot het Einde van de 16e Eeuw*, The Hague, 1908.

onward; and likewise, the greatest defect in canonistic theories of poor relief at the end of the Middle Ages was their failure to deal with this problem.[88]

Just Price

Before the Scholastics there was no significant discussion of the criteria of a just price. The canon law codes simply adopted the doctrine of the early Fathers that to sell at a higher price than that at which one had bought was unlawful. To some this doctrine seemed equivalent—quite wrongly, the economist would be obliged to say— to the view that a fair exchange involved an exchange of two things of equal value. If there was not to be radical conflict between moral teaching and the elementary requirements of economic process in an economy in which goods were produced for a market and in which middlemen were an essential link between the grower or craftsman and the ultimate user, it was necessary for moral theologians to discover the social usefulness of the middleman's activities and to recognize that the middleman's incentive to render his vital services depended on a margin between the price at which he bought and the price at which he sold, without which it would be impossible for him to meet his incidental costs and subsistence. The Scholastics gradually performed this task of economic analysis by recognizing the legitimacy of the seller's expectations that the prices he could obtain would on average cover all the cost elements which a modern economist would list—with the exception of certain kinds of interest regarded by the Scholastics as usurious.[89]

Whatever measure of economic understanding of the price-making process the Scholastics achieved was as an incidental by-product of

---

88. *Medieval Poor Law*, p. 132. W. J. Ashley, *op. cit.*, p. 350, had long before reached a similar conclusion that the poor law of Elizabeth "was but the English phase of a general European movement of reform. It was not called for by anything peculiar to England either in its economic development up to the middle of the sixteenth century, or in its ecclesiastical history."

89. There are accounts of the contribution of the Scholastics to the economic analysis of price determination in all the references given in note 52 above, and also in the standard histories of economic doctrine. Special studies of value are Henri Garnier, *De l'idée du juste prix*, Paris, 1900; Lewis Watt, S.J., "The Theory Lying Behind the Historical Conception of the Just Price," in V. A. Denant, ed., *The Just Price*, London, 1930, pp. 60–75; Selma Hagenauer, *Das justum pretium bei Thomas von Aquino*, Stuttgart, 1931 (some highly speculative interpretations are presented); Armando Sapori, "Il giusto prezzo nella dottrina de San Tommaso e nella pratica del suo tempo," *Archivo Storico Italiano*, 7th series, XVIII (1932), 1–56; A. Sandoz, "La notion du juste prix," *Revue Thomiste*, XLV (1939), 291 ff.; John W. Baldwin, "The Medieval Theories of the Just Price . . . in the Twelfth and Thirteenth Centuries," *Transactions of the American Philosophical Society*, n.s., XLIX (1959), Part IV.

their concern with "commutative justice." Thus St. Thomas discusses just price in the *Summa* under the heading of "cheating"; that is, in a section in which he is primarily interested in violations of the "just price," as one of four kinds of sin connected with "voluntary commutations" or transactions concerning temporal goods between pairs of individuals, the other three being usury, rapine, and theft. As before, it will be convenient to concentrate on the exposition of the relevant doctrine by St. Thomas.

With respect to the lawfulness of selling a good above its original purchase price, St. Thomas says that the intended gain from trading becomes licit if directed to some necessary or even virtuous end. "Thus, for instance, a man may intend the moderate gain which he seeks to acquire by trading for the upkeep of his household, or for the assistance of the needy, or . . . for some public advantage, for instance, lest his country lack the necessaries of life, and seek gain, not as an end, but as payment for his labour." He interprets St. Augustine's comment on Psalm LXXI.15[90] as a condemnation of the vices of men and not of trading activity as such.[91]

For the non-tradesmen—those who had not originally bought in order to resell—he lists other conditions, not related to subsequent ends or intentions, but economic in character, which legitimate sales at higher than buying prices:

> Not everyone that sells at a higher price than he bought is a tradesman, but only he who buys that he may sell at a profit. If, on the contrary, he buys not for sale but for possession, and afterwards, for some reason wishes to sell, it is not a trade transaction even if he sell at a profit. For he may lawfully do this, either because he has bettered the thing, or because the value of the thing has changed with the change of place or time, or on account of the danger he incurs in transferring the thing from one place to another, or again in having it carried by another.[92]

If St. Thomas is here expounding a strictly economic justification for profit by the non-professional trader, and a strictly non-economic justification for profit by the professional trader, resting on the moral quality of the merchant's intention, then I cannot find that later Scholastics followed him in this distinction except in accepting Aristotle's simple distinction between the pure middleman and the craftsman or processor.

90. See above, Ch. 1, p. 35.
91. *Summa Theologica*, II–II, q. 77, a. 4.
92. *Ibid.*, ad 2.

It is also, of course, a condition of lawful gain from trade that the means used shall be honest. To the objection that the civil (i.e., Roman) law permits the buyer and seller to "deceive" one another, and that therefore "it is lawful to sell a thing for more than it is worth," St. Thomas replies that it is impracticable for human law to forbid all that is contrary to virtue. "Accordingly, if without employing deceit the seller disposes of his goods for more than their worth, or the buyer obtains them for less than their worth, the [civil] law looks upon this as licit [within limits]."[93] Under divine law, however, "he who has received more than he ought must make compensation to him that has suffered loss." Since, however, the just price of things is not fixed with mathematical precision, but rather depends on a kind of estimate, "the compensation is required only if the loss be considerable."[94] Again, this last qualification reconciles moral law with civil law.

Commenting on a passage in St. Augustine, at one point, St. Thomas encounters a "scale of value" issue with reference to just prices. St. Augustine had acknowledged that market prices conform to the usefulness to man of the things sold rather than to "their degree of nature," so that a horse sometimes fetches a higher price than a slave. St. Augustine stated this as a fact of life, and as shown by the earlier quotation from the relevant passage,[95] apparently accepted it, both as just and inevitable. With express acknowledgment to St. Augustine, St. Thomas accepts this reasoning, thereby, in effect, postulating the ethical priority of the market scale of values, or the scale of usefulness to man, over the ontological scale according to "degree of nature":

Hence it is not necessary for the seller or buyer to be cognizant of the hidden qualities of the thing sold, but only of such as

93. *Ibid.*, a. 1, with a reference to I–II, q. 97, a. 2, where, as elsewhere, St. Thomas accepts the practical limits of what civil law can achieve as proper limits to what it should attempt, even in the interests of virtue. "Deceit" is probably used here to mean mistaken evaluation as well as, or rather than, deliberate deception. In the Roman law of sales, deliberate deception was at least as much condemned as in modern systems of law, but the exercise of trading skill was not interfered with. See F. De Zulueta, *The Roman Law of Sale*, Oxford, 1945, p. 19; W. W. Buckland and Arnold McNair, *Roman Law and Common Law*, 2nd ed., Cambridge, Eng., 1952, p. 211. St. Thomas seems to have understood this perfectly. He is appealing to practical good sense and is not being "lax." For St. Thomas' essentially friendly attitude toward Roman law as expounded by the glossators of his time, see Jean-Marie Aubert, *Le Droit romain dans l'œuvre de Saint Thomas*, Paris, 1955, pp. 131–139.

94. *Summa Theologica*, II–II, q. 77, a. 2.

95. See above, pp. 55–56.

render the thing adapted to man's use, for instance, that the horse be strong, run well and so forth.[96]

St. Thomas did not discuss by what means buyers and sellers could determine the just price. He stated that the civil authorities must "determine the just measures [i.e., units of weight, volume, etc.] of things saleable, with due consideration for the conditions of place and time"; and that it was not lawful to disregard such measures. Given just measures, he thought that buyers and sellers could readily discover the qualities of commodities that were relevant to their value.[97]

St. Thomas' doctrine that commutative justice requires equality of value between the things exchanged by individuals in commercial transactions is often interpreted as requiring "equal benefit to both parties" or "equal advantage."[98] No confirmation of this, I think, is to be found in the writings of St. Thomas or other Scholastics, all of whom expected prices to be the same for all buyers. An equality of objective value, or value "by common estimation," is all that commutative justice requires.[99] To require equality of benefit would demand knowledge that is not accessible, with any notable precision, to anyone. It would call for differences in prices for the same commodity in the same market according to the personality and needs of the individual buyer and seller. Thus it would make the "common estimate" of the market irrelevant and would be utterly unenforceable. The Scholastics were better economists than those who attribute such doctrine to them.

Some of the early Scholastics, perhaps especially nominalists, held that the just price must reap a sufficient yield to the craftsman or the merchant to maintain his customary standard of living, and some of them advocated official fixing of prices in accordance with this criterion. Until fairly recently, it was commonly believed that this was the prevailing doctrine among the Scholastics. It has been convincingly demonstrated, however, that, at least for the later Scholastics, the dominant criterion of the just price was the "common estimate," which was the price that would be reached under normal

96. *Summa Theologica*, II–II, q. 77, a. 2, ad 3. This became standard doctrine for the later Scholastics, and economic value theory, as later developed by economists, takes its validity for granted.

97. *Ibid.*, ad 2 and ad 3.

98. As one of many examples, see Kenneth E. Kirk, *Conscience and Its Problems*, London, 1927, p. 198.

99. St. Thomas' most precise definition of commutative justice in market transactions seems to be that given in *Scriptum Super Sententiis Magistri Petri Lombardi*, super lib. iii, dist. 33, q. 3, a. 4, solutio 5, M. F. Moos, ed., Paris, 1956, XXX, f 1101.

conditions in a competitive market as a result of the bids and offers by buyers and sellers. In keeping with this doctrine, the Scholastics uniformly condemned all private monopolies and were unenthusiastic about official ones. Advocacy of price regulation thus gave way to advocacy of regulation of the functioning of market institutions in the interest of fair competition. In this way, the doctrine of the just price lost most of whatever practical importance it may have had earlier as a justification for state, guild, or ecclesiastical interference with routine free-market, or competitive, processes. It retained doctrinal importance and practical value as a restraint on monopoly and as a guide for dealing with disputes in cases where there was no ascertainable market price, and where abnormal conditions, such as famine or siege, seemed to justify interference with ordinary market processes. But, except in the case of usury, the traditional questioning of the legitimacy of ordinary trading profits and of the role of the middleman had almost completely disappeared from treatises on moral theology by the seventeenth century.[100]

Usury

Throughout the Scholastic period, and thereafter until the first half of the nineteenth century, when socialism became an urgent problem, the usury issue was by far the most important and most debated economic issue in Catholic doctrine.[101] It was the only church doc-

---

100. On "just price" as competitive market price, see Joseph Höffner, *Wirtschaftsethik und Monopole*, Jena, 1914, and *ibid.*, "Statik und Dynamik in der scholastischen Wirtschaftsethik," *Arbeitsgemeinschaft für Forschung des Landes Nordrhein-Westfalen Geisteswissenschaften*, Cologne, 1955, Heft 38; Raymond de Roover, "Monopoly Theory Prior to Adam Smith: A Revision," *Quarterly Journal of Economics*, LXV (1951), 492, 524, and *idem*, "La doctrine scolastique en matière de monopole," a paper to be included in a forthcoming volume of essays in honor of Amintore Fanfani, an advance copy of which the author has kindly made available to me [editors' note: The exact reference is "La doctrine scolastique en matière de monopole et son application à la politique économique des communes italiennes," *Studi in onore di Amintore Fanfani*, Milan, Dott. A. Giuffrè, 1962, I]; Wilhelm Weber (a student of Höffner), *Wirtschaftsethik am Vorabend des Liberalismus*, pp. 99–143. Abbé Manuel Rocha, *Travail et salaire à travers la scolastique*, Paris, 1933, presents material which seems to me to justify a similar interpretation of "just wages" as those competitively set in a well-functioning market. Vernon A. Mund, *Open Markets: An Essential of Free Enterprise*, New York, 1948, p. 46, cites an English tract of 1636 as appealing to the maxim, *emporium est optima aestimatrix rerum*. It would be interesting to know the origin of this maxim.

101. As Victor Brants has said, the theory of usury in a manner dominated the economic life of the Middle Ages (*L'Economie politique au moyen-âge*, p. 31). It is not surprising, therefore, that the literature, primary and secondary, on the Scholastic doctrine on usury is of immense proportions. The references given above in n.52 all deal with the Scholastic texts, and some of them deal also with sections of the more recent secondary literature. An extensive bibliography, of both primary sources

trine with important economic relevance which gave rise to serious tension between the Church and the world of commerce and finance. On practically all other matters relating to commercial activity, church doctrine was stated in such abstract or general terms as would not in practice give rise to problems for respectable businessmen. The Church either tolerated practices sanctioned by the civil law, even when it did not expressly or implicitly approve of them, or it spoke in terms of counsel and not precept. This was not the case with usury, where the Church was able to make its precepts effective in practice by bringing about changes in the form, if not always the economic substance, of transactions with explicit or implicit time-dimensions.

The moral theologians based their condemnation of usury first, on biblical texts with a clear or imputed rigorist bias; second, on church tradition; third, on "natural law" as expounded by the Greek and Roman pagan philosophers and thereafter by the doctors of the Church; and fourth, though in a lesser way, on reasoning as to the economic consequences for society of the practice of usury.

The biblical texts to which appeal was made were, with one exception, all in the Old Testament. The exception can be found in Luke VI.35, translated in the Vulgate as "Lend, hoping for nothing thence" (Mutuum date, nihil inde sperantes); it was interpreted as precept and as signifying that loans should be interest-free. With respect to the Old Testament, the Church did not exercise its customary discretion in deciding which Old Testament precepts continued to be mandatory under the new covenant. In the thirteenth century, Aristotle first became directly available through translation of some of his works into Latin, and as far as the form of presentation of the usury doctrine was concerned, he at once became a powerful and, as far as I can see, completely unfortunate influence.

Taken from Roman law were the concept of a *mutuum*, or a loan contract with interest stipulations attached, sometimes called a *foenum*, and the distinction between "fungibles," which lose their identity in or are destroyed or transformed by use, and "non-fungibles," which are not destroyed or transformed by use. In modern discussions of the Scholastic doctrine of usury the distinction between

---

and lay and clerical commentaries, is given in Benjamin N. Nelson, *The Idea of Usury*, Princeton, 1949, pp. 167–220. The most useful survey of the Scholastic doctrine, combining thorough acquaintance with the primary source material and familiarity with modern economic analysis, is John T. Noonan, Jr., *The Scholastic Analysis of Usury*, Cambridge, Mass., 1957. E. Van Roey (later a cardinal), "La monnaie d'après Saint Thomas d'Aquin," *Revue Néo-Scolastique*, XII (1905), 27–54, 207–238, is to my mind the most ingenious and subtle of the modern defenses of St. Thomas' usury doctrine on analytical or intellectual grounds.

fungibles and non-fungibles is often identified with the distinction between consumers' goods and producers' goods. Moreover, on the assumption that those who borrow for consumption are typically poor, the medieval doctrine is interpreted as being chiefly concerned with loans by rich men to the needy poor. There is no basis for this view in the Roman law use of the terms, nor, as far as I have been able to determine, in the Scholastics' interpretation of their own doctrine. Not only consumption goods but also some kinds of production goods, such as seed corn, feedstuffs for beasts of burden, and fuel, are destroyed or transformed by use. Roman law and the Scholastics both regarded grain, for example, as a fungible, whether it was used as seed corn, as feedstuff for work cattle, or as food for man. The Scholastics did not base the distinction between fungibles and non-fungibles on the view that it corresponded, even roughly, to the distinction between poor and rich, or between use for consumption and use in production. They emphasized, instead, that fungibles could not, whereas non-fungibles could, ordinarily be the subject of a lease as distinguished from a sale. In a transaction involving a non-fungible, a house, say, or a horse, there can be transfer of possession (with right of use) without transfer of ownership (*dominium*); but in the case of fungibles, grain, for example, transfer of possession (with right of use) normally is inseparable from transfer of ownership. A house, therefore, can be either leased or sold, but the right to use grain can be transferred only by sale or by gift of the grain, or else by a loan in kind where repayment will not be in the identical kernels of grain lent, but in their equivalent in weight or volume. The unique feature of Scholastic usury doctrine, therefore, is the tremendous moral significance attached to the form of transaction as between a sale, a loan, and a lease.[102]

A key element in the Scholastic doctrine of usury was the classification of money as normally a "fungible." Money could be loaned, but not leased. If a house was leased, the same house would be returned to its owner at the termination of the lease; when money was lent, what was returned was a generically equivalent amount of money, but not the identical coins that had been lent, as would be the case if money could be "leased." Also, money, like fungibles in general, was "destroyed" or "transformed" immediately upon its receipt by the borrower, that is, it normally did not remain unaltered

102. For the distinction in Roman law between "fungibles" and "non-fungibles," see Charles P. Sherman, *Roman Law in the Modern World*, Boston, 1917, II, 143–144.

in his possession as a house he had rented would.*

The Roman law distinctions between ownership and possession, sale and lease, fungibles and non-fungibles were presumably developed to serve a practical purpose, namely to help in framing convenient and uniform legal rules for the identification of rights and obligations under contracts and implied contracts. The Scholastics thus took distinctions peculiar to Rome law, and originally designed to provide a uniform basis for legally determining ownership of particular assets, and used them as criteria for deciding whether particular transactions were just or moral, irrespective of mutual profitability to the parties directly involved or the impact on third parties or the community at large. Some modern economists of high standing, most notably Lord Keynes and Joseph Schumpeter, have found economic significance in the distinctions of the Scholastics. But the reasons they give seem strange to me and I venture to say would not have been less so to the Scholastics. There may be a sound economic or ethical case against what the Scholastics condemned as usury, but if so, this case weighs equally against a whole array of practices involving implicit interest to which Scholastic doctrine gave full or qualified sanction. Leaving dogma aside, in their usury doctrine the Scholastics either condemned too much or condemned too little.

I will base my exposition of the Scholastic usury doctrine almost wholly on St. Thomas' formulation, which represents the doctrine at an advanced, though not at its fully developed, stage. Except for the material available in the *Summa*, I will rely in the main on secondary sources.

Based on the distinction between fungibles and non-fungibles, St. Thomas constructed what, according to Noonan, was an original argument to the effect that to charge interest on a loan of fungibles is to require two payments for one thing, or to require payment for a non-existing thing. In effect, the argument is that a money loan is a sale of money, for which the repayment of the loan is full compensation. To charge interest, therefore, is to demand payment both for the thing sold and for its use.[103] In the nature of such transactions, however, the borrower pays for the "use" only as long as he has failed to

---

* Editors' note: N. 104 makes it clear that J. V. does not subscribe to this statement himself. The assertion evidently means that the borrower ordinarily spends any borrowed money immediately.

103. In the *Summa* the doctrine is barely indicated (II–II, q. 78, a. 1, ad 3) but it is acknowledged that the civil law sanctions this double payment, as a matter of expediency. Noonan calls it St. Thomas' "chief argument" and gives a translation of a fuller statement of it in *De Malo*, q. 13, a. 4c (*The Scholastic Analysis of Usury*, pp. 53–54).

pay for the "purchase"; he and the lender regard the interest as a payment for the lapse of time during which the lender of the money has surrendered the use of it to the borrower without receiving *anything* in return, unless there is interest.[104]

St. Thomas presents as another argument for the unlawfulness of interest on loans of money that the transaction involves an "unnatural" use of money:

> Now money, according to the Philosopher . . . was invented chiefly for the purpose of exchange; and consequently the proper and principal use of money is its consumption or alienation whereby it is sunk in exchange. Hence it is by its very nature unlawful to take payment for the use of money lent, which payment is known as usury.[105]

This is an "ontological" or "finalistic" type of argument, directly derived from Aristotle. Aristotle's doctrine is that "Nature" makes each separate thing for a separate end; nothing contrary to nature is right; and the use of a thing for something other than its purpose in nature is "improper." The proper function of money is to act as a medium of exchange. To use it to acquire more money is therefore an improper use. An example of this impropriety is its use in trade ("retail trade") in order to acquire more money (or wealth in general). Lending of money at interest is an extreme form of the improper use of money to acquire more money. As an additional argument, Aristotle held that the introduction of money opened the way to the unlimited pursuit of wealth, or avarice. This argument was also adopted by the Scholastics, but their main borrowing from Aristotle was the argument that each commodity had a single proper use. Aristotle's statement of the argument is as follows:

> Of everything which we possess there are two uses: both belong to the thing as such, but not in the same manner, for one is the

104. For the Scholastic treatment of the special case where money was borrowed to be held for display (*ad pompam*) instead of to be exchanged for something else, see below, p. 90. Another use of money which does not involve immediate transfer to someone else by the borrower is its use for "liquidity" or "cash balance" purposes, which is economically as "productive" a use as any other use of other kinds of capital assets. This was not recognized by the Scholastics and is overlooked even by many modern critics of the Scholastic usury doctrine. Even in terms of its own logic, the Scholastic case against interest on money loans would collapse if interest was charged only on such part of the loan as was left as a liquidity balance in the hands of the borrower. Perhaps "liquidity" is what St. Thomas meant when he included "security" as one of the objectives of loans *ad pompam*.

105. *Summa Theologica*, II, q. 78, a. 1.

proper, and the other the improper or secondary use of it. For example, a shoe is used for wear, and is used for exchange; both are uses of the shoe. He who gives a shoe in exchange for money or food to him who wants one, does indeed use the shoe as a shoe, but this is not its proper or primary purpose, for a shoe is not made to be an object of barter.[106]

St. Thomas silently deviated from Aristotle's doctrine on two points of some importance. Aristotle had condemned usury as an extreme example of trade for profit, or an activity which was improper as a whole. St. Thomas, helped perhaps by an error in the first Latin translations of Aristotle, which gave "money changing" as the meaning of the Greek word for trade, confined to usury the condemnation which Aristotle levelled at all trade for profit. Secondly, whereas Aristotle stated as a general rule that each thing had only a single "proper" use, St. Thomas followed him in this as far as money was concerned. With respect to other things he frequently, perhaps universally, accepted as lawful, though inferior, "secondary" or "subsidiary" uses. Even in the case of money, St. Thomas recognized one secondary use as licit, namely, its use by the borrower for purposes of display (ad pompam), and hence accepted the levy of a charge for such use as lawful.[107]

Aristotle's special application to usury of his "ontological" doctrine about the use of money is as follows:

The most hated sort [of "unnatural" moneymaking], and with the greatest reason, is usury, which makes a gain out of money itself, and not from the natural use of it. For money was intended to be used in exchange, but not to increase at interest. And this term usury (tokos), which means the birth of money from money, is applied to the breeding of money because the offspring resembles the parent. Wherefore of all modes of making money this is the most unnatural.[108]

106. *Politics*, I.9, 1257, Benjamin Jowett, tr., *The Politics of Aristotle*, Oxford, 1885, I, 15. The word "barter" in Jowett's translation varies in its meaning: "barter" may be sometimes employed improperly to mean "use for purpose of profit or gain."

107. *Summa Theologica*, II–II, q. 78, a. 1, ad 6. Noonan reports a passage in *De Malo*, q. 13, ad 15, which apparently makes it clearer than the passage in the *Summa* (at least as translated) that not only is it licit to lend money for a secondary use such as display but also to treat it as a lease for which a charge can be made (*The Scholastic Analysis of Usury*, pp. 55–56). Does this mean that if the borrower diverts the money to another use, a "fungible" one, the lender must cancel the "rental" charge?

108. *Politics*, I.10, 1258b. According to Jowett, *The Dialogues of Plato*, New York, n.d., II, 257, *tokos* has the meaning both of "offspring" and interest, and Plato played with this double meaning. If Aristotle also did so, such play with words has had an unusually important role in usury doctrine, as have also mistranslations.

It should be noted that Aristotle does not say that money is "barren"—that it cannot "breed"—but that breeding is "unnatural" for it. In the history of usury doctrine, the dictum appears in either form,[109] and St. Thomas uses both.[110]

The "proper use of money" argument against loans at interest became standard in Scholastic doctrine.[111] It was taken over by many who were neither Scholastics nor sympathetic to them: Pascal used it against the "laxists"; some early Protestant theologians accepted it; and as an application of "natural law" reasoning, it still carries weight with some when applied in other fields. I have found only one instance of rejection by a Scholastic of this mode of reasoning on the ground that it was not rational. Soto, in the sixteenth century, ridiculed Aristotle's use of the argument, including his shoe illustration of the "natural" and "unnatural" uses of things.[112] In addition to Soto, a few theologians in the Scholastic period, and a larger number later, have adhered to the condemnation of usury on dogmatic grounds while conceding that they found no support for the condemnation on natural law grounds. These authors were presumably not persuaded of the validity of the Aristotelian mode of argument, or at least of the correctness of its application in the case of usury.[113]

---

109. See Edwin Cannan and others, "Who said 'Barren Metal'?" *Economica*, II (1922), 105–111.

110. Thus, St. Thomas says, in *Summa Theologica*, II–II, q. 78, a. 1, ad 3: "The Philosopher, led by natural reason, says that 'to make money by usury is exceedingly unnatural.'" Edward Schreiber, *Die volkswirtschaftlichen Anschauungen der Scholastik*, p. 101, reports St. Thomas as speaking of the sterility of money in *In commentum in . . . Sententarium*, and *Summa* II–II, q. 61, a. 3c.

111. In what Noonan calls the first special treatise on usury, Gilles of Lessines, an immediate disciple of St. Thomas, made use of the argument in its Aristotelian and Thomist form, but also gave it what may have been an original twist by applying it to the act of lending as distinguished from the money lent: a loan is an act of "liberality" by its nature, and it is therefore illegitimate to exact an interest payment for it from the borrower (*De usuris*, in *Opuscules de Saint Thomas d'Acquin*, Vedrine, etc., trs., Paris, 1858, VII, 575–581, 641. This work was often published in collections of St. Thomas' works in the belief that it was by St. Thomas). Concerning Gilles of Lessines, see Noonan, *The Scholastic Analysis of Usury*, p. 62.

112. I depend here on William T. Cortelyou, *Banking Profit*, Washington, D.C., p. 135.

113. The impropriety of using things for other than their "natural purpose" has also been one of the elements of the Catholic case against birth control. The symposium "Birth Control: The Perverted Faculty Argument," *Ecclesiastical Review*, LXXXI (1929), 54–79, illustrates an extreme use of this form of argument and includes a questioning of its validity. As I understand it, "perverted faculty" and Thomist and Aristotelian "improper use" are identical ideas. In his exposition of the "perverted faculty" argument at this symposium, an English Jesuit, H. Davis, insisted that it obscures the issue to give consideration to "love, justice, economics, hardships, overburdened wives, and devitalized mothers" (*ibid.*, pp. 54–55). An

92

In Aristotle's treatment of usury the implication is that there is an exclusive association of "productivity" with fertility, biologically conceived, in a sense which makes it morally or economically meritorious. This implication probably antedates Aristotle. It is easily understood as the outcome of naive or unsophisticated observation, and it survives to the present day in much popular economic thinking. In fact, of course, "productivity" in the sense of contribution to either private or community material wealth or income, has no simple, unidirectional relationship to biological fertility. Much of "production" takes the form of suppressing, restricting, or countering the deleterious effects of biological fertility; as, for example, in campaigns against weeds, brush, pernicious insects, and malignant bacteria. As in the case of human "labor" or "work," biological fertility contributes to a useful social product only if it takes, or is forced into taking, appropriate forms, degrees, location, and timing. The progress of economic analysis has consisted in substantial measure in the fuller perception of this fact, and in the appreciation of its many and complex ramifications. The Scholastics made some contribution to this progress, but it would have been greater and come sooner if they had followed the lead of the Roman jurists in recognizing both *fructus civiles* and *fructus naturales*, instead of following Aristotle in making a morally significant distinction between "natural" and "unnatural" fertility.

St. Thomas accepts the legitimacy of a return on investment in a "society" or partnership on the grounds that there is no transfer of ownership by the investor and that he shares in the risk:

> [Unlike the lender of money] he that entrusts his money to a merchant or craftsman so as to form a kind of society, does not transfer the ownership of his money to them, for it remains his, so that at his risk the merchant speculates with it, or the craftsman uses it for his craft, and consequently he may lawfully demand as something belonging to him, part of the profits derived from his money.[114]

To maintain that ownership (*dominium*) of the actual money is not transferred when an individual invests in a "society"—especially a society of many members—requires a "legal fiction" of the kind

American participant in the symposium replied: "The perverted faculty argument is intrinsic and metaphysical. If its force is not immediately and intuitively perceived it cannot be made convincing through any processes of argumentation" (*ibid.*, p. 70).

114. *Summa Theologica*, II–II, q. 78, a. 2, ad 5.

which the Scholastics, and St. Thomas in particular, firmly refused to apply to loans. But "money" invested in a partnership or society is at least as "fungible" as money lent at interest. The investor in a society acquires in return for his "money" another kind of property, an equity in the assets of the society (which predominantly do not consist of "money"), and a contractual share in the profits. In practice, moreover, the sharing of the profits and risks was not then, and is not today, strictly proportional to the investment, even after deducting an allowance for the services of the active managers and operators of the enterprise from the "profits."[115] Besides neglecting this point, the Scholastics commonly leave out of account both the risk to the lender that he will not regain his principal, and the fact that the lender, unlike the investor in a partnership, accepts a ceiling to the amount of gain he can receive.

St. Thomas treats the just price as identical for cash sales and credit sales. On this ground, he holds that the sale of commodities for deferred payment at a price higher than the cash price is usury, though he finds no usury on the part of either seller or buyer in the grant of a rebate by the seller in order to induce earlier payment.[116]

Scholastics prior to and after St. Thomas argued that to charge a higher price on sales for future payment than for cash sales was to "sell time," and that "time" was a free gift of God to all, a common good for which it was usurious to make a charge. The idea may stem from Seneca, who exclaimed with reference to the legal documents used in credit transactions: "but these bills of thine, what are they? What the computations and the sale of time and the bloodthirsty

115. E. Van Roey, "La monnaie d'après Saint Thomas d'Aquin," p. 231, agrees with St. Thomas here, but silently substitutes for non-transfer of ownership of the *money* invested in a partnership, non-transfer of ownership of "capital." Had he followed the same procedure in dealing with loans, he would have found it difficult to maintain that a loan involves a complete transfer of ownership.

To distinguish the partnership from the loan, St. Thomas argues in effect that ownership and risk bearing must be closely associated. There is no obvious principle which leads to this result, and in practice, especially with the development of a wide range of insurance devices, distribution of risks can be widely different from the distribution of ownership. Even in the Middle Ages, there was often a wide divergence between the pattern of investment and the pattern of risk bearing in partnership contracts. See Florence Edler, "Eclaircissements à propos des considérations de R. Davidsohn sur la productivité de l'argent au moyen-âge," *Vierteljahrschrift für Sozial- und Wirtschaftsgeschichte*, III (1937), 378; Raymond de Roover, "The Story of the Alberti Company," *Business History Review*, XXXII (1958), 38–39; Paul Vinogradoff, *Roman Law in Medieval Europe*, 2nd ed., Oxford, 1929, p. 92.

116. *Summa Theologica*, II–II, q. 78, a. 2, ad 7, and *De Emptione et Venditione ad Tempus*, Alfred O'Rahilly, tr. and ed., *Irish Ecclesiastical Record*, XXXI (1928), 164–165.

twelve percent?"[117] St. Thomas makes no use of this argument in the *Summa*, but in his letter on credit-sales he thrice repeats that selling time is "usury."[118]

St. Thomas rejects the defense of interest on the basis of a voluntary contract. "He who gives usury does not give it voluntarily simply, but under a certain necessity in so far as he needs to borrow money which the owner is unwilling to lend without usury."[119] In response to the uncritical view that free contract demonstrates unconstrained freedom of choice, this is a valid argument. But logically it is as applicable to non-loan contracts in general as to loans. St. Thomas may, however, have believed that lack of bargaining power was more prevalent among borrowers than among other categories of participants in economic transactions. If so, he may have followed his frequent practice of deliberately formulating in universal terms what he knew in fact to be true only in the majority of cases: "in contingent matters, such as human and natural things, it is enough for a thing to be certain [to be treated as certain?] as being true in the greater number of instances, though at times and less frequently it fails."[120]

St. Thomas concedes that a lender may justly contract for compensation for any loss which he incurs—presumably in the form of impairment of capital—as a result of making a loan (this title was later called *damnum emergens*). But he condemns requests for compensation for surrendering the possibility of gain which otherwise might have been procured through the use of the money lent (later to be called *lucrum cessans*). "He must not sell that which he has not yet and may be prevented in many ways from having."[121]

St. Thomas declares that it is not sinful to borrow at usury, since acceptance of injury (i.e., undertaking to pay interest) is not a sin. It

---

117. On Benefits, Book VII, Ch. 10, § 4, *Moral Essays*, III, Loeb Classical Library, Cambridge, Mass., 1925, p. 481.

118. *De Emptione*, pp. 164–165.

119. *Summa Theologica*, II–II, q. 78, a. 1, ad 7.

120. *Ibid.*, I–II, a. 96, a. 2, ad 3.

121. *Ibid.*, II–II, q. 78, a. 2, ad 1. The argument turns on certainty in the one case and uncertainty in the other. In practice there would be uncertainty in both cases, but in different degree. The logical procedure would seem to be to treat the two cases alike in terms of *ex ante* probabilities, and this is what in effect St. Thomas himself does in connection with restitution for injury. See *ibid.*, II–II, q. 62, a. 5.

Van Roey, "La monnaie," p. 219, in support of St. Thomas' rejection of *lucrum cessans* as a valid title to interest, asks why compensation for the surrender of an opportunity for gain should be more applicable to a loan than to a sale. But surely there is no parallel between the two cases if the sale is for cash. If a farmer sells a plow for cash, he loses the opportunity of gain from the use of the plow, but he acquires the opportunity of gain from the use of the cash. He might indeed use the cash immediately to buy another plow.

is not lawful to induce a man to sin, "yet it is lawful to make use of another's sin for a good end." It is therefore permissible to borrow for a good end from a professional usurer. The good end, however, must be "such as the relief of his own or another's need." Borrowing for the purpose of making a profit (presumably in excess of what the borrower "needed") would not be covered by this, as one would then "be giving a sinner [i.e., the usurer] matter for sin, so that one would be a participant in his guilt." On the other hand, it is permitted to deposit one's money for safekeeping with a usurer if he has other means of practicing usury, "since this is to use a sinner for a good purpose."[122]

In another work, St. Thomas recognizes the validity of a second title to interest in addition to *damnum emergens*, namely, a payment by the borrower of a penalty for failing to repay a loan at maturity in order to compensate the lender for any consequent loss. He reconciles this view with his rejection of *lucrum cessans* as a valid title by using the argument that the loss of opportunity for gain during the agreed loan period was foreseeable when the lender entered voluntarily into the loan contract.[123]

St. Thomas never expressly accepts the sanction by civil legislation as a valid title to interest, but he speaks tolerantly of such legislation, conceivably as a lesser evil than what legal prohibition might involve. By implication at least, therefore, he recognizes the possibility of conflict between temporal welfare and "justice":

Human laws leave certain things unpunished, on account of the condition of those who are imperfect, and who would be deprived of many advantages, if all sins were strictly forbidden [that is, by civil law] and punishments appointed for them. Wherefore human law has permitted usury, not that it looks upon

---

122. *Summa Theologica*, II–II, q. 78, a. 4. In *De Emptione*, p. 165, St. Thomas holds it unlawful for a merchant to reimburse himself for interest he has paid to a usurer by raising his selling prices. For he had sinned by paying usury and thus had given the usurer an occasion for sin when he was not under extreme necessity to do so.

123. *De Malo*, 13.4, ad 14, as reported by Gunther Steuer, *Studien über die theoretischen Grundlagen der Zinslehre bei Thomas v. Aquin*, Stuttgart, 1936, pp. 103–104. See also John T. Noonan, Jr., *The Scholastic Analysis of Usury*, pp. 109 ff. for fuller treatment of St. Thomas' position on the legitimacy of interest as a penalty for delay in payment. It is to be noted that when St. Thomas considers that the lender acts with free discretion and in the light of prudential considerations, he is in effect making the usury issue turn not on the distinction between lending interest-free and lending at interest but between non-lending and lending at interest.

usury as harmonizing with justice, but lest the advantage of many should be hindered.[124]

Other medieval writers expounded the same view or went even further in the same direction. John Gerson, for instance, is reported as having written:

The civil law, when it tolerates usury in some cases, must not be said to be always contrary to the law of God or the Church. The civil legislator, acting in the manner of a wise doctor, tolerates lesser evils that greater ones may be avoided. It is obviously less of an evil that slight usury should be permitted for the relief of want, than that men should be driven by their want to rob or steal or to sell their goods at an unfairly low price.[125]

This reasoning raises some fundamental issues. First, is usury contrary to natural law or natural reason? Second, if not, what effect should this have on church doctrine? The medieval writer most frequently cited as questioning whether natural law condemns usury was Francis de Mayronis, who wrote: "On the basis of natural law, it does not appear that usury is illicit . . . . If usury is illicit it is so on the basis of supernatural law."[126] Most medieval writers apparently held that even if it could be shown that usury served the public good, or that it could not be condemned on natural law grounds, it was nevertheless illicit because condemned by divine law.[127] In the seventeenth century and later, the laxists tended to question the social usefulness of the usury prohibitions; they argued that divine law must be presumed not to condemn what is useful to mankind.[128] Further-

---

124. *Summa Theologica*, II–II, q. 78, a. 1, ad 3. St. Thomas expresses the same idea in other places. See Abbé Deville, *Le Droit canon et le droit naturel*, Lyon, 1880, pp. 100–105.

125. *De Contractibus*, II–17, as cited by George O'Brien, *An Essay on Medieval Economic Teaching*, London, 1920, pp. 197–198. Charles Jourdain, "Mémoires sur les commencements de l'économie politique," pp. 38, 40–42, reports Gerson as holding that the Church should adapt its position on usury to social needs; further that a moderate rate of interest does not conflict with natural reason, and also that a rigorous policy would even compromise the revenues of many churches. He reports Buridan as holding that the criterion deciding when interest is permissible is whether it is socially useful.

126. *Sent.* IV, dist. 16, as reported by, among many others, Hedwig Brey, *Hochscholastik und Geist des Kapitalismus*, Leipzig, 1927, p. 73n.

127. See T. P. McLaughlin, "The Teaching of the Canonists on Usury," *Mediaeval Studies*, I (1939), 105 ff.

128. See, for instance, [Gabriel Daniel], *Réponse aux Lettres Provinciales . . . ou Entretiens de Cléandre et d'Eudoxe*, Cologne, 1696, p. 124.

more, adopting a seemingly moderate stand, Pope Benedict XIV in 1745 argued that since revelation teaches us that justice promotes the welfare of mankind, Christians must infer that those types of contracts which the Church has condemned as usurious are not requisite for the extension of commerce which serves the public good.[129]

The Church in time gave its sanction to or tolerated a longer list of titles to interest than St. Thomas expressly conceded. *Lucrum cessans* came to be accepted as a valid title. The receipt of interest on loans to governments was given papal approval, as were *montes pietatis*, or charitable lending institutions (pawnshops) charging moderate rates of interest on loans to the poor, secured by chattels. Many types of interest-bearing loans in the form of *rentes* and mortgages on real estate were approved, and monasteries and other church institutions were often the major investors in such loans. Pure interest, however, never received explicit official sanction from the Catholic Church, and *poena conventionalis*, or a penalty for delayed payment stipulated in the loan contract, though widely practiced and defended by some casuists, and *periculum sortis*, or a charge in the guise of insurance for the risk of non-repayment of the principal because of the bad faith, insolvency, or death of the debtor, apparently were never officially accepted by the medieval Church as valid titles.

Of the extrinsic titles to interest accepted as valid after St. Thomas' time, especially interesting was the sanction of interest-charging *montes pietatis*. They were first established in Italy at the end of the fifteenth century, but they continued to give rise to bitter controversy within the Church even after the issue was presumably settled in favor of their legitimacy by the Lateran Council of 1515. Practically the sole argument on behalf of the *montes pietatis* was the need of the poor, but this was not a characteristic type of argument in the debate on usury within the Church. Some notable theologians, as, for example, Cajetan and Soto, continued to deny the legitimacy of these establishments, and rejected any subordination of the traditional interpretations of divine law to humanitarian or utilitarian considerations. The success of the advocates for *montes pietatis* is the sole instance I know of in the history of the usury doctrine where the official position of the Church was expressly modified on the basis of humanitarian considerations. It was clear that for the poor the only conceivable alternatives were borrowing from professional money-lenders, borrowing at moderate rates from ecclesiastically managed

129. See his encyclical *Vix pervenit*, Nov. 1, 1745, J-P. Migne, *Theologia cursus completus*, XVI, cols. 1059 ff.

institutions, or not borrowing at all. Traditional doctrine was set aside to make the second alternative available.[130]

The multiplication of the accepted or tolerated "extrinsic" titles to interest not only facilitated willful evasion of the prohibition of usury but increased the range of doubtful and debatable cases. By the seventeenth century many factors made the maintenance of a rigorous position increasingly difficult, both subjectively and in terms of the prestige and general influence of the church teaching and the retention of the loyalty of its members. These factors included the increasing legitimization of interest by civil legislation even in Catholic countries; the competition of Catholic merchants and communities with Protestant merchants and communities not subject to the Catholic usury restrictions; economic rivalry between Catholic towns, when the advantage went to those towns where civil and ecclesiastical authorities were more tolerant of usury; and the growing scepticism, even among theologians, as to the strength of the natural law arguments against usury. The doctrinal position of the Church, moreover, was increasingly compromised by its own heavy involvement, as creditor and debtor, in financial transactions in which interest was either explicit or faintly obscured from the general view.[131]

In response to the many pressures towards liberalization, in the eighteenth century the Church began a gradual retreat from its traditional position, without explicit acknowledgment of a change in basic doctrine, as distinguished from application and interpretation. The major formal steps were first, the encyclical *Vix Pervenit* of Benedict XIV in 1745; second, a papal circular of 1838 which instructed confessors not to disturb penitents who confessed to accepting interest at current rates; and third, the Canon 1543, of the recodification of the Canon Law, promulgated in 1918, which contained an express legitimization of the charging of interest on the loan of fungible goods,

---

130. For the early history of the controversy, see P. H. Holzapfel, O.F.M., *Die Anfänge der Montes Pietatis (1462–1515)*, Munich, 1903. Nicolas Bariani, an Augustine who continued to oppose the lawfulness of *montes pietatis* after the papal decision in their favor, entitled his tract *De Montes Impietatis*. See Léon Lallemand, *Histoire de la Charité*, III, 363.

131. There is an extensive literature on the Church as moneylender from the Middle Ages on. Representative scholarly items in this literature are Robert Génestal, *Rôle des monastères comme établissements de crédit—XI à XIII siècle*, Paris, 1901; E. Allix and R. Génestal, "Les opérations financières de l'Abbaye de Troarn du XI au XIV siècles," *Vierteljahrschrift für Sozial- und Wirtschaftsgeschichte*, II (1904), 616–640; U. Gottlob, "Päpstliche Darlehenschulden des 13. Jahrhunderts," *Historisches Jahrbuch*, XX (1899), 665–717; X. Mossman, "De L'épargne au moyen âge, de son emploi et de ses effets," *Revue Historique*, X (1879), 55–67; Fedor Schneider, "Das kirkliche Zinsverbot und die kuriale Praxis im 13. Jahrhundert," in *Festgabe für Heinrich Finke*, Münster i. W., 1904, pp. 127–167.

money included, at a rate permitted by civil law, as long as the rate was moderate, and at a rate higher than the civil law maximum when a "just and proportionate" title could be claimed. Some modern Catholic writers insist that there has been nothing more than normal "development" in the Catholic doctrine on usury since St. Thomas, and that no basic dogma has been abandoned.[132] But the distinction in Catholic terminology between "development" and "change" of doctrine is a technical one without a clearly perceivable counterpart in secular verbal usage.

Coinage and Taxation

The Scholastics regarded it as within their province to lay down moral principles which princes or rulers were bound to follow under divine and natural law in their economic dealings with their subjects. It was the duty of the prince to serve the "common good" in a sense which clearly included the temporal welfare of the community as a whole. The chief economic transactions of princes with their subjects were in the fields of coinage and taxation. As far as coinage was concerned, the Scholastics found several issues which were "moral" in character and therefore fell within their province.

The Scholastics, following Aristotle, regarded coins as a "measure," specifically, of the relative value of commodities. It was the duty of the prince to see to it that all "measures" used in commercial transactions should be honest ones, that is, should be what they purported to be. For the protection of the unwary and ill-informed, they should be uniform and constant through time. As part of this duty, the prince should ensure that the coins he issued were of full weight and purity of content.[133]

According to the so-called "feudal theory of coinage," the prince had an exclusive right to coin as part of his feudal privileges, and he was not answerable to anyone for his manner of using it. Some economists held, however, that the authority over the coinage belonged properly to the community, and all economists and theologians maintained that the prince must accept certain restraining principles.

132. See, for example, Otto Schilling, *Die Staats- und Soziallehre des hl. Thomas v. Aquin*, 2nd ed., Munich, 1930, p.306, and Auguste Dumas, "Intérêt et usure," *Dictionnaire de droit canonique*, Paris, 1953, cols. 1475–1518.

133. I do not know of any discussion of coinage in an authentic work of St. Thomas. There is some discussion of coinage in Book II, Chs. 13 and 14 of *De Regimine Principum*, generally included in collections of St. Thomas' works. But it is now generally agreed that the section of this work containing these chapters was not written by St. Thomas. See St. Thomas Aquinas, *On Kingship to the King of Cyprus*, Toronto, 1949, the Introduction by I. Th. Eschmann, O.P., pp. ix–xxvi.

For example, he should not operate the coinage for his personal benefit and therefore must either bear from his own resources the cost of coinage ("brassage") or limit his seigniorage charge at most to a moderate excess over the minting cost. As some of the Scholastics realized, this principle would mean that (except for wear and tear, which was probably substantial in those times, but was apparently ignored) coins would normally circulate at or near parity between the coined and the uncoined metal.

Toward the end of the thirteenth century, and especially from 1295 on, during the reign of Philippe le Bel, the rulers of France "altered" the official coins by reducing their metallic content without changing their denominations, that is, their "nominal" or "legal" value. In that period, and in fact for several centuries after, it was commonly taken for granted that when a ruler or minter reduced the metallic content of a coin or raised the denomination of a coin of unchanged content or changed the nominal or legal valuation of silver relative to gold coins of a given metallic content, he was in effect and intent stealing from the national currency, which was the property of the community, not of the ruler. Separation, either in thought or in practice, of the personal finances of the prince from the "public" or "government" treasury was as yet unknown; it was thus not recognized that an "alteration" of the currency might be in the interest both of the ruler and the community. It was also wrongly taken for granted that "alterations" of the coinage were always, at least in the case of reductions in metallic content, directly profitable to the prince. Above all, the Scholastics appraised coinage changes only in terms of their consequences for the purchasing power of the standard coins over the monetary metals or over foreign coins. They either did not consider at all the effects of "alterations" on the purchasing power of the standard coins over goods in general, or, in the case of alterations which lowered the money-metal equivalent of a standard monetary unit, they took for granted that the result would be a rise in the prices of commodities. Discussion of monetary issues in terms of the general price level, inflation and deflation, were to make their first appearance in the sixteenth century, after the inflow of the precious metals from newly discovered America. It may be that, given the practices of the rulers of this period, the assumption that "alterations" of the coinage were generally made in the private interest of those who controlled the coinage was valid. In any case, moral theologians and canonists united in condemning alterations of the coinage which involved a reduction in the money-metal equivalent of a standard monetary unit, regardless of whether it took the form of a reduction of the metallic content of a particular coin or a rise in the nominal monetary denomination of a coin of unchanged metallic content.

The first important criticism of alterations of the coinage resting on moral and economic analysis was by John Buridan, who was rather a philosopher and moralist than a theologian.[134] Buridan made the following objections against alterations of the currency: they caused unrest and disturbance among the people; they constituted exactions from the public to the benefit of the treasure chest (treated as personal) of the prince; they disturbed the proper functioning of the standard coin as a measure of value; they constituted an "innovation," and every innovation which was not necessary was an evil; and they constituted a sacrifice of the common good to the private good of the prince.

While much of this would now be regarded by most economists as obsolete and unenlightened, especially in the light of the absence of essential qualifications, it nevertheless represented a forward step in the use of economic analysis as a basis for economic and moral judgments.

The next major step in the use of economic analysis as an important element in the moral appraisal of alterations of the currency was made by Nicholas Oresme, a French cleric who became a bishop towards the end of his life, in his *De Moneta*, written some time in the 1350's.[135]

Oresme wrote his treatise avowedly from "a philosophical and Aristotelian" point of view.[136] Apart from his use of biblical passages of questionable relevance to support his case that it is unjust for princes to make a profit from coinage or to tamper with the coin in its function as a unit of measure, his discussion is conducted mainly along non-theological lines. He concedes the legitimacy of a seigniorage charge, not exceeding the cost of minting; but in other respects he

134. Buridan presented his views on coinage in his commentaries on Aristotle's *Politics* and *Ethics*. For his views, I rely mainly on Constantin Miller, *Studien zur Geschichte der Geldlehre*, Stuttgart, 1925, pp. 99–114.

135. Oresme has been extensively discussed, but almost wholly either from a purely technical economic point of view, or from the point of view of coinage technology. The most valuable accounts for present purposes are Emile Bridrey, *La Théorie de la monnaie au XIVe siècle, Nicole Oresme*, Paris, 1906 (741 pages, with no index!); Adolphe Landry, "Notes critiques sur le 'Nicole Oresme' de M. Bridrey," *Le Moyen Age*, XXII (1909), 145–178; *idem*, *Essai économique sur les mutations des monnaies dans l'ancienne France*, Paris, 1910; Constantin Miller, *Studien*, pp. 115–120. For the text of *De Moneta*, I have used the translation by Charles Johnson, in his *The De Moneta of Nicholas Oresme and English Mint Documents*, London, 1956, pp. 1–48.

136. That these "experts" were coinage experts or other secular wise men appears more clearly in an addition to the Prologue to *De Moneta* included in some of the early manuscripts. See Emile Bridrey, *La Théorie de la monnaie*, pp. 55 ff., 443, 678.

shares Buridan's views. He treats making profit out of the coinage as analogous to making money breed money through usury and thus as being "monstrous and unnatural." Altering the coinage for purposes of profit is even worse than usury; the latter at least involves free will on both sides, and the borrower at least enjoys the use of the money lent to him as an offset to the interest he pays. On the other hand, the altered coins are forced on the public and yield them no benefit.[137]

Oresme's rigor, however, moderates when he considers whether it is ever proper for a *community*, as distinguished from a "prince" or ruler, to alter the coinage. On this subject he concedes that some of his objections to alterations are no longer applicable, and that as a form of taxation for public purposes alterations have important merits:

> Such an alteration seems to unite almost all the good conditions required by any tollage or contribution. For it brings in much profit in little time, is very easy to collect and assess or share without employing a large staff or risking fraud in collection, and is cheap to collect. Nothing, either, can be devised more fair or proportional, since he who can afford most pays most. And it is, for its amount, less seen or felt and more endurable without danger of rebellion or popular discontent. For it is universal: neither clerk [cleric?] nor noble can escape it by privilege or otherwise, as many try to escape other contributions, causing envyings, dissensions, litigation, scandals and many other evils which do not arise from such an alteration of the coinage [*De Moneta*, p. 36].

It would even be proper for the community to make the prince its agent in carrying out an alteration of this kind. But Oresme maintains that this method of finance should not be used except where there is a major need for funds. It would involve sending the extra coins out of the country, so that, as I interpret him, there would be no increase in the nominal amount of money within the country.[138]

In the light of these concessions, it seems reasonable to interpret Oresme as mainly condemning alterations of the coinage for improper purposes, and especially challenging the right of the prince to use it for his personal profit or as an exercise of absolute jurisdiction. That there was a political basis for his objections which was essentially

---

137 *De Moneta*, pp. 25–26, 28.

138. *Ibid.*, pp. 35–37, 39–42. Oresme's criteria of a good tax stand up quite well in comparison with Adam Smith's famous, and largely unoriginal, four canons of taxation.

democratic, or at least anti-absolutist, is further borne out by his reported response to the argument that the community had conferred unlimited rights over the coinage to the prince:

> A community of citizens, which naturally is free, and tends to liberty, would never knowingly submit to servitude or lower itself to the judgment of tyrannical power . . . . God forbid that the courage of the French should be so debased that they would voluntarily become serfs.[139]

Another monetary phenomenon which, reasonably enough, some of the Scholastics regarded as presenting a moral problem was the impact of alterations of the coinage on parties to long-term rental or other contracts, and receivers of customary wages, rents, and other payments. Writers often recognized that injustice could arise when claimants were obliged to accept settlement of their claims in terms of a debased monetary unit. In some cases they held that such claimants had a right to compensation for the reduction in the value of the standard monetary unit, though they do not appear to have solved the problem of formulating a general rule whereby this could be managed without overwhelming administrative complications.[140]

In the 1520's, there developed in the Electorate of Saxony a controversy between the two branches of the ruling house about the desirability of altering the mint ratio between gold and silver coins. The ruling family had divided into two branches in 1485, each holding separate territories, but with some rich silver mines remaining as jointly owned property, and with the minting of coins also carried on as a joint activity. With the advent of the Reformation, one branch, the Ernestine, became Protestant, while the other branch, the Albertine, remained Catholic. In 1524 the Ernestine branch supported a proposal to raise the monetary value of silver as compared to gold, but, after some hesitation, the Albertine branch rejected it. The Ernestine branch, in consequence, withdrew from the joint operation of the coinage and began to mint a new silver coin at the old nominal price relative to the gold coin, the gulden, but with its silver content reduced by about 6 per cent. In 1530 an anonymous tract appeared on behalf of the Albertine side, *Gemeine Stymmen von der Müntze*,

---

139. Cited by Alfred O'Rahilly, *Aquinas versus Marx*, p. 24, from V. Meunier, *Essai sur la vie et les ouvrages de N. d'Oresme*, 18, p. 79.

140. Accounts of the treatment of this issue, mainly by economists and civilians as distinguished from "theologians" proper, are to be found in Wilhelm Endemann, *Studien in der romanisch-kanonistischen Wirtschafts- und Rechtslehre*, II, 184–197, and Walter Taeuber, *Geld und Kredit im Mittelalter*, Berlin, 1933.

which attacked the alteration of the coinage. A reply to this from the Ernestine side, *Die Müntze Belangende*, came out in the same year, which in turn led to a rejoinder in 1531 entitled *Apologia und Vorantwortung*.[141]

Alfred Müller-Armack points out that the Albertine tracts followed the traditional Catholic position that the coinage must be maintained at its full metallic value. In doing so, these tracts simply took for granted that a "good" money would have favorable economic consequences. The Ernestine, or Protestant, tract based its support for alteration solely on the ground of the desirable economic consequences for Saxony.[142] This reading is undoubtedly substantially correct. However, there is very little if anything in the tracts themselves or, as far as I know, in the history of the controversy, which gives credibility to Müller-Armack's suggestion that the difference in religion was an important factor underlying the difference in monetary policy of the two groups. I have been unable to find any evidence, moreover, of a general tendency in the sixteenth century or later for Protestant countries to resort more readily to alterations of the coinage than Catholic countries. A thorough investigation might result in interesting findings.

To understand the Scholastic treatment of taxes one must bear in mind that taxation, as we now know it—namely, as a routine, normal, and respectable method of providing for the financial needs of government—is a comparatively modern phenomenon. In feudal times, on the other hand, rulers derived their revenues mainly from personal estates, customary tributes and dues paid by their vassals, tolls on strangers and on traffic on roads and rivers, war booty, rapine and piracy, and, in times of special need, from "aids," subventions, donations, etc., in form at least voluntarily granted to them, by the "consent" of the people. In a number of countries, the greatest political crises in their history arose out of alleged abuse by rulers of their powers in the fiscal field. It is with this in mind that one should interpret Scholastic texts which deal with taxation in terms of "extortion," "robbery," "acts of tyranny," "exactions," and so forth.

All of St. Thomas' references to taxation that I know of treat it as

---

141. Walther Lotz, *Die drei Flugschriften über den Munzstreit der sächsischen Albertiner und Ernestiner um 1530*, Leipzig, 1893, gives an account of the history of the controversy and also presents the texts of the three tracts both in the original form and in transcriptions into modern German. Jean-Yves Le Branchu, *Ecrits notables sur la monnaie, XVI siècle*, Paris, 1934, Vol. I, Introduction, pp. xxxiv–xxxix and pp. 31–47, also gives an account of the controversy, as well as a translation of the Ernestine tract *Gemeine Stymmen* into French.

142. *Genealogie der Wirtschaftsstile*, 3rd ed., Stuttgart, 1944, pp. 197–199.

a more or less extraordinary act of a ruler which is as likely as not to be morally illicit. In the *Summa* he distinguishes taxation from robbery only if it is "due to them [the rulers] for the safe-guarding of the common good"; it is licit then, he says, even if the rulers use "violence" to exact it. But the context suggests that a milder term such as "coercion" or "compulsion" or "power" would more accurately reflect his meaning.[143] Elsewhere, in answer to the question whether a ruler may justly levy taxes, he replies that general utility must be the basic criterion. However, the presumption is that taxes are not routine measures and therefore are legitimate only with the consent of the people and as a last resort when other resources are unavailable.[144] In another work he writes that princes sin with reference to taxes if the levy is not made for the good of the people, if the princes take more by "violence" than is sanctioned by the law (which is a pact between ruler and people), or if what the princes exact exceeds the capacity of the people to pay.[145]

A medieval papal bull, *In Coena Domini*, which apparently continued to be republished each year until late in the eighteenth century, threatened with excommunication all rulers "who levied new taxes or increased old ones, except for cases supported by law, or by an express permission from the pope." In a defense of the record of the Papacy, first published in 1819, de Maistre refuses to concede that there was anything to criticize in this bull.[146] Later casuists added as a criterion of permissible taxation the need to conform with distributive justice, which they interpreted as requiring the distribution of taxes in accordance with ability to pay. Some of them added that where taxes were unjust or were obstacles to taxpayers in meeting the necessities of daily life, it was not a strict moral duty to pay them. In some instances, casuists condemned outright certain specific types of taxes, as, for example, export and import taxes and road and bridge tolls, on the grounds that though originally levied to finance the protection of travelers and merchants, they were now irrelevant for these purposes. When a taxpayer was convinced that a tax was unjust or too high, some casuists held that it was not sinful for him to evade the

---

143. *Summa Theologica*, II–II, q. 66, a. 8, ad 3: ["etiamsi violentia adhibeatur, non est rapina"].

144. *De Regimine Judaeorum, ad Ducissam Brabantiae*, *Opuscula Omnia*, Mandonnet, ed., Paris, 1927, I, 488–494. An English translation is available in A. P. D'Entreves, ed., *Aquinas: Selected Political Writings*, Oxford, 1948, pp. 85–98.

145. *In Epistola ad Rom. Expositio*, lect. 1, as quoted in Abbé Léon Godard, *Les Principes de '89 et la doctrine catholique*, Paris, 1863, p. 178.

146. *Du pape*, Book II, Ch. 15, in *Œuvres*, J.-P. Migne, ed., Paris, 1841, cols. 396–399.

tax if he could, even by trickery, and in such cases he was not obligated in conscience to make restitution. This was a phase of the late medieval "lax" casuistry which was to be subjected to severe criticism by the seventeenth-century "rigorists."[147]

Medieval Social Heresies and Deviations

The medieval moral theologians accepted responsibility for providing moral guidance to rulers, clerics, and the public at large, but except for the issue of usury their guidance did not call for any sharp break with the existing patterns of social behavior or existing social institutions: feudalism in the rural areas; the market, the gild system, and private property in the towns. The Church itself had become the greatest of the feudal landlords and clung to feudalism even during the latter's decline and decay under the impact of internal and external pressures. As investor, creditor, and debtor, the Church was engaged in major financial operations. To conduct them it followed the common procedures and instrumentalities of the market-place. Church and social structure became so tightly intermeshed that major conflict between them could not have occurred without resulting in civil commotion or radical change in the ecclesiastical structure.

Inside and outside the Church, however, an undercurrent of opinion held that the Church was in too close alliance with the world, and that the true mission of the Church was either to keep itself free from worldly entanglement or to refashion the world on the model of New Testament teachings. In the early Christian Church, the withdrawal of the zealots to the desert and later the establishment within the Church of monastic institutions were modes of escape for individuals from the entanglements of the Church with the world without breaking with the Church. But worldly corruption had crept into the monasteries, and there was a period before the Reformation and the Counter-reformation when moral criticism of the Church by the world was perhaps as common as moral criticism of the world by the clerics. For this and/or other reasons, some of the heretical sects of the Middle Ages believed that the existing forms of monastic life, even where they were available to them, were unacceptable; they sought either to remake or

147. The most useful guides to the taxation doctrines of the later Scholastics that I have found are Rudolph Amberg, *Die Steuer in der Rechtsphilosophie der Scholastiker*, Berlin, 1909; Franz Hamm, *Geschichte der Steuermoral in der Kirche*, Trier, 1907; and Wilhelm Weber, *Wirtschaftsethik am Vorabend des Liberalismus*, pp. 194–204. J. Laures, "Ideas fiscales de cinco grandes jesuitas españoles," *Razón y Fe*, LXXIV (1928), 200 ff., 307 ff., 365 ff., cited as important by Wilhelm Weber and others, was not available to me.

withdraw from the Church in order to establish communities of saints living as "islands of righteousness in an ocean of iniquity."

It is often said of these heretical sects that they constituted movements of social protest by the lower classes as much as or more than movements of religious reform. But these sects were not confined to the lower classes, and the pioneers and leaders of these heretical movements often seem to have come from the upper rather than the lower social levels. Especially in the West, where educated laymen were few, the pioneers were often clerics whose own economic and social status was a comfortable one.[148]

Many heretical sects, from the twelfth to the sixteenth centuries, attained some degree of regional importance, and most of them espoused radical social doctrine or had extreme wings who did so. I have no acquaintance with the relevant primary sources, and the voluminous secondary literature is usually directed to other aspects of these sects than the doctrinal relation of their theological and social doctrine, which is our sole interest here. The numerous older "dictionaries of heresies" concentrate on the purely theological elements of the doctrines of the sects. Many of the modern accounts are written by men of socialist sympathies who are not interested in the theological foundations of the sects' social doctrines. My comments, therefore, will be limited to a few points.

Some of the sects, and also individual heretics, made the economic structure and practices of the Church a major target of attack. This seems to have been true, for instance, of Joachim of Floris (twelfth century), a precursor of the Franciscan Order,[149] of Wat Tyler, John Ball, and Jack Straw (all of them priests or friars involved in the Peasants' Revolt of 1381 in England), of Wycliffe, and the "Minorite" wing of the Franciscan Order. Walter Map (or Mapes), Archdeacon of Oxford, had attacked some of the richer orders of the Church at the end of the twelfth century, especially the

148. See Georges de Lagarde, *La Naissance*, 1st ed., 1934, I, 102–103 (the Waldensians); Peter Brock, *The Political and Social Doctrines of the Unity of Czech Brethren in the Fifteenth and Early Sixteenth Centuries*, The Hague, 1957, pp. 103, 117, 183; Austin P. Evans, "Social Aspects of Medieval Heresy," in *Persecution and Liberty, Essays in Honor of George Lincoln Burr*, New York, 1931, p. 113n.; Roy Pascal "Communism in the Middle Ages and Reformation," in Lewis, Polanyi, and Kitchin eds., *Christianity and the Social Revolution*, New York, 1936, p. 136 (the Cathars); Arno Borst, *Die Katharer*, Stuttgart, 1953, pp. 44–45, 137–138, 243. For advocacy of communism in fourteenth-century Byzantium by laics and opposition to it by clerics defending the social *status quo*, see Ernest Barker, *Social and Political Thought in Byzantium*, Oxford, 1957, pp. 184–193, 196–206.

149. See Max Beer, *Social Struggles in the Middle Ages*, J. J. Stenning, tr., London, 1924, pp. 97–101.

Cistercians but also the Templars and the Hospitallers, for their alleged attachment to wealth. Distinguishing between the "black monks," or the clergy following a life of austerity and poverty, and the "white monks," or the Cistercians and other orders allegedly living in luxury, he charged that while the God of the black monks "saith, 'No man can serve God and Mammon,' theirs [the white monks'] saith, 'No man can serve God without Mammon.' "[150]

As was the case in the first centuries, the Church directed its official censure of the heretical sects, not to their social doctrines as such, but to their theological doctrines and schismatic activities. Thus Innocent III, in condemning the Waldensians in 1208, prescribed to them the abjuration, not of their communistic doctrines, but of their claim that the possession of private property was a barrier to salvation. He asked them to affirm: "We believe and confess that those who remain in the world and possess their own wealth, by practising alms, and other benefits from their possessions, and by keeping the commands of the Lord, are saved."[151] On the insistence of John Gerson, the Council of Constance in 1477 condemned the doctrine of Mathieu Grabou (Grabow), a Saxon Dominican who held that possession of some property was essential for the performance of one's worldly duties and that no one, therefore, could surrender without sin what was needed for a moderate level of living. He also held that only in an approved religious order, under monastic discipline, is life without private property possible; and that except within such an order, to abandon one's entire property on religious grounds and to live in communist communities or voluntarily to make oneself dependent on alms is heresy.[152] In attacking Grabou, the Church thus defended voluntary communism as permissible for laics or clerics, even outside the monastic orders.

Max Beer and other socialist historians have interpreted the "historical role" of St. Thomas and his Scholastic successors as that of whittling away the communist element in natural law and providing a moral justification for the new urban economic order which came into

---

150. *Master Walter Map's Book De Nugis Curialium (Courtier's Trifles)*, Frederick Tupper and Marbury B. Ogle, tr., London, 1924, p. 56.

151. Denzinger, *The Sources of Catholic Dogma (Enchiridion Symbolorum)*, No. 427, p. 164.

152. See Jacques L'Enfant, *The History of the Council of Constance*, tr. from the French, London, 1730, II, 255–258; C. Ullman, *Reformers Before the Reformation*, Robert Menzies, tr., Edinburgh, 1855, II, 163–169; J. B. S. Schwab, *Johannes Gerson*, Würzburg, 1858, pp. 763–765; George C. Powers, *Nationalism at the Council of Constance*, Washington, D.C., 1927, p. 170n.; Father Ducatillon, "Doctrine communiste et doctrine catholique," in *Le Communisme et les chrétiens*, Paris, 1937, pp. 112–113.

being during the Crusades. Accordingly, these historians interpret the role of the heretical sects as that of a protest against the processes of accommodation of the Church to this new economic order.[153] The case of Grabou, however, suggests that the Church was not aware of this "historical role" or at least did not feel free to follow it without restraint.

The tension within the Church between the appeal of the early doctine of hostility or coldness to a social system resting on private property and the late medieval acceptance by the Church for the community at large of a sharp distinction between rich and poor (made conspicuous by the wealth of some of the Church's own ecclesiastical institutions) is probably a part of the explanation of the appearance of communistically oriented utopias written by devout Catholics, notably those of Sir Thomas More and Campanella.[154] In the case of More's *Utopia*, interpretation is difficult and varies as between commentators. The book is written in a humanist as distinguished from a specifically Christian tone and embodies some aristocratic features. It does not seem possible confidently to attribute to More any of the radical views with respect to property expounded in the dialogue. Thomas More may perhaps have accepted communism as a Christian ideal, but one that was not realizable in the existing historical state of man. He may have used the dialogue form as an exercise in exploring the outlines of an ideal state, framed in accordance with reason alone, abstracting both from religious dogma and practical limitations.[155] In other works More defended private property in general and defended the Church against threatened spoliation. "I doubt not," he wrote, "but that there are at this day holy saints in heaven, of such as are spiritual and of such as were temporal too, that had while they lived here as great possessions as hath spiritual or temporal within the realm of England."[156] The communistic elements

---

153. See: Max Beer, *Social Struggles in the Middle Ages*, p. 96; Ernst Werner, *Pauperes Christi: Studien zu Sozialreligiösen Bewegungen im Zeitalter des Reformpapsttums*, Leipzig, 1956, pp. 81, 204.

154. See Alfred Müller-Armack, *Genealogie der Wirtschaftsstile*, pp. 175–180.

155. See August Rüegg, "Des Erasmus 'Lob der Torheit' und Thomas More's 'Utopie,' " in *Gedankschrift zum 400. Todestage des Erasmus von Rotterdam*, Basel, 1936, pp. 75–78; P. Albert Duhamel, "Medievalism of More's Utopia," *Studies in Philosophy*, LII (1955), 99–128; Edward L. Surtz, S.J., "Thomas More and Communism," *PMLA*, LXIV (1949), 549–564; and by the same author, *The Praise of Pleasure: Philosophy, Education and Communism in More's Utopia*, Cambridge, Mass., 1957.

156. *The Apology of Sir Thomas More, Knight, 1533*, Arthur I. Taft, ed., London, 1930, pp. 86–87. See also *A Supplication of Soules*, in *Works*, 1557, pp. 304–305; *Dialogue of Comfort*, appended to Everyman ed. of *Utopia*, pp. 255–258; and *Thomas Morus' Utopia*, Berlin, 1922, Hermann Oncken's Introduction, p. 42.

in the *Utopia* seem, however, to have been interpreted by his friends, without correction by More, as expressing his views.[157]

Campanella, the author of *Civitas Solis*, an account of a utopian state, communist and totalitarian, suffered many years of imprisonment by the Church and the State for his religious views, his hostility to Spanish rule in Italy, and perhaps also his social views. In 1634, late in life, he escaped to France, where, as an enemy of Spain, he received the friendly protection of Louis XIII and Richelieu and where he died in 1639. In his last years he had a period of regret for his utopian writings, and in a "Song of Repentance" he confessed that they had manifested "pride" and that he had been impious in imagining that without the aid of revelation the human mind could design a better social order. The lesson he drew from this, as stated in his poem, was as follows:

> Man, observe the laws under which you were born. Look upon the princes and the priests as representatives of divinity, and their commands as divine commands even if at times they seem unjust to you, as well as to all the people. If God permits floods, conflagrations, and wars, He who reigns over all; if he suffers in silence these agents of his anger, remain you likewise silent and obey his will. Fatigued by your journey, in making your vows, hope that you will reach the harbor without casting yourself on the reefs.[158]

On the basis of the foregoing discussion of the social aspects of medieval moral theology, it seems possible to find some fairly clear difference in doctrine and emphasis between the Scholastic treatment of economic questions and that of the Christian Fathers. As compared with the earlier Fathers, the Scholastics reveal no influence of eschatological or chiliastic expectations in their social doctrines, though such influence was present in some of the heretical sects. The Scholastics also adopted a more tolerant attitude towards economic in-

---

157. A letter critical of private property, written in 1516 by his friend, Jerome Busleyden, was printed during More's lifetime within editions of *Utopia*, although perhaps not with his approval or knowledge. The letter is added as an appendix to the edition of *Utopia*, J. H. Lupton, ed., Oxford, 1895, pp. 313–319. For views critical of private property by other members of More's circle, see above, as regards John Colet, p. 69, and as regards Erasmus, Edward Surtz, *The Praise of Pleasure*, pp. 171–174, and pp. 69–70 above. For praise of Utopia by other friends of More, see Thomas Stapleton, *The Life and Illustrious Martyrdom of Sir Thomas More* (Part III of *Ires Thomae*, Douai, 1588), Philip E. Hallett, tr., London, 1928, pp. 32–34. None of the quotations cited by Stapleton take any issue with More's book.

158. *Œuvres choisies de Campanella*, Louise Colet, ed. and tr., Paris, 1844, pp. 146–151, at p. 147.

equality and the pursuit of profit and did not question the possibility of engaging in commerce without recourse to sinful practices. The doctrine of just price was substantially a Scholastic product, but it was for the most part formulated and applied in such fashion as not to conflict with current trade practices, provided they did not involve monopoly, fraud, exploitation of emergency situations for abnormal profit, or overt usury. The Scholastics made more systematic appeal to natural law (in effect, to non-theological reasoning) in the exposition of their social doctrine than did the Fathers, and by the use of a wide and elastic range of methods of interpretation of biblical texts they succeeded in finding a greater degree of harmony between revealed dogma and the current economic practices of the world. The Scholastic treatment of usury, however, constitutes, I repeat, something of an exception in this respect. Here, biblical texts, strictly interpreted, played an important role. Natural law was used in support of rigorous instead of accommodating doctrine, and what the early Church had presented as counsel, at least as far as laics were concerned, was presented by the Scholastics as precepts whose violation would involve mortal sin.

The Scholastics, however (though with exceptions on the part of the "laxists"), showed little more interest in temporal prosperity for its own sake than did the Fathers. Where they took a moderate attitude towards economic activities in pursuit of gain, they were moved rather by the necessity of tolerating irremediable human weakness than by concern for the material consequences in wealth and income of such activities. They recognized, as had the Fathers, that extreme poverty as well as extreme riches could bring moral dangers, and that wealth was the source of alms to the poor as well as gifts to the Church. The Scholastic doctrine, from the sixteenth century onwards, had to meet the impact of new ideas and interests, whether stemming from the Renaissance, from "humanism," Christian or libertine, from the Protestant Reformation, or from the writings of a new lay middle class, numerous, educated, articulate, powerful, and with views of their own. The clergy in the seventeenth century, especially in France, were in violent dispute among themselves on the issue of "rigorism" versus "laxism." Catholic moral theology was nevertheless still being expounded in substantially similar terms at the end of the seventeenth century as in the thirteenth century, even on economic matters. Part of the explanation for this stability of doctrine was, no doubt, the fact that in doctrine as well as in practice Catholicism was more tightly bound to tradition, less responsive to changing external forces, intellectual and social, than was Protestantism. The latter was almost completely free to adopt for itself or to reject at its discretion the content of Scholastic economic doctrine insofar as it went beyond the basic moral principles, freely interpreted, of Christianity as embodied in the Bible. While within Christianity the lay world was responding to and making its own contribution to the new secular trends of thought, Scholastic moral theology was increasingly becoming a frozen and lifeless relic of an earlier age, still studied reverently in theological seminaries but steadily losing its influence on social behavior in the outer world. It was increasingly being replaced—in Protestant countries almost completely, in Catholic countries largely[159]— by a secularized moral philosophy with a different and weaker type of attachment to formal theology and by an economic and political doctrine which paid only lip service to traditional moral theology.

By the seventeenth century, mercantilism, as a political and economic doctrine which stressed national power and national prosperity, dominated the lay world. Although it was about as prevalent in Catholic countries as in Protestant ones and used "political cardinals" heavily as exponents and administrators in the Catholic countries, mercantilism penetrated much less into Catholic than into Protestant theology. Catholic doctrine as such was universalist by tradition, and papal ambitions, ecclesiastical and political, encountered a formidable obstacle in strongly nationalistic policies, which operated especially to strengthen the position of Gallican movements within the national branches of the universal Catholic Church. Mercantilism, which was nationalist in essence and stressed national objectives as against the moral claims of individuals or other peoples, found an easier entry into the doctrinal teaching of clergymen belonging to the various state-established, state-supported, and largely state-dominated churches of Protestantism than into the corpus of doctrine of the tradition-bound and supra-national Catholic Church. Although in its struggle against Gallicanism and Protestantism, the Papacy did not hesitate to make use of national rivalries for power and wealth, it escaped deep entanglement with mercantilism as *doctrine*, as some of the established churches of Protestantism did not.[160]

159. See Ph. Delhaye, "La Théologie morale d'hier et d'aujourd'hui," *Revue des Sciences Religieuses*, XXXVII (1953), 114–118.

160. Very pertinent in this respect is Emil A. Fischer's explanation as to why Giovanni Botero was not "nationalist" in his economics and politics, *Giovanni Botero, ein politischer und volkswirtschaftlicher Denker der Gegenreformation*, n.d. (ca. 1955), p. 23: "Botero's indifference with respect to national considerations may to a not small extent arise out of the fact that he was a cleric, a member of a universal spiritual organization, which particularly in his time was bidding for new possibilities of world-wide expansion. In contrast to the mostly national-church-oriented Protestantism, the Catholic Church was certainly not organized on a national basis. This

The new forces, however, found less resistance among those late Scholastics who later were labelled by their critics as "laxists." These Scholastics developed for casuistic purposes and for relief of conscience from what they regarded as excessive scruples a modification of the old moral theology which, though not concerned with nationalism and mercantilism, did in effect sanction a new degree of freedom from religious constraints on individual enterprise and individual aspirations for economic betterment. The controversy between the "laxists" and their critics, the "rigorists," which took place during the seventeenth century and later is the subject of the next chapter.

---

was especially so in Counterreformation Italy. The administrative center of the Catholic Church, it is true, was in Italy, but the water which drove the mills of the Counterreformation had its source in Spain. If it is possible at all to speak of Botero's attachment to any nation-state, it is of a friendliness to Spain resting on the obvious ground of the tight alliance of the Catholic Church with Spanish imperialism."

Chapter Three

Secularizing tendencies in Catholic social thought from the Renaissance to the Jansenist-Jesuit controversy

The Concept of "Secularization"

The wide range of meaning given to the term "secularization" in literature on the relation of theology to social ethics makes it urgent that I explain in advance, with as much precision as possible, the meaning I give to it in this study. Whether my meaning is the "correct" one or not seems an unimportant question, provided I have made my meaning clear. I will use the term to mean either or both of two closely related but distinguishable ideas: first, the elimination from ethical discussion, or from the formulation of moral codes of behavior, of reliance on dogmatic theology invoking revelation; second, the shifting of emphasis from transcendental values to temporal values held on temporal grounds. As I will use the term here, it will signify a process, or tendency, which may or may not culminate in full substitution of temporal for transcendental considerations.*

The secularization process can manifest itself in many different ways. It is clearly in operation when an argument based on rationalism, naturalism, or temporal expediency ("utility") is substituted for an appeal to theological dogma in presenting a case for or against a particular social practice—as when usury is condemned not because it is sinful but because it has a net injurious effect on the temporal welfare of the individuals or the community. This phenomenon may be characterized as the "desanctification" of an argument hitherto conducted on theological grounds. It manifests itself most clearly when a type of behavior hitherto condemned on theological grounds is approved on temporal grounds, with tacit or express rejection of the relevance of theological considerations. An intermediate form of the process is the transfer of a particular issue from the domain

* Editors' note: In the 1966 Jayne Lectures, Viner defines "secularization" as "a lessening of the influence on ethical and economic thought of ecclesiastical authority and traditional church creeds, and a shifting of weight from dogma and revelation and other-worldliness to reason and sentiment and considerations of temporal welfare" (*The Role of Providence in the Social Order*, p. 55).

of dogma to the area of "adiaphora," or "things indifferent."[1] St. Thomas may have had "adiaphora" in mind when he says that outside the life of internal grace where faith acts through love of God, "to each one it is free to decide what he should do or avoid; and to each superior, to direct his subjects in such matters as regards what they must do or avoid."[2] But it should not be taken for granted that when a theologian declares a certain matter to be in the area of "adiaphora" he means that it is free from ethical significance; he may mean merely that while it remains an issue for "civil righteousness" or for natural ethics, it is not a question of sin or salvation, of theological precept or even counsel.

The process of "secularization" manifested itself most significantly through the emergence of differentiated intellectual disciplines, each with its own expertise and, in time, with its own special experts. During the period when the Church had a virtual monopoly of learning all of these experts would be clerics, but many of them would have no pretensions to be "theologians," and some might in fact rival the theologians proper for jurisdictional authority over particular classes of problems of conduct. Such specialization occurred fortuitously in the age of the Fathers, when pagan "philosophy" was absorbed into Christian theology, but had perforce to accept, although in a qualified way, the intellectual authority of the great Greek philosophers and Roman moralists. One of the characteristics of the later Renaissance was that it brought into existence secular-minded philosophers, both lay and clerical, who had confidence in their own capacities for independent thought and who rejected outright or evaded important elements of traditional theological doctrine, includ-

---

1. The concept of "things indifferent" is apparently of Stoic origin. It has been used to mean things without ethical significance of any kind, so that in the absence of relevant provisions of positive law, and where public scandal would not result, the individual was completely free to follow his personal inclinations. It has also been used, both in Catholic and in Protestant moral theology, to mean things unrelated to theological mandates or to salvation but not necessarily indifferent as far as "civil righteousness" was concerned. Such things come under the jurisdiction of civil but not of religious authorities in their religious capacity. It is the latter of these meanings which is relevant here. I have not found any comprehensive history of the concept. Some historical material is provided in the following: R.G. Bury, tr. and ed., *Sextus Empiricus, Against the Ethicists*, Cambridge, Mass., 1936, pp. 415–419; Edward F. Meylan, "The Stoic Doctrine of Indifferent Things and the Conception of Christian Liberty in Calvin's *Institutio Religionis Christianae*," *Romanic Review*, XXVIII (1937), 135–145; W. Gordon Zeeveld, *Foundations of Tudor Policy*, Cambridge, Mass., 1948 (see index, under "Adiaphora"). The term "imperfection" (*re* behavior) in Post-Thomist Catholic theology seems to be a variant of the concept of "adiaphora"; see Hugueny, "Imperfection," in *Dictionnaire de théologie catholique*, VII[2], Paris, 1927, cols. 1286–1298.

2. *Summa Theologica*, I–II, q. 108, a. 1.

ing the Scholastic sanctification of Aristotelian philosophy. These philosophers offered instead a blend of theology, philosophy, and human "wisdom" which was more secular than Scholastic doctrine, and provided methodological foundations for subsequent fuller secularization of philosophy and ethics.[3]

Traditional Catholic theology had incorporated a great deal of classical wisdom: Aristotelian and Platonic metaphysics, Aristotelian dicta, Greek and Roman "natural law" doctrine, Roman civil law. In their original form these were predominantly non-transcendental in character and dependent on one species or other of "reason" for their persuasiveness or further development. The extent to which these divergent materials lent themselves to coherent synthesis was already a matter of controversy for the Fathers, who differed among themselves in the degree of welcome they gave to pagan "philosophy." Later controversy within the Church turned on the choice between Aristotelian and Platonic metaphysics, between Stoic ethics and the ethics expounded or implied in the Bible, and between Roman law and other systems of law. In each case, these controversies partially turned, whether consciously or not, on the issue of how far it was legitimate to go in accepting naturalistic as opposed to transcendental, rational as opposed to fideistic, temporal as opposed to spiritual, approaches to the formulation of Christian ethics. When specialized experts emerged in the various fields of philosophy and law, they tended, by professional pride, training, and aptitude, to shift the weight of emphasis and authority from faith to human reason, from considerations of salvation and sin to considerations of temporal welfare and terrestrial happiness. In time, these experts succeeded in largely pre-empting these fields for themselves, and in so doing increased the role of secularized thought, even if such was not their conscious purpose.

No sharp lines of distinction were drawn between theologians proper and civil or canon lawyers, and later between theologians and philosophers, so that secularizing tendencies were able to operate within theology proper. The development of distinctions between "perfection" (or superogatory virtue), counsel, precept, and adiaphora, made it possible to discuss ethical issues at different levels or degrees of transcendentalism without a breach with orthodoxy. This was also the case with the distinctions between the "two tables" of the Decalogue and (dating from the threshold of the thirteenth century) between the "cardinal" and "theological" virtues. Some held that "cardinal" virtues were sufficient as a guide to external behavior

3. See below, pp. 123–30.

and the conduct of temporal affairs; such virtues had been made known, even to the heathen, by unaided human reason prior to and independent of the Christian revelation.[4]

There was danger of heresy, of course, in claiming too much scope for reason at the expense of revelation and faith. One device used to free reason from the authority of theology and sanctified metaphysics, while professing merely to protect religion from any vulnerability to the criticisms of reason, was the doctrine of the "twofold truth," each valid in its own field, one operating *per modum credendi* or on the basis of revelation and authority, the other operating *per modum intelligendi*, or on the basis of unaided human reasoning.[5] Writing in 1516, four years after the doctrine of the twofold truth had been condemned by the Lateran Council, Pompanazzi claimed that a superior morality could be established if the mortality of the soul were accepted. He treated it as "a neutral problem" as far as "natural reasons" are concerned, whether the soul is in fact immortal and asserted that the immortality of the soul is an article of faith, "to be proved by what is proper to faith." On the ground of revelation and faith, however, he conceded—whether sincerely or not has been debated ever since—that "we must assert that beyond doubt the soul is immortal."[6] Even if Pompanazzi was sincere, his demonstration of the possibilities of developing an ethical system without relying on supernaturalism helped to prepare the way for a later fully secularized ethics.

It was in jurisprudence and political philosophy, rather than in metaphysics, moral philosophy, economics, or even natural science, that "human reason" first gained a large measure of autonomy from theology and the effective exercise of ecclesiastical authority. This was not, I would suggest, because of any inherent quality of these disciplines. In the case of civil law, the Romans had already achieved marvels of systematization; they had constructed a smoothly functioning, self-coherent system which could only be operated by experts and upon which it was difficult to impose innovations stemming from alien sources. Roman law has in many respects proved more stable

4. See Dom Odon Lottin, "La théorie des vertus cardinales de 1230 à 1260," *Bibliothèque Thomiste*, XIV (1930), 233–259, and Phyllis Doyle, *A History of Political Thought*, new ed., London, 1949, pp. 94–95 (*re* Dante).

5. See F.C. French, "The Doctrine of the Twofold Truth," *Philosophical Review*, X (1901), 477–487; Max Maywald, *Die Lehre von der zweifachen Wahrheit*, Berlin, 1871; W. Betzendörfer, *Die Lehre von der zweifachen Wahrheit bei Pomponatius*, Tübingen, 1919.

6. *De Immortalitate Animae: On the Immortality of the Soul*, W. H. Hay, tr., in *The Renaissance Philosophy of Man*, Chicago, 1948, pp. 280–393 (see especially pp. 376–380).

and less susceptible to change than religious dogma; and where the two have come into conflict it seems to have been religious dogma that has more often been the one to yield. In the case of politics, the temporal rivalry between Church and State led to the development of a corps of "legists" and "politiques," which, with the help and protection of the princes, could operate as an autonomous discipline, in opposition to the Church and immune from its disciplinary powers and intellectual tutelage. It was centuries before there were metaphysicians, moralists, or economists similarly situated. Gentilis, an Italian international lawyer and convert to Protestantism teaching law at Oxford, speaking as if lawyers had lost the autonomy they once enjoyed, regretfully recalled the days when "an imperious voice," confident in its power to make clear to theologians their fundamental lack of jurisdiction in the legal field, could say: "Be silent, theologians, in this matter which does not concern you!"[7] Before the end of the Middle Ages, no one but a ruler, or the lawyers operating under his protection, could safely have dealt with theologians in this manner, even if the issue was an astronomical one.

With some exceptions, overt secularization proceeded faster, of course, in the thought and writings of laymen than in the formal theological treatises. These treatises, in fact, sometimes manifested a tendency which, perhaps more in form than in substance, was the exact opposite of secularization, namely, the sanctification of what had hitherto been secular doctrine. This process entailed the provision of transcendental support for prevalent secular doctrine and established social institutions. The beneficiaries in this process of sanctification have included at times slavery, feudalism, capitalism, monarchism, social stratification, imperialism, socialism, and corporatism.

In the conceptual field, the outstanding example of the sanctification of the secular is "natural law." Natural law as "right reason," of universal, unvarying, and everlasting application, had already been expounded by the ancient Greeks and Romans, sometimes, as in the case of Cicero, as law derived from God. For the Christian theologians who incorporated "natural law" into their theology, however, it raised a number of problems of principle and application. Their

---

7. *"Silete theologi, in munere alieno."* See G.H. van der Molen, *Alberico Gentili and the Development of International Law,* Amsterdam, 1937, p. 210. Cf. Richard McKeon, "The Development of the Concept of Property in Political Philosophy," *Ethics,* XLVIII (1938), 338: "By the sixteenth century the philosopher and the priest had largely disappeared as serious contestants for the place of the statesman, and the problems of politics were oriented to the consideration of the necessities of life and the powers that do or should control them."

own definitions of "natural law" did not bring it obviously within their own jurisdiction. The emphasis placed on reason as the judge of what was good and bad gave rise to the necessity of either postulating the impossibility of conflict between reason and faith, or of finding a valid rule for deciding between them in cases of conflict. The more territory assigned to natural law and the greater the effectiveness ascribed to it as a course of moral discipline, the less would seem to be the need for a moral theology with sanctions of future rewards and punishments—all the more so when civil law with its provisions for temporal rewards and punishments was treated as a reflection or declaration of natural law. For Augustinians, as later for Protestant predestinarians, there were logical difficulties in harmonizing the "justice" of natural law with the doctrine of original sin and of the fewness of the elect. Many found it difficult to reconcile the doctrine of a prevalent natural law, including its expression in positive law, with the observed variations in mores and legislation at different times and places. Moral theologians were never completely agreed on the proper answers to these problems, all of which were a standing invitation to secularization, either in the form of a natural law freed from theological entanglements or some other species of naturalistic explanation of the origin and obligatory character of moral principles and sentiments.

The inherent tension between theological dogma and natural law doctrine is perhaps brought out most clearly by the contrast between two extreme positions, each with its following. Some medieval theologians, especially Scotists and nominalists, held that to ascribe to human reason, unaided by revelation, the capacity to judge between good and evil was to challenge God's absolute sovereignty. It was God who determined by inscrutable processes what was good or bad.[8] At the opposite extreme was the doctrine that natural law was independent of divine sanction and was binding even on God himself. Accordingly, the principles of natural law had a binding force of their own and were intrinsically necessary and founded in the nature of things. Acts are not good because commanded by God, but are commanded by God because they are good. The origin of this doctrine is commonly attributed to Grotius, and it has its widest circulation in Arminian Protestant circles. Its roots were ancient, however. It has been attributed to Clement of Alexandria, and Lactantius rebutted it

<hr>

8. See Alois Dempf, *Sacrum Imperium*, Munich, 1929, pp. 508–509 (as regards William of Ockham); A.H. Chroust, "Hugo Grotius and the Scholastic Natural Law Tradition," *The New Scholasticism*, XVII (1943), 109 ff. (as regards the Scotists in general). This doctrine was later to be expounded also by strict Calvinists.

as an erroneous pagan doctrine.[9] It was invoked by jurists in the Middle Ages as an argument against papal claims that the temporal jurisdiction of the Church was essential to the exercise of moral discipline.[10]

There is a vast and learned literature, still flowing in undiminished volume, on the relations between natural law doctrine and Catholic moral theology. The one phase of the history of these relations which needs to be noted here is the threat posed by any emphasis on natural law, and human reason as the source of knowledge of natural law, to the authority of dogma and the jurisdictional claims of theologians. One way of dealing with this problem was to reduce the authority ascribed to an autonomous natural law by invoking the doctrine of the corruption of human nature by original sin, with the implied consequence that the competence of this corrupted human nature to distinguish good from bad without the aid of revelation had been seriously impaired. Another method of dealing with this problem was to distinguish between the intuitive and discursive ways in which human reason operated and to stress the need for trained and disciplined minds if the discursive way was to be competently used. As long as the Church had a near-monopoly of learning, this last position would logically serve to give it special jurisdiction in the interpretation of natural law. More important, however, was the doctrine of St. Thomas and other medieval theologians that while human reason had some capacity to determine what is just without the aid of revelation, faith sharpened the perceptive power of reason.[11] The implication was, perhaps, that the theologian, with his special dedication to faith, would have an especially sharp perception of what was just.

A more radical approach was that of Pascal, and before him, Henry Cornelius Agrippa,[12] both of whom, as Christians defending

9. See M. -L. Boutteville, *La Morale de l'église et la morale naturelle, études critiques*, Paris, 1866, pp. 459–460.

10. See Walter Ullman, *The Growth of Papal Government in the Middle Ages*, London, 1955, pp. 455–457.

11. See Etienne Gilson, *L'Esprit de la philosophie médiévale*, 2nd ed., Paris, 1944, pp. 10–11, 16, 37, 223, etc., and M.-D. Chenu, "La théologie comme science au XIIIe siècle," *Archives d'Histoire Doctrinale et Littéraire du Moyen Age*, II (1927), 31–71; see also the encyclical letter of Leo XIII, Aug. 4, 1879, and especially its citation from the Vatican Synod, "Faith frees the reason from error, and guards it, and instructs it with a manifold knowledge," in the English Dominican translation of St. Thomas Aquinas, *Summa Theologica*, American ed., New York, 1947, Vol. I, Introduction, p. x.

12. Pascal rejected natural law in his *Pensées*, published posthumously, where he was echoing Montaigne. Pascal's Jansenist friends were much disturbed by this, and Antoine Arnauld apparently suspected that Pascal's manuscripts had been tampered with or misinterpreted by their editor. See Antoine Arnauld, *Œuvres*, Paris, 1775, I,

faith as against reason, joined a long line of sceptics—or at least men of uncertain faith—stretching from Callicles in Plato's *Gorgias* and Sextus Empiricus to Montaigne and Charron, in discrediting natural law. According to Lagarde, some medieval theologians also opposed the marriage of classical natural law and traditional Christian theology. This opposition had the paradoxical result of promoting secularization by intensifying the search for an autonomous natural law by the exponents of "naturalism."[13]

Opponents of "secularization" have often charged it with being indifferent or hostile to religion. No doubt "secularizers" have often been anti-clerical or schismatic and have sometimes been avowed or, more likely, concealed sceptics, agnostics, or even atheists. Secularization may stop with questioning or rejection of the virtues of asceticism, monasticism, the cloistered life of contemplation, as compared to an active though not undisciplined participation in worldly activities and worldly pleasures. Alternatively, it may go on to reject or minimize revelation and substitute "natural theology" or "deism" or "rational religion" for traditional dogma. The rejection of deism and the adoption of agnosticism or atheism—and especially of crusading atheism—are "secularization" carried to an extreme which before the eighteenth century probably only a very few had reached and which no one could then openly avow without extreme peril. On one point, moreover, the most sceptical and the most devout could enter into a paradoxical alliance, namely, in denying the possibility of attaining positive knowledge of transcendental matters by means of unaided human reason. The most devout have at times rivalled or surpassed the sceptics in insisting on the independence of faith from human reason and of reason from faith. Intellectual sceptics have often proclaimed their unquestioning faith in traditional dogmas while insisting on the impossibility of providing a rational foundation of them. Whether the professed fideism of men like Pompanazzi, Agrippa, Montaigne, Charron, Bayle, and Mandeville may have been a protective disguise for unbelief, no one will ever know for certain. In any case the historical record justifies the assumption that secularization, even when patently heretical, is not always anti-religious or even anti-clerical.

In the long-standing moral controversy between secularizers and exponents of an orthodox dogma it has been a frequent practice of the

---

644–648 (a letter of Dec. 29, 1668). For Agrippa, see his *Sur l' incertitude aussi bien que la vanité des sciences et des arts* [1537], De Guedeville, tr., Leyden, 1726, Vol. III, Ch. 91, p. 1191.

13. *La Naissance de l'esprit laïque*, 1st ed., III, 404–406.

latter to treat the issue as one between morality and immorality (or at best amorality) and not as a question of rival systems of ethics, rival moral evaluations of particular practices or institutions, or the use of innocent abstraction to simplify analysis. As an extreme manifestation of this uncharitable procedure, I cite the following statement by Jacques Maritain, written in condemnation of "secularized" economics:

> The economic has as its end the acquisition and increase without limit of material riches as such. And all which can promote this end—even an injustice, even oppressive and inhumane conditions of life—is *economically* good. Justice, friendship, and all truly human values become strangers to the structure of political and economic life as such and if morality intervenes with its own requirements, from the start it will enter into conflict with political and economic reality, with political and economic science. A *homo oeconomicus* is imagined whose sole function is to accumulate material goods. If one seeks to add to this man a man subject to the regulations of morality, a man truly human, this linking will remain ineffective. In reality the economic man, whose appetite is insatiable, will devour his moral replica and all the rest, and he will work to pulverize, in the fashion of a bloody machine, the poor true humanity which suffers in the undergrounds of history.[14]

"Secularists" also resort too frequently and inexcusably to biased semantic procedures. They often write as if their own value systems have exclusive claims to the label "humanist" or "scientific," as if dogmatic moral theology, "humanism," and "science" were necessarily in conflict. The supply of terms is more limited than the range of ideas, but at least in intellectual discussion there is a great deal to be said for relying as little as possible on the eulogistic or pejorative associations of unavoidably ambiguous terms to carry the weight of one's argument.

The term "laicization" is often used, especially by French authors, as the equivalent of what I have here labelled as "secularization." Such use is made both with regard to questions of doctrine and where the transfer of authority over the formulation and enforcement of moral principles from the Church to civil officials is involved. I have no doubt that the general historical tendency has been for a shift of

---

14. *Religion et culture*, Paris, 1930, pp. 43–45.

authority or influence from Church to State, or from clerics to lay moralists, to be associated with a secularizing shift in doctrine. But this association is not a logical necessity. All of the "secularizing" tendencies can conceivably be operating within an established church, and some of them have at times been strongly defended by some clerics while strongly resisted by many laics. Heresy, schism, and dissent have often been a revolt against secularizing tendencies within an established church. "Erastian" ecclesiastics have often supported the secularizing activities of rulers to the discomfort of their more "orthodox" flocks. "Enthusiast" and "fanatic" are terms which have often been applied by clerics as labels for lay opponents of secularization. An additional reason for not identifying secularization of doctrine with laicization is that the distinction between cleric and laic has sometimes been blurred or even obliterated. This was the case with the political cardinals of seventeenth and eighteenth century France; with the "enlightened" abbés of eighteenth-century France, who were as "lay" and "secular" as they could be in everything except their *pro forma* celibacy, their costume, and the source of their income; and it was true of the "lay preachers" of some of the dissenting Protestant sects in England.

The Italian Renaissance

The Italian Renaissance is undergoing a close reexamination by modern scholars. Some of these are pressing hard the thesis that the period in question was not marked by any substantial break in continuity of adherence to traditional medieval patterns of belief. The "humanism" of the Renaissance, they claim, was not predominantly an anti-religious or sceptical humanism, but was a "Christian humanism."[15] Most of this literature touches only glancingly, if at all, on the less literary expositions of moral philosophy, and on those writings which reflect or discuss codes of behavior operating in the economic field. On general principles I would expect it to be possible to show that there was a large measure of continuity with earlier medieval thought in the Renaissance period, and that such changes as did occur largely entailed a new distribution of emphasis and a new

15. For expositions of this point of view, see Charles E. Trinkhaus, *Adversity's Noblemen: The Italian Humanists on Happiness*, New York, 1940; Paul O. Kristeller, "Humanism and Scholasticism in the Italian Renaissance," *Byzantion*, XVII (1944–1945), 369 ff.; *idem, The Classics and Renaissance Thought*, Cambridge, Mass., 1955, especially pp. 22, 72; and, for an objective report on the literature taking this position, W.K. Ferguson, *The Renaissance in Historical Thought*, Cambridge, Mass., 1948, pp. 342–358, 380–382.

degree of elaboration of a stock of ideas inherited from the past. But my concern here is a more limited one, and in any case I do not have either the knowledge or skills to identify the problem raised, let alone judge the degree to which the centuries involved represent a distinct stage in the cultural history of Italy—or of western Europe—entitled to a label which marks it off from preceding and following centuries.

Nevertheless, I think it can be demonstrated that in at least two areas relevant for this study the Renaissance was associated with views which, though not absolutely original, were in their emphasis, degree of elaboration, and in terms of the importance of their exponents, phenomena without close parallel in earlier periods in Italy or elsewhere. These two areas are, first, the formulation by or on behalf of successful businessmen of a defense or even eulogy of their pattern of life, and, second, the formulation by more philosophically minded men of a fairly systematic moral doctrine which was both different from and specifically critical of Scholastic moral theology, its conclusions and method of argument.

There was in the flourishing Italian cities, and especially in Florence and Venice, a novel expression of respect for the status in society, and a novel justification of the ideals and pattern of life, of the rich merchant. For the first time there was a merchant class of great wealth, politically dominant, and rivalling the clerics in culture and education. Articulate, talented, with no inferiority complex with respect to their dignity, social usefulness, and morality, these merchants and the lay philosophers, jurists, and litterateurs who shared their views openly challenged the moral teachings and intellectual procedures of the Scholastics.

These patricians paid tribute to the excellence of man instead of stressing the degradation resulting from original sin. They maintained that the life of virtue was within the reach of the ordinary run of mankind and was a pleasurable one; that virtue was to be pursued for its own sake or for its benefit to others, independently of its contribution to religious salvation or its obligatoriness as a religious duty. They claimed that both the activities by which their wealth had been acquired and the manner in which they used their wealth were beneficial to their communities. They rejected the doctrine that striving for enrichment and the ambition to rise in social status were sinful *per se*. Perhaps most important of all, they insisted that material things, magnificence in expenditure, spectacles, sacred and profane art, fine craftmanship, the embellishment of their palaces, their churches, and their cities, luxurious living accompanied by liberal giving—all these were good things in their own right, and that lives of useful activity were more to be admired than an ascetic life of passive contemplation or pious resignation.[16]

It would not be easy, I think, to match by comparable quotations from an earlier period in Italy or elsewhere the secular character of the opinions of a representative Florentine humanist, Coluccio Salutati, written towards the end of the fourteenth century:

> In fleeing the world, you may fall from heaven, whereas I, by remaining in the world, can raise my heart to heaven. If it is to serve your family, your children, your neighbor, and your city, which embraces all, if it is this which you make provision for, which you serve and devote your thought to, you cannot then fail also to raise your heart to heaven and please God. Perhaps you may even please Him more in these occupations; for you will not presume that you can procure by yourself alone peace in God, but you will unite yourself to Him, who concerns Himself with the things necessary to the family, cherished by friends, and useful to the community; and you will be acting with the power which He will have given you.[17]

> To tell the truth, I will boldly affirm and openly confess that I will willingly and happily give up to you and to those who lift their speculation to the sky all other truths, if only the truth and reason of things human are left to me.[18]

Eulogy of this kind of the successful merchant and of his role in society may well have made its first appearance in Renaissance Italy. It was later to be encountered also in France,[19] Germany, and no

---

16. I rely almost wholly on secondary sources. For general accounts, see especially, Amintore Fanfani, *Le origini dello spirito capitalistico in Italia*, Pubblicaz. della Univers. Cattolica del Sacro Cuore, 3rd series, Scienze Sociali, XII (1933); *idem*, *Storia del lavoro in Italia dalla fine del secolo XV agli inizi del XVIII*, Milan, 1943, pp. 23–24; Hans Baron, "Franciscan Poverty and Civic Wealth as Factors in the Rise of Humanistic Thought," *Speculum*, XIII (1938), 1–37; Yves Renouard, *Les Hommes d'affaires italiens du moyen âge*, Paris, 1949; Eugene F. Rice, Jr., *The Renaissance Idea of Wisdom*, Cambridge, Mass., 1958, pp. 38–44; Carlo Curcio, *La politica italiana del '400*, Florence, (1932), pp. 131–160; Friedrich Engel-Jánosi, "Soziale Probleme der Renaissance," *Beihefte zur Vierteljahrschrift für Sozial- und Wirtschaftsgeschichte*, IV. Heft, 1924; E. Garin, *L'Umanesimo italiano*, Bari, 1952. For individual authors, see Ernst Walser, *Poggius Florentinus Leben und Werke*, Berlin, 1914, p. 130, *re De Avaritia*, ca. 1428, a dialogue in which one of the speakers defends the rich burghers and their economic activities; P. H. Michel, *La Pensée de L.B. Alberti (1404–1472)*, Paris, 1930, pp. 318–322.

17. Cited in a French translation by Enrico Castelli, *Les Présupposés d'une théologie de l'histoire*, Paris, 1954, pp. 171–172.

18. As cited by Eugene F. Rice, Jr., *The Renaissance Idea of Wisdom*, p. 40. Rice explains that by "things human" Salutati meant "man and his individual, family, and social activities."

19. See the eulogy of the merchant, attributed to La Planche, in "Le Livre des

doubt elsewhere. An outstanding instance was in the writings of Konrad Peutinger, Catholic jurist, humanist, and counsellor of the Fuggers, Welsers, and other wealthy business families of Augsburg. From 1522 to 1530 Peutinger prepared a series of briefs in which the merchant striving for gain, big business, and free enterprise in general were defended, on moral, political, and especially economic grounds, against attacks of a traditional moral-religious kind, as well as against charges of monopolistic practice.[20]

It does not seem necessary to probe deeply into the cultural history of the Middle Ages to find an explanation for these developments. It would seem inevitable that a wealthy, politically dominant, and highly literate commercial aristocracy would either formulate for itself or find others to formulate for it a justification of its role in the community as a response to the critical attitude to business of the medieval Church. The attitudes of the businessmen and the secularizing tendencies of the literary humanists would naturally have much in common even if, in some respects, they could conflict with each other.

There is no mystery, either, in the prior development in Florence and Venice of an impressive apologia for the businessman's place in the world. Given the wealth and power of these cities, their political autonomy, and the cultural superiority of the patricians over the bucolic landlords of the countryside, everything falls into place. Where these conditions were approximated elsewhere, substantially similar phenomena occurred, with such divergences as did manifest themselves being plausibly explained by obvious differences in the location of political power and the degree of subordination to the temporal power of the Church. Outside Italy, the landed aristocracy and ecclesiastical princes retained a large measure of political authority over the cities; or there were strong national governments to hold in check the power and to lower the prestige of the urban upper classes, or else such commercial development as took place did not produce a top group of businessmen of great wealth and influence in

marchants," appended to Louis Régnier, Sieur de la Planche, *Histoire de l'état de France* [1576], Ed. Mennechet, ed., Paris, 1836, cols. 405–480, especially cols. 421–422.

20. See Erich König, *Peutingerstudien*, Freiburg i. B., 1914, pp. 130–142; Léon Schick, *Un Grand Homme d'affaires au début du XVIe siècle, Jacob Fugger*, Paris, 1957, pp. 561–571; Clemens Bauer, "Conrad Peutingers Gutachten zur Monopolfrage," *Archiv für Reformationsgeschichte*, XLV (1954), 1–43, 145–196; *idem*, "Conrad Peutinger und der Durchbruch des neuen ökonomischen Denkens in der Wende zur Neuzeit," *Augusta 955–1955, Forschungen and Studien zur Kultur- und Wirtschaftsgeschichte Augsburgs*, 1955, pp. 219–228.

setting the pattern of thought and living for their urban communities. In the southern cities of pre-Reformation Germany, where the closest parallel to the Italian development took place, though with a lag, this lag is attributable in part to the slower rate of economic growth, the lesser degree of urban autonomy, and the stronger political power and prestige of the Church and the landed aristocracy.[21]

Stress on the dignity of the individual and his moral, intellectual, and cultural potentialities, the laudatory treatment of what theologians labelled as the sin of "pride," criticism of the intellectual credentials of Scholasticism—these were common to the humanism of both the Italian merchants and the literati. But in Renaissance Italy, as in other periods and climes, theologian and intellectual could join in despising the avarice of the merchant and his pattern of life as compared to that of the agrarian aristocrat or the rural peasant. Despite claims to the contrary, mixed with approbation or censure, as regards such Renaissance theologians as Antonius of Florence, Bernardino of Siena, and Cardinal Cajetan, I have been able to find only meager scraps of evidence to indicate that theologians had any part in the favorable reappraisal of the merchant and in allaying the traditional medieval suspicion of urban types of gainful activity. Urban "magnificence" was admired by all. But it was not until the latter part of the sixteenth century that a specialized economic literature first made its appearance. Appropriately enough, this occurred in Italy; it threw a fairly clear light on the processes whereby the growth of civil wealth, the embellishment of cities, and the favorable opportunities for artistic creation were directly or indirectly the products of the striving of merchants for private enrichment.[22] Earlier there had only been Scholastic economics and Utopian dreaming.

21. For material confirming the existence of parallel tendencies in some German cities and the greater power of ecclesiastical and agrarian civil rulers over German than over Italian cities as restraints on these tendencies, see: K. Hagen, *Deutschlands literarische und religiöse Verhältnisse im Reformationszeitalter*, Frankfurt a. M., 1868, I, 17 (cited by W. K. Ferguson, *The Renaissance*, p. 157; Heinrich Werner, *Die Reformation des Kaisers Sigmund, Die erste deutsche Reformschrift eines Laien vor Luther*, Berlin, 1908; Helmut Weigel, "Die Entstehung der sog. Reformation Kaiser Sigmunds," in *Politik und Geschichte. Gedächtnisschrift für Georg von Below*, Berlin, 1928, pp. 128–145; Peter Nolte, *Der Kaufmann in der deutschen Sprache und Literatur des Mittelalters*, Göttingen, 1909, pp. 16, 21–23, 48–49, 57, 93; Alfred Schultze, *Stadtgemeinde und Reformation*, Tübingen, 1918, pp. 23–26; Heinrich Bechtel, *Wirtschaftsstil des deutschen Spätmittelalters (1350–1500)*, Munich, 1930, pp. 349–356; Erwin Gustav Gudde, *Social Conflicts in Medieval German Poetry*, University of California Publications in Modern Philology, XVIII (1934), No. 1; Alfons Dopsch, *Herrschaft und Bauer in der deutschen Kaiserzeit*, Jena, 1939, pp. 203, 211.

22. For the beginnings of systematic economic thinking in Italy, see Supino, "La scienza economica in Italia della seconda metà del secolo XVI alla prima del XVII," *Memorie della Reale Accademia delle Scienze di Torina*, 2nd series, XXXIX (1889).

It seems clear, however, that Renaissance humanism prepared the way in a much more fundamental manner than the patrician merchants for the fuller secularization of social life and thought later to be associated with the Enlightenment.[23] Renaissance humanism did so, even when criticizing or ignoring the practices, attitudes, and patterns of life of the patrician merchants, by its advocacy of the uninhibited pursuit of knowledge and of a life of activity instead of one of contemplation or torpor, and through its reappraisal of traditional doctrine in all fields in the light of freedom of thought and respect for temporal values.

In the sixteenth century there were humanists outside Italy who were much influenced by Renaissance thought. They were critical of Scholasticism and medieval theology and ardent exponents of the dignity of man and the worthiness of temporal values, but they were also aesthetically, morally, or religiously critical of what they regarded as the avarice of the bourgeois merchant. Erasmus was one example, and Ulrich von Hutten another. Erasmus was decidedly conservative in his attitude towards the morality of profit seeking, basing his opposition to Scholastic moral theology on other grounds than the need to strengthen the incentives for private profit. Despite his refusal to take the Scholastic argument against usury seriously and his shrewdness in protecting his own economic interests, Erasmus was more hostile to the business mentality than were the late Scholastics.[24] Humanist though he was, Hutten remained loyal to the social views of his knightly class and shared to the full its agrarian

23. I have found difficulty in locating systematic discussion of the influence of Renaissance social thought on the social thought of later centuries. To the references to modern studies of the Renaissance given in previous bibliographical notes in this section, there should be added the admirable study of Léon Blanchet, *Campanella*, Paris, 1920, which provides an impressive survey of the general intellectual trends in Italy toward the end of the Renaissance period. Especially useful for my purposes is Part V, Chs. 3–4, pp. 376–488. "La morale et la religion," which is in effect a study of the secularization of moral philosophy from Pomponazzi to Campanella. For the ethical views of Pomponazzi, see Jacques Matter, *Histoire des doctrines morales et politiques des trois derniers siècles*, Paris, 1836, I, 56–93; Andrew H. Douglas, *The Philosophy and Psychology of Pietro Pomponazzi*, Cambridge, Eng., 1910, pp. 248–269.

24. See A. Renaudet, "Erasme économiste," in *Mélanges offerts à M. Abel Lefranc*, Paris, 1936, pp. 130–141; Edward Surtz, S. J., *The Praise of Pleasure . . . in More's Utopia*, Cambridge, Mass., 1957, pp. 157–158, 170–180; Erasmus, *The Education of a Christian Prince*, Lester K. Born, tr. and ed., New York, 1936, pp. 217–218; Heinrich Wiskemann, *Darstellung der in Deutschland zur Zeit der Reformation herrschenden Nationalökonomischen Ansichten*, Leipzig, 1861, pp. 6–13; Wilhelm Maurer, *Das Verhältnis des Staates zu Kirche nach humanistischen Anschauung vornehmlich bei Erasmus*, Giessen, 1930, pp. 15–19.

biases.[25] In the southern Germany of his time the landed aristocracy, the peasants, and the urban poor were all hostile to the great city merchants, the Fuggers, the Welsers, and so forth, whom they regarded as monopolizers and usurers. It was a historical accident that the Fuggers were devout Catholics, bankers for the Church, and deeply involved in its economic affairs, so that the agrarian-minded Luther could make the Church and the Fuggers a common target for his invective; and similarly an accident that Hutten, whose criticism of the Church did not quite carry him to the point of schism, could make the Church and Fuggerism common targets, while Peutinger, like Hutten, a humanist, could be the leading apologist for the Fuggers and unqualifiedly loyal to the Church.[26] While it seems to be true that the humanists of the Italian Renaissance and those elsewhere who had been strongly influenced by it were critical of the Catholic Church of their time, and especially of the medieval blend of Aristotelian metaphysics and Scholastic logic, few if any of them were critical to the point of schism, and even fewer found early Protestantism an attractive alternative. The Renaissance was a bridge to the Enlightenment, to deism, to religious toleration, to a naturalistic ethics, but not to orthodox Lutheranism, to Calvinism, to casuistry, or to Jansenism.

In the French Catholic literature of reaction to the French Revolution, the Renaissance is often charged, together with the Protestant Reformation, the Enlightenment, and "rationalism" in general, as bearing major responsibility for the evils of the modern world: socialism, "liberalism," scepticism, rationalism, anti-clericalism, mammonism, and so forth. An extreme specimen of this literature is the history (in twelve volumes) of the origins of the French Revolution written by Msgr. Jean Joseph Gaume, whose central theme was that all these evil trends were initiated by the Renaissance and especially by the revival of pagan classicism, which thereafter became dominant in higher education.[27] But despite his backing in Rome and

25. See Hajo Holborn, *Ulrich von Hutten and the German Reformation*, New Haven, 1937, pp. 45, 187; Heinrich Wiskemann, *op. cit.*, pp. 13–25.

26. See August Kluckhohn, "Zur Geschichte der Handelsgesellschaften und -monopole im Zeitalter der Reformation," *Historische Aufsätze dem Andenken an Georg Waitz gewidmet*, Hanover, 1886, pp. 666–703.

27. *La Révolution: Recherches historiqr es sur l'origine et la propagation du mal en Europe*, Paris, 1859. Gaume initiated the controversy with his *Le Ver rongeur*, Brussels, 1851, which I have not seen. See also, R.B.V., "The Gaume Controversy on Classical Studies," *Dublin Review*, VII (1866), 200–228. For present-day criticism on religious grounds of Renaissance thought, see the (critical) account by Herbert Weisinger, "The Attack on the Renaissance in Theology Today," *Studies in the Renaissance*, II (1955), 176–189.

a strong following in France, Msgr. Gaume also had many Catholic critics who regarded his thesis as extreme and unbalanced. There can be no doubt that the Renaissance exerted an important influence on subsequent ethical and social thought. It was a delayed influence, however; neither the early Protestant reformers nor the Counter-reformation were receptive to it, except in limited ways, and the further progress of secularization of ethical and economic thought, such as it was, showed no clear indebtedness to Renaissance thought until the seventeenth and, more markedly, the eighteenth century, when, indeed, both Catholic and Protestant moral theology were profoundly influenced by it. It seems to me also that via Renaissance humanism the influence of Cicero and Seneca contributed appreciably to some of the intellectual developments of the Enlightenment that Msgr. Gaume so intensely disliked.

The Jansenist-Jesuit Controversy
in Seventeenth-Century France

There waged in seventeenth-century France, continuing into the eighteenth century, with repercussions in all Catholic countries and with echoes persisting to the present day, a bitter controversy between the upholders of two opposed doctrines as to the theological foundations or criteria of virtue and sin. Originating in issues which were almost purely theological in character, the controversy also became embroiled in personalities, rivalries and jealousies between different Catholic orders, questions relating to the authority of the Papacy over the Gallican Church, and of the pope over the bishops. Because of the closeness of the relationship of Church and State in seventeenth-century France, the controversy also had important political connotations. The two sets of doctrines involved were commonly labelled, by the respective opposition and by more-or-less neutral observers, as "rigorism" and "laxism." Because the leaders on the rigorist side, who belonged to the group associated with the convent at Port-Royal, were disciples of Jansenius, a Louvain theologian, and used his book, *Augustinus* (1640), as an authoritative doctrinal guide, the exponents of rigorism were commonly called Jansenists. The chief targets of the rigorists as exponents of laxism were the Jesuits, so that the controversy was regarded, and to a large extent correctly so, as a controversy between Jansenists and their followers, on the one hand, and Jesuits and their supporters, on the other hand. It is important, however, to bear in mind that there was some range of doctrinal difference even among the Jansenists, that the Jesuits did not take a position in the name of their Order, and that there were important Jesuits, notably Bourdaloue, whose doctrine was in some respects more rigorous than that of some of the Jansenists.[28] The controversy was carried on with passionate zeal, frequently sank to incredibly low standards of debate on normal criteria of historical objectivity and scholarly fairness, and constitutes a notorious example of the lengths to which *odium theologicum* can be carried.[29] The most famous item in the controversy, because of the personality and the fame of its author, its literary quality, and its devastating effectiveness as polemic, is Blaise Pascal's *Lettres provinciales*, 1656-1657. There continues to the present day to be extensive, more or less biased, somewhat bitter, and inconclusive debate as to the scholarly quality and the fairness of Pascal's attack on the laxists. But for the limited purposes of this study the *Lettres provinciales* are not an important source. Pierre Nicole and Jean Domat were the only writers to apply the doctrine of rigorism to specific economic issues at all systematically. Therefore, to simplify my task of exposition, I will concentrate on the general doctrine as presented by Nicole and confine my survey of those aspects of the controversy which have a bearing on the question of the secularization of economics ethics to the writings of Nicole and Domat.

Underlying all the differences between rigorists and laxists were differences with respect to the doctrine of grace. The intricacies of this doctrine are unlimited, and there were subtle differences among the Jansenists, as also among their opponents. The rigorist doctrine of the Jansenists was derived from St. Augustine, via Baius in the sixteenth century,[30] and Jansenius. Its essence, for present purposes, was that as the result of the Fall of man and original sin, man was so depraved that in the absence of special grace he could not free himself sufficiently from vice to escape eternal damnation. Indeed, only a few, even among the Christians, were predestined to receive such

28. The literature of the controversy is of immense proportions. The outstanding formal bibliography, Leopold Willaert, *Bibliotheca Janseniana Belgica*, Namur, 1949–1951, although selective in its references to non-Belgian publications, lists over 14,000 items.

29. As samples of polemical contributions on the Jansenist side which are marked by distorted quotations of texts, exaggerated interpretations, and irrelevant arguments *ad hominem*, there may be cited, from the long list available, *La Théologie morale des jésuites*, 1659; *La Morale pratique des jésuites*, 1669; *La Morale des jésuites*, 1667. As one example of a reply in kind by an enemy of the Jansenists, see Louis Hennepin, *La Morale pratique du jansenisme*, Utrecht, 1698. Hennepin was not a Jesuit, but a member of the Recollet order. For the circumstances under which this book was written, see Hugolin Lemay, "Etude bibliographique et historique sur la *Morale pratique* du P. Louis Hennepin, Recollet," *Proceedings and Transactions of the Royal Society of Canada*, 3rd series, XXXI (1937), Sect. 1, pp. 127–149.

30. For Baius, see F.X. Jansen, S.J., *Baius et le baianisme, essai théologique*, Louvain, 1927.

grace. "True Virtue" was the doing of good from the pure love of God ("charity," *caritas*); all that was not virtue was vice, or, in St. Augustine's terms, *aut caritas, aut cupiditas*. This doctrine was common to all the Jansenists, and it will generally not be necessary to explore the subtle differences between Nicole and other Jansenists in interpretation and distribution of emphasis.

Nicole labelled as vice all behavior motivated by self-interest (*amour-propre*), and he maintained that very nearly all human behavior, regardless of its external appearance, if closely examined, would be found to have roots in self-interest, in desires other than that of serving God. An act, moreover, was not truly virtuous if it was not performed solely out of virtuous motives, even though virtuous motives might be present and the act be irreproachable. Nicole spent much effort in exploring the various devices and psychological practices by which the self-interest which underlay objective behavior was commonly concealed not only from observers but from the agent himself. He carried his hunt for sin into the subconscious and the dream and found the dominance of *amour-propre* even in the idealism of the Christian mystic, in the shape of pride and pleasure in a rare experience, disguised by use of a false mystical language.[31] The Jansenists were aware that this was difficult doctrine "not in harmony with human thought,"[32] and made some effort to qualify it in order to stay within the limits they understood to be set by the Scriptures, the early Fathers, especially St. Augustine, and the Councils of the Church.[33] The following passage is representative of Nicole's usual position:

31. The bulk of Nicole's writings is most readily available in the collected editions extending to some twenty-five volumes, and published, in part, under the covering titles of *Pierre Nicole, Essais de morale* and *Continuation des essais de morale*, [1730]. I have used the Paris 1755 (Vols. I to VIII) and 1767 editions (Vols. VIII² to XIII). I will document only direct quotations and material not to be found repeatedly in Nicole's writings.

For Nicole on subconscious sinning, on *pensées imperceptibles*, dreams, etc., see the references in Paul Bénichou, *Morales du Grand Siècle*, 3rd ed., Paris, 1948, pp. 88 ff., and F.J. Tanquerey, "Le Jansénisme et les tragédies de Racine," *Revue des Cours et Conférences*, 1st series, XXXVIII (1936–37), especially Part 4, pp. 457–461.

32. Nicole, in a letter to Pasquier Quesnel, *Essais de morale*, VIII², 211.

33. Arnauld's doctrine appears at times to have been somewhat less austere than that of Nicole. Arnauld emphasized the difference in the degrees of sin, and criticized Protestantism for rejecting this doctrine. Venial sins, involuntary or minor sins, were not barriers to salvation. There was such a thing as imperfect or incomplete good, which was insufficient for heaven, for attainment of blessedness, but consistent with avoidance of the torments of hell. The *honnête homme* could presumably attain this intermediate status. See Jean Laporte, *La Doctrine de Port-Royal, exposition de la doctrine (d' après Arnauld)*, Vol. II, Part II, 1851, first portion, p. 71; second portion, pp. 150–151. See, however, pp. 137–38, below.

Without charity one is nothing. A man may have all the talents, internal and external, all temporal and spiritual grandeurs; he may add to these acts of the most dazzling virtue; he may thereby draw the admiration of his fellow-men; he may have suffered martyrdom or may be prepared to suffer it; he may have given all his goods to the poor; nevertheless, he must not take confidence in all this, because he may, despite all these things, be wholly without true virtues and in an abyss of miseries. Whether one is everything or one is nothing depends on an unknown foundation of which we can never have entire assurance.[34]

The opposing doctrine, labelled by those hostile to it "laxist," or "Molinist" after one of its leading expositors, Luis de Molina, a Spanish Jesuit (1535–1601), was a modified form of the Pelagian and "semi-Pelagian" doctrines which in the early days of the Church had been declared heretical. Its essential principles were that original sin had not totally corrupted human nature; that man still retained some capacity for attaining virtue; that imperfect virtue—for example, "attrition" as distinguished from "contrition"—would suffice for salvation, though not for perfection; that God spread his saving graces generously; and that those who out of ignorance were unacquainted with the mandates of Christian moral theology were not thereby excluded from all chances of salvation.[35]

The account of the controversy between rigorism and laxism has been confined so far to its more purely theological characteristics and to the subjective or "internal" criteria of virtue. The controversy, however, extended to the level of practical morality—to criteria for the moral appraisal of objective behavior, whether by "acts" of omission or commission, of men living in contemporary society. To compare the positions of Jansenists and Jesuits on this level, I find it convenient to distinguish between "rigorism" with respect to subjective morality and rigorism with respect to objective morality. With

34. *L'Esprit de M. Nicole,* 2nd ed., Paris, 1771, pp. 324–325. This is a collection of extracts from Nicole's writings.
35. For accounts of the conflict between rigorism and laxism, see Ignaz von Döllinger and Fr. Heinrich Reusch, *Geschichte der Moralstreitigkeiten in der römisch-katholischen Kirche seit dem sechzehnten Jahrhundert,* Nördlingen, 1889, I, 68–116; Albert de Meyer, *Les Premières Controverses jansénistes en France (1640–1649),* Louvain, 1919; and, as a sample of a Jansenist reply to Molinist polemics [Matthieu Petit Didier], *Apologie des Lettres Provinciales . . . contre . . . [P. Daniel], Entretiens de Cléandre et d'Eudoxe,* Rouen, 1697. For modern defense of the record of the Jesuit casuists, see Alexandre Brou, S.J., *Les Jésuites de la légende,* Paris, 1906, I, 413–430; J. Brodrick, S.J., *The Economic Morals of the Jesuits,* London, 1934.

respect to subjective morality there can be no doubt that the Jansenist doctrine was unambiguously more "rigorous," more austere, than the Molinist doctrine. But with respect to moral appraisal of objective behavior or to the moral code for external behavior, the comparative degree of rigor of the two schools is much less clear. A further complication arises from the fact that neither group had an absolutely uniform doctrine and that in the course of protracted controversy, polemical strategy led to a measure of adaptation and modification, as well as a revision of convictions.

A Marxist student of Jansenism, Lucien Goldmann, has claimed that there was an extremist group led by Martin de Barcos, abbé de Saint-Cyran, consisting of *gens de robe*, a socially discontented class in revolt against the monarchy whose motto was, in effect, "hate the world," and a "centrist group, including Nicole and Arnauld, not so embittered against the world, who held merely that one should not love the world."[36] I am not in a position to judge the validity of Goldmann's view. It is clear, however, that there were minor differences between individual Jansenists in the degree of severity with which they dealt with what I here distinguish as "objective" morality. Many Jansenists, moreover, showed no interest in questions of "objective morality" except where they provided material for their attack on what appeared to be vulnerable aspects of Jesuit casuistry.[37]

Nicole, and perhaps the Jansenists in general, addressed his rigorist, "subjective" moral theology to a spiritual élite, the "gens du bien," regarded as being few in number.[38] The rest of the world

36. "Remarques sur le jansénisme; la vision tragique du monde et la noblesse de robe," *XVIIIe Siècle*, No. 19, 1953, pp. 190 ff.

37. I have found only two studies which have as their central theme the social doctrines of the Jansenists: Paul Honigsheim, *Die Staats- und Soziallehren der französischen Jansenisten im 17. Jahrhundert*, Heidelberg dissertation, 1914, and E. Préclin, "Les conséquences sociales du jansénisme," *Revue d'Histoire de l'Eglise de France*, XXI (1935), 355–391. Neither is of much help for my present purposes. Préclin, who is concerned mostly with the eighteenth century, neither deals in detail with Nicole, nor distinguishes between "subjective" and "objective" morality.

For comments on Pascal's position in relation to other Jansenists indicating that he was more rigorous with respect to "objective" morality, see Jean Laporte, "Pascal et la doctrine de Port Royal," [1923], reprinted in his *Etudes d'histoire de la philosophie de Pascal*, Vol. II, Neuchatel, 1947; Gilbert Chinard, *En lisant Pascal*, Lille, 1948. Charles Droulers, *La Cité de Pascal*, Paris, 1928, manages somehow to picture Pascal as an optimist and an admirer of mankind.

38. For evidence of the Jansenists' restriction of their doctrine of subjective morality to a spiritual élite see: Mlle Paule Réguron, *Les Origines du mouvement anti-janséniste*, Grenoble, 1914, pp. 173–175; Nicolas Fontaine, *Mémoires pour servir à l'histoire de Port-Royal*, Utrecht, 1736, II, 78–79 (*re* Singlin); Duvergier de Hauranne, Abbé de Saint Cyran, "Pensées sur le sacerdoce," in *Lettres chrétiennes* [1645], 1744, I, 361, as quoted in Jean Laporte, *La Doctrine de Port-Royal*, Paris,

consisted, in effect, of *honnêtes hommes*, good citizens, though *méchants* from a subjective point of view, for whom the life of subjective morality was largely irrelevant because it was beyond their reach. It also consisted of rascals, criminals, dissolute characters, and libertines, about whom Nicole's only concern was that the civil authorities should punish them and protect the rest of the community from them. Nicole was sufficiently interested in the temporal world to have respect for the morality of the *honnêtes hommes*, not because of any religious "merit" for purposes of salvation, but because this morality was admirable in its external or objective manifestations and contributed to a temporally flourishing society.[39]

Nicole presents his view of the ethics of "enlightened self-interest" (*amour-propre éclairé*) in greatest detail in "De la charité et de l'amour propre," and in "De la grandeur," Ch. 6.[40] He writes under the influence of Hobbes, but expounds more explicitly than Hobbes ever did the objective attractions of a society flourishing temporally under the motivation of self-interest, criticizing Hobbes only for treating such a society as legitimate and unblamable.

Enlightened self-interest, through the medium of commerce resting on mutual exchange of services, meets all the needs of earthly life without any intervention of charity. Thus we find that in countries where charity has no point of entry because the true religion is banned, life is carried on with as complete peace, security, and ease as if one were in a community of saints. Self-interest gives the same answers as charity to most of the questions put to it. It can correct all the external faults of the world and bring into existence a well-

---

1923, I, 102; Antoine Arnauld, in a letter to the Landgraf of Hesse, 1683, *Œuvres*, Paris, 1775, II, 334.

39. There is a large literature on the concept of the *honnête homme*, but much of it overlooks the fact that the term underwent a gradual evolution of meaning during the seventeenth and eighteenth centuries. (See Pierre Villey, *Montaigne devant la postérité*, Paris, 1935, p. 339.) The term was used freely by Nicole and other Jansenists to mean respectable citizens who observed all the prevailing moral standards of their class and occupation, but whose internal or subjective morality was below the minimum standards required for salvation. The *honnêtes hommes* and the outright rascals together constituted the *méchants* and accounted for the great bulk of mankind. Other terms used occasionally by Nicole as approximately synonymous with *honnêtes hommes* were *gens du monde*, *demi-pêcheurs*, and *demi-chrétiens*.

The Jansenists were anti-Scholastics, and in developing their moral doctrines they deliberately bypassed five centuries of Scholastic doctrine. Nevertheless, if one may read "wicked" in the passage which follows from St. Thomas, *Summa Theologica*, I-II, q. 114, a. 10, ad 4, to correspond to Nicole's *honnêtes hommes*, the passage does represent a basic element in Nicole's doctrine: "All things happen equally to the good and the wicked, as regards the substance of temporal good or evil; but not as regards the end, since the good and not the wicked are led to beatitude by them."

40. In *Essais de morale*, III, 134–193; II, 172–181.

ordered society if only it is universally enlightened. However corrupt such a well-ordered society would be internally and in the eyes of God, there would be nothing in its external appearance which could be more civil, more just, more peaceful, more honest, and more generous. If the foundation of this society in self-interest were not visible, the society would take on a most attractive appearance. Totally devoid of charity though it would be, to an outside observer it would manifest only the characteristics of charity.

Common charity, in fact, could not do as well as far as external appearance was concerned. It is cupidity which leads persons in the countryside to serve the traveller from the city, to prepare a lodging for him, to obey his commands, and to do so with such grace that thanks are given. But one thing more is necessary if cupidity is to render the great services of which it is capable; something must prevent it from being carried to excess. The political order provides the essential art of regulating cupidity, restraining it through fear of punishment, and directing it to things which are useful to society. It is this political order which gives us merchants, doctors, craftsmen, and generally all those who contribute to the pleasures and relieve the pains of life.[41]

It seems clear from Nicole's writings as a whole that he regarded the "subjective" code as too exacting for all except a small élite; that for the ordinary run of mankind he thought the prevailing moral code was about as good as could be attained; and that, even when counselling the devout on their behavior, he did not ask them to adhere scrupulously in all details to the prevailing objective code and rarely advised them to improve on it. It is easy to see how his readers, by skipping over his subjective doctrine and placing all the weight on his exposition of the admirable external features of a society moved by enlightened self-interest and regulated by civil government, could interpret him as an accommodator of moral theology to the world instead of an intransigent critic of the world. The particular *essais* in which he most systematically expounded his "objective" moral sys-

---

41. Bernard Mandeville, in his *Fable of the Bees*, took over much of Nicole's system, including the association of lavish praise on objective grounds and radical condemnation on subjective grounds of a society moved by self-interest and regulated by government. But the sincerity of Mandeville's claim to reject such a society on moral grounds is highly questionable, and in treating the rascals as at least as serviceable to society as the honest and respectable citizens, Mandeville not only deviates from Nicole, but must be interpreted as being wilfully provocative for all schools of morality, in a spirit of libertine fun-making. See my "Introduction" to Bernard Mandeville, *A Letter to Dion* (1732), Augustan Reprint Society Publication 41, 1953, reprinted in my *The Long View and the Short*, Glencoe, Ill., 1958, pp. 332–342.

tem went through over fifty editions in France alone in the seventeenth century and were frequently translated. It may be conjectured that this peculiar combination of a subjective morality of extreme rigor applicable only to a spiritual élite and an objective morality of almost complete conformity to a routine respectability considered as the most that was subjectively within the reach of ordinary people (and objectively quite good enough even for the élite) met a widespread need for a rationalization of the actual code of the *honnête homme* which would not require an overt rejection of the subjective requirements of rigorism. At the same time, it met the devout Jansenist's standards of subjective morality without demanding any higher standard of objective behavior than was required by the code of the *honnête homme*. As Duvergier de Hauranne, abbé de Saint Cyran, commented in a letter to Arnauld, the rigorists "should lead a life like the others in appearance, but as different from theirs in spirit as the Son of God is from his creatures."[42] This meant in practice that Jansenism uncritically accepted the *status quo* as far as current political and social issues were concerned. As one writer has penetratingly commented:

> For them [the Jansenists], to seek to organize a government adapted to leading all men to salvation would have constituted, strictly speaking, a heresy. All men belonged to the realm of nature. A small number belonged at the same time to the realm of grace. Mankind in general, therefore, needed to be governed by natural laws, not at all by the laws belonging to the domain of grace. As in the first centuries of the Church, the true Christians were in the minority. No more than under the Roman emperors, it was not for them to take over government in order to make of it a Christian government. It was necessary to give to Caesar what belonged to Caesar.[43]

Concessions to human frailties, even on behalf of the spiritual élite, and accommodation of Jansenist moral doctrine to the requirements of comfortable living in a society of *honnêtes hommes* are to be

42. See Jean Laporte, *Etudes d'histoire*, p. 141.
43. Charles Droulers, *La Cité de Pascal*, pp. 40–41. The leading lay Jansenists were "bourgeois," but on the fringes of the aristocracy—officials, magistrates, and lawyers. It does not appear that the Jansenist theologians obtained or sought a following among businessmen, merchants, financiers, foreign traders, and the like. See Paul Bénichou, *Morales du Grand Siècle*, 3rd ed., Paris, 1948, pp. 112–130, "Le parti janséniste."

found scattered throughout Nicole's writings.[44] This was true also of Antoine Arnauld, the "great Arnauld." While, for example, he warned that luxury was evil insofar as it served vanity and pride and kept men from paying their debts and helping the poor, he said that to wear expensive clothing or jewels was not condemnable if done in order to behave like the rest of the world in conformity with existing custom or to make apparent one's status in society out of respect for the established order. It was even permissible to pray for riches for these purposes. While the stratification of society into different social classes began only with the Fall of man, given the state of sin to which man had thereby been reduced, it had become quasi-necessary ("comme nécessaire"). The Christian religion therefore did not seek the abolition of classes, but contented itself with pointing out the duties of each class and insisting on the spiritual equality of all Christians. Expenditures on luxuries, moreover, gave employment to the poor.[45]

It was, however, Jean Domat, a distinguished jurist and close associate of Nicole, who most systematically reconciled Jansenist theological rigorism with the practical requirements of a temporally well-ordered and flourishing society such as he considered the France of his time to be.[46] For the most part Domat's doctrine follows closely the lines of Nicole's argument, but with greater stress—in keeping with his vocation as jurist and a magistrate—on the role of government in producing a flourishing civil society.

Domat starts from the proposition that self-interest (*amour-propre*), though an evil and the principle underlying all evils, has been made by God the source of an infinity of good effects. Self-interest produces only corrupt fruits for those moved by it, but for society it yields genuine benefits. Fear brings obedience of subjects to their rulers; avarice is the great stimulus to commerce; pride, curiosity,

---

44. See Henri Brémond, *Histoire littéraire du sentiment religieux en France*, IV (1920), 466–468.

45. *Œuvres*, Paris, 1775–1783, II, 644–649; III, 237. Pascal, in his ninth Provincial Letter was very severe in criticizing luxury. H. Baudrillart, *Histoire du luxe privé et public*, Paris, 1880, IV, 187, is wrong, therefore, at least as far as Arnauld is concerned, when he says that "the Jansenism of Arnauld and of Nicole did not show itself in this respect more tolerant than that of Pascal." In his notes to his Latin translation of Pascal's *Provincial Letters*, a polemical enterprise against the laxists, Nicole takes no issue on any point with Pascal, but nothing, I think, can be inferred from this as to what Nicole's own position was. I have not found any discussion of luxury in Nicole's other writings.

46. For Domat's career and doctrines in general, see Henry Loubers, *J. Domat philosophe et magistrat*, Paris, n.d. (c. 1873); Th. Funck-Brentano, "Le droit naturel au XVIIe siècle," *Revue d'Histoire Diplomatique*, I (1887), 491–505.

and the love of luxury, condemnable as they are *per se*, are responsible for most of the progress in arts and sciences. Thus, by the design of Providence, those passions which tend by their nature to destroy the divine order are made to contribute to its conservation. But since the passions if left to themselves would not stay within the limits of their serviceability to society, but often lead to usury, frauds, theft, murder, and other crimes, God has provided for the protection of society from these excesses by establishing, and permitting mankind to establish, laws for the suppression of offenses against the public order arising out of the unrestrained operation of self-interest.[47]

In another work, Domat lists four "natural foundations" of social order which operate alongside self-interest, keeping it from working to the ruin of society: (1) religion; (2) "the secret action of God on society in all the universe"; (3) the authority which God gives to "powers," that is, the family and "police," or civil power; and (4) "that light which remained with man after his Fall, by which he knows the natural rules of equity." Another benefit to society emphasized by Nicole was the element of reciprocal benefit in the operations of "enlightened" self-interest. Although Domat does not include this benefit in his list, it is implicit in his argument.[48]

If an abstraction is made from the Jansenist stress on the presence of subjective sin in objectively virtuous behavior, and if the emphasis on the role of government is interpreted to refer primarily to the enforcement of commutative justice or the suppression of crime, the Nicole-Domat social doctrine becomes a striking anticipation of Adam Smith's economic philosophy. Furthermore, if the Jansenist stress on providential design is laid aside, the doctrine often sounds like an anticipation of nineteenth-century economic liberalism. Nicole and Domat, however, accepted uncritically the whole contemporary range of French governmental activity, and in its objective phase Jansenist social doctrine was in full harmony with at least the domestic aspects of contemporary French mercantilism.[49] Whatever may have been the Jansenists' intentions, therefore, they prepared the way for, rather than obstructed, all the later modes of substituting criteria of temporal benefit for religious dogmas, transcendental goals, or traditional maxims in the moral appraisal of social behavior. Jansenism, despite its rigorism on the subjective level, was thus a part of

47. *Harangue prononcée aux assises de 1679*, in *Œuvres complètes*, Paris, 1830, IV, 96–97.
48. *Traité des loix*, Ch. IX, *ibid.*, I, 26–27.
49. I am not aware that any of the Jansenists dealt with international relations.

the secularizing trend.[50] The Enlightenment needed little more in order to absorb Jansenist doctrine than to ignore its subjective morality. Writing in 1765, Helvétius remarked that Nicole, La Rochefoucauld, and Pascal had accustomed the French public to take the word *amour-propre* always in a bad sense; "it was only recently that a small number of men commenced to refrain from necessarily attaching to it ideas of vice, pride, etc."[51] In 1672 Jacques Esprit, a Jansenist, had published a book with the title *Faussetés des vertus humaines*, whose central theme was that most of the "virtues" held in esteem by the worldly were tainted by self-interest and therefore were not true virtues. Jeremy Bentham, in a work written in the 1790's—or perhaps the editor of its published version, Etienne Dumont—commented that Esprit's book would require only a few slight verbal alterations to convert it into a work on the genuine presence of human virtues, since only as virtue serves human interests has it any reality.[52] Some modern writers have indeed interpreted the Jansenists' social doctrine as if its rigorist foundations were non-existent or of no consequence even for the Jansenists themselves.

My argument has been that on the level of "objective" morality, the Jansenists, or at least some of them, were not "rigorous." This calls for explanation as to why the controversy between the Jansenists and the Jesuits took place and continues to be interpreted as a debate between rigorist and laxist doctrines of practical morals. The explanation lies in the special character and the limited functions of Jesuit "casuistry."

The Jansenist Attack on Casuistry

In its original meaning, casuistry in the Catholic Church is the application by experts of the general principles of orthodox moral theology to specific and concrete cases of human behavior in order to determine whether they fall within the limits of permissible behavior.

50. J.P. Zimmermann, "La Morale laïque au commencement du XVIIIe siècle," *Revue d'Histoire Littéraire de la France*, XXIV (1917), 49–50, comments that while Nicole no doubt looked at motives and not at effects and therefore must have been convinced that self-interest was opposed to salvation, his doctrine came at a time when "the notion of social utility was being substituted for the Christian ideal of individual perfection, and consequently [his doctrine] was often misinterpreted." De Crousaz-Crétet, *La Morale et les moralistes sous l'ancien régime*, Paris, 1885, pp. 155–156, concludes his account of Nicole's doctrine with the comment: "Let us therefore be grateful to Nicole for having managed the transition from vice to virtue, perhaps at the cost of a slight contradiction, by utilizing that worldly *honnêteté* which elsewhere he took so sharply to task."

51. In the article "Intérêt," in the *Encyclopédie*, Berne edition, 1783, XVIII, 889.

52. Bentham, *The Rationale of Reward*, London, 1825, p. 126.

It is regrettable that a neutral term, say "casuistics," was not used to describe this general procedure, reserving "casuistry" as a pejorative term for its misuse or abuse. Soon after its establishment the Jesuit order made the preparation of manuals of casuistry an important item in its program of activities, and in the seventeenth century Jesuit manuals were the most widely used. They were intended primarily for use in the training of candidates for the priesthood, by spiritual counsellors in advising their clients, and above all by priests as guides in the execution of their judicial functions in the confessional. For the most part they were published in Latin, but one or two at least were published in French or Spanish. Latin, moreover, was not the barrier to wide circulation which it would be today, and some of the more controversial manuals were used as textbooks in the French schools.[53] The Jansenist charge that these manuals expounded a lax morality ("une morale relâchée"), which was broadcast in innumerable tracts, was the most prominent feature of the rigorism-laxism controversy and made it a public controversy instead of merely a technical debate between professional theologians.

The manuals were in effect guides as to how far a Christian could go without becoming liable to penitential penalties or risking salvation;[54] a seventeenth-century cleric called them "peccameters."[55] There were occupational dangers in their preparation, and obvious reasons why it might have been regarded as unwise to allow them to circulate freely. Even if it were not true, as was alleged, that rivalry between the orders in attracting penitents to their confessionals acted as a stimulus to lax doctrine, a relaxing tendency would have arisen from the humane wish to make the burden of compliance with the requirements of the faith rest as lightly as was permissible on the consciences of the members of the Church, and to avoid imposing a discipline more severe than the ordinary man could bear. In any case, some of the general principles contained in many of these manuals exercised a pervasive relaxing influence, most notably through the "probabilist" doctrine that if any authority of standing could be found who held that a particular practice was permissible, his opinion could be followed even if the majority of the authorities held otherwise, and even if the priest making the decision himself believed that a more

---

53. Cf. André Schimberg, *L'Education morale dans les collèges de la compagnie de Jésus en France sous l'ancien régime (XVIᵉ, XVIIᵉ, XVIIIᵉ siècles)*, Paris, 1913, p. 88.

54. On the function of casuistry in the Catholic Church, see Joseph Mausbach, D.D., *Catholic Moral Teaching and Its Antagonists* (translated from the 6th German ed.), New York, 1914, pp. 69 ff.

55. See Ph. Delhaye, "La théologie morale d'hier et d'aujourd'hui," *Revue des Sciences Religieuses*, XXVII (1953), 119.

rigorous opinion was more probably true.[56] There was also the almost inevitable chance that among the many authors of manuals who were engaged in constructing hypothetical cases dealing with the whole range of moral problems, there would be an occasional one without good judgment or with some mental or moral twist, and that there would be occasional lapses of judgment even on the part of the most solid authors.

A Jesuit, Térillus, writing in 1660 when the controversy was at its height, condemned the faults of the casuists in language as vigorous as that used by the Jansenists:

> For thirty years the libraries have been filling with their cases of conscience, which spread out as fodder for the vulgar to feed on, in order to capture their goodwill, opinions progressively more lax. . . . I have not been able to observe without horror how some men trample under foot, by the most frivolous or arguments, the laws of God and of the Church based on the most solid of proofs. There have been some who have made collections of these immoral opinions to present them to the public as a guide to consciences. These they call a collection of probable opinions. Satan found this field of theology planted with sober and severe opinions; he has sown among this wheat the tares of laxism and then gone off, convinced that it would not be possible to pull up the tares without damage to the wheat.[57]

---

56. See Thomas Slater (an English Jesuit), *A Short History of Moral Theology*, New York, 1909, and *idem*, *Cases of Conscience for English-Speaking Countries*, New York, 1911–1912, for a history of the doctrine of "probabilism" and a defense of it in "moderate" form. See also De Blie, "La théologie morale dans la compagnie de Jésus," in *Dictionnaire de théologie catholique*, VIII (1924), cols. 1074 ff. The founder of "moderate probabilism" was Saint Alfonso de Liguori, who in the 1750's introduced the distinction between degrees of probability: "less probable," "equally probable," and "more probable." While adhering to the principle that "an uncertain law cannot entail a certain obligation," he held that it was a mistake of some probabilists to teach that when there were two contradictory opinions each of which was probable one could choose the laxer one while suspending one's judgment as to which was correct. See *Œuvres complètes*, Paris, 1838. Vol. XXIX, "Réponse apologétique . . . à une lettre d'un religieux sur l'usage de l'opinion également probable," pp. 351–378, and *idem*, "De l'usage modéré de l'opinion probable," Ch. IV, pp. 178–215. De Liguori wrote that many of the opinions of casuists had been rightly condemned by the Church, and that a mass of others, in his opinion, should have been condemned, but that in his day the problem was not one of undue laxity but of undue rigorism in casuistry ("Réponse apologétique," p. 362). For the life and works of Liguori, see Berthe, *Saint Alphonse de Liguori*, 1696–1787, Paris, 1900, especially, I, 473–489, "La 'Théologie morale,'" and Abbé Th. Gousset, *Justification de la théologie morale du B. Alfonse Marie de Ligorio*, Besançon, 1832.

57. Cited by Berthe, *Saint Alphonse de Liguori*, I, 475.

Given the great mass of casuistical literature, its special function in determining the limits of permissible conduct, the malice and bias with which the enemies of the Jesuits combed it, the possibilities of misinterpretation, mistranslation, and quotation out of context, it hardly seems surprising, and not necessarily significant, that plausible indictments could be made against the literature as a whole, especially in the absence of a measure of the degree of laxness, innocence, or rigor in the material[58] and in the absence of genuinely objective appraisal by qualified persons not involved in the animus of the Jansenist-Jesuit controversies. For present purposes, however, if it be granted that there was a general laxist tendency in the Jesuit manuals, there remains the question of whether that laxity had a systematic pattern in regard to issues of economic behavior, and in particular the question whether there was a contrast between the casuists' decisions in this area, on the one hand, and the "objective" moral standards of the Jansenists and the *honnêtes hommes*, on the other.

To test the extent of conflict between Jansenist and casuist doctrine on questions of practical morality, I will consider the two significant economic questions on which there was sharpest controversy, namely, usury and the permissible limitations to the giving of alms. As before, I will give special attention to the views of Nicole.

Arnauld, Nicole, and Domat all condemned the charging of interest on loans as illicit. But both Arnauld and Nicole conceded that if natural reason alone were consulted, a convincing general case could not be made against usury; that it was only on the basis of Scripture and Church decrees that usury could be condemned.[59] No casuist, as far as I know, ever conceded that there was no case in natural law against usury. Jansenist criticism of the position of the casuists on the usury issue mainly turned on the latter's defense of such devices as the so-called Mohatra contract. This entailed the substitution of a loan at interest by the sale of some merchandise to a would-be borrower for deferred payment and repurchase at a lower cash price—a device which could easily be regarded as a legalistic trick with no function except that of evading the prohibition of interest on a pure loan.[60]

---

58. My own limited acquaintance with the literature of seventeenth-century casuistry suffices to persuade me that the defenders of the casuists have missed a gambit by not making a collection of the *rigorous* decisions to be found in the manuals.

59. For Arnauld, see Jean Laporte, *La Morale d'après Arnauld*, I, 64 ff., and Arnauld, *Œuvres*, I, 711 ff; for Nicole, see what follows in the text.

60. Cf. the comment of H.F. Stewart, ed., *Les Lettres Provinciales de Blaise Pascal*, Manchester, 1920, pp. 280–281, on the casuists' opinions with respect to usury which were ridiculed by Pascal. "Their ingenious suggestions are in no sense

When discussing the question of usury in his anti-casuist polemics, Nicole adheres to the traditional doctrine in all its rigor and without any qualifications.[61] But in his only significant discussion of usury outside the Jansenist-Jesuit controversy[62] he not only takes a position which is decidedly "laxist" in certain respects but presents an argument for giving weight to economic or "utilitarian" considerations in reaching moral decisions which is as explicit and elaborate as any I have encountered in the work of earlier Catholic moral theologians.

In this tract Nicole discusses two issues: first, whether by selling at a higher price for credit than for cash constitutes "usury," and second, whether it is a morally and religiously licit practice. He begins by quoting approvingly a statement by St. Thomas Aquinas which, as he interprets it, maintains that where there is not complete certainty, there is more moral danger in deciding that an action involves mortal sin than the opposite,[63] a proposition quite in the spirit of "laxist" casuistics. He accepts without question that usury is a sin, but claims that what makes this certain is not natural reason but divine law as interpreted by Church tradition. By the aid of reason alone, he says, it would be difficult to persuade anyone that there is evil in charging 5 per cent for a loan to a merchant who expects to gain much more from the loan and who would be disappointed if the lender were to share in the risk and thus were entitled to a corresponding share of any gain. Similarly, where the borrower saves 10 per cent as a result of the loan without incurring risk, reason alone would not suggest that the lender is imposing an injustice on the borrower by charging him 5 per cent.[64]

Where divine law speaks clearly, says Nicole, the preceding considerations are without relevance. But he holds that they suffice to oppose any condemnation of usury going beyond the Scriptures and their explanation by the Fathers. Such condemnation is particularly perilous where the form of contract involved is not expressly condemned by any law, ecclesiastical or civil. In fact, no instance can be

---

fraudulent. Yet they are immoral because they are subterfuges invented for the purpose of evading the law which they pretend to keep."

61. *Les Provinciales, ou lettres écrites par Louis de Montalte* [i.e., Pascal] . . . *avec les notes de Guillaume Wendrock* [i.e., Nicole]; Nicole's "Notes" III and IV on Pascal's Eighth Letter, I, 430–435. The use of pseudonym was common in both camps.

62. "Si c'est usure que de vendre plus cher à crédit," *Essais de morale*, VI, 112–148.

63. The reference is to *Quodlib*. 9, a. 5.

64. Some Scholastics would have replied that even if usury were not an injustice against the borrower, it could be unjust to a third party, or to the community, to whom the interest burden is transferred in the form of higher prices.

found of a Father—presumably also of a civil law—condemning the sale at credit at a higher price than for cash, though such transactions must have been very common, since commerce is practically impossible without resort to credit.

Nicole next argues that the credit-sale contract, whether licit or not, does not properly come under the category of "usury" as found in Church decrees and canon law, where usury is restricted to loan transactions. Where the contract has been condemned by the Church, it has been because the charge for deferment of payment was excessive. He concedes that St. Thomas Aquinas did condemn such contracts as usurious.[65] But he replies, first, that one is not obliged to follow Aquinas where he cannot be supported by citations from Scripture, from the Fathers, or from canon law. Secondly, he argues that St. Thomas is not persuasive when he concedes that it is lawful for a seller to reduce his price in order to obtain cash payment, while insisting that it is usurious to demand a higher price for deferred payment. Thirdly, lest this last point should be construed as resort to "subtlety," Nicole claims that both prices, the lower price for cash and the higher price for deferred payment, are "just prices" if the just price is regarded as the price the merchant must receive not only to avoid loss but to gain an honest income in serving the public faithfully and worthily. He cites in support the words which St. Augustine attributes to a merchant justifying the sale of goods above the purchase price if the gain is not excessive.[66] Nicole then claims that the merchant who sells on credit has troubles, losses, and dangers. As proof that the merchant does not exceed the just price merely by charging a higher price for deferred payment, he also cites the probability that the merchant would much prefer to make all his sales for cash at the lower price.

Nicole finds additional justification for a higher price for sales at credit in the loss which the seller incurs because he is temporarily deprived of his money. In many cases, heavy investment is necessary several years before the merchandise is available for sale, as in the case of goods imported from the Indies or of the publication of a work in many volumes. No one, he says, would regard it as unreasonable for the just price to include compensation for the privation from the money advanced prior to sale; why then is it not also reasonable to include in the just price of the merchandise sold at credit a compensation for the privation from use of the money during the period intervening between sale and final payment?

---

65. In *Summa Theologica*, II–II, q. 78, a. 2, and 7; see Ch. II, p. 93 above.
66. See Ch. I, p. 35 above.

Nicole concedes that if an appeal is made to reason, a similar case can be made for usury, that is, for loans at interest. He argues, however, that a fundamental distinction can be made between the two cases; one involves a sales contract and the other a loan contract. According to divine, civil, and canon law the loan contract is a free contract, whereas the sales contract is one which can legitimately be profitable. In sanctioning the profitability of the sales contract, the law must be regarded as sanctioning also the admission of every permissible element of compensation.

The fact that the law, divine and civil, requires lending to be an act of liberality and not a means of earning a living, whereas it not only tolerates but approves the merchant's profession in all countries as necessary for life, results in a different moral code in the two cases. The sins of the usurer are professional sins; those of the merchant are, as St. Augustine said, sins of the man, not of his profession.

Condemning loans at interest makes loans less frequent, but not impossible; condemning selling for credit at a higher price would make trade impossible. Most buyers are unable to pay cash; if wholesalers refused to sell at credit their sales would shrink; if they sold at credit at the cash price, they would fail; if they charged all buyers a price intermediate between the cash price and the deferred-payment price, it would be unfair to those who paid cash, and no one would pay cash. It follows, therefore, that all wholesale merchants would go out of business or would give up hope of salvation if it was not permitted (that is, *in foro conscientia*) to sell at a higher price for credit than for cash.

He concludes with a passage in which he insists that in formulating moral doctrine full consideration must be given to the requirements of secular life subject to the limits expressly set by divine law:

> This rigor, which would ruin commerce, would work strongly against the re-establishment of true morality, since it would provide an opportunity to say with some color of truth that doctrine is carried to such extremes that one could not observe the rules which it is proposed to lay down without abandoning every kind of profession, and even those most necessary for the conservation of states. One should despise such objections when one is only proposing what is clearly ordered by Scripture and by tradition, and therefore rightly one gives them no consideration when it is a question of open and formal usury, which is the gain which one derives from a loan. But one should consider them when one passes these limits, and one should then rely only on reasoning

and on consequences, so as not to impose on men without un-avoidable necessity burdens that would crush them.[67]

Nicole here parallels, both in method and conclusion, the casuists whom he elsewhere so harshly condemns. There are some differ-ences, but there is more resemblance than contrast with the casuists' treatment of usury if the outcome of the discussion is what matters.

In 1720 a book entitled *Traité de l'usure, ouvrage très utile à tous les chrétiens* was published under Nicole's name, though it was not by Nicole, and was a reprint, under a new title, of a book by L. Bulteau, [*Le Faux Dépôt*], first published in 1674. It is a routine rigorist treatment of the usury issue and there is no evidence that Nicole had any connection with it. It contains a passage, however, which is of interest both for its partial agreement and partial conflict with Nicole's position with respect to the appropriate roles of official dogma and socio-economic reasoning in the formulation of moral doctrine:

> People are easily persuaded that what is useful is also permitted.
> . . . As to the utility which is attributed to these contracts [deposits at interest], . . . I leave it to the *politiques* to treat . . . . I speak of things only as they relate to conscience . . . let it be what one wishes with respect to secular policy, it is not from this point of view that I am considering it here. My design is only to make it known for what it is according to the law of God. As however this sovereign law prohibits usury without any excep-tions, I have no hesitation in giving assurance that the dispensa-tions which men allow themselves, however reasonable they ap-pear, are not at all exempt from sin.[68]

Nicole and Bulteau were in agreement that where there is au-thoritative dogma, further argument is out of place. They probably differed, however, as to what constituted authoritative dogma, and Nicole, unlike Bulteau, showed real concern for the dictates of reasoning, as opposed to Bulteau's trust in the *politiques*. If it may be assumed that appeal to reasoning of a socio-economic kind generally leads to less rigorous doctrine than passive search for and acceptance of dogma, Bulteau was more of a rigorist here than Nicole.

Another concrete issue on which the Jansenists sharply criticized

---

67. *Essais de Morale*, VI, 156–157.

68. L. Bulteau, *Le Faux Depôt, ou, réfutation de quelques erreurs populaires, touchant l'usure* (1st and 2nd ed., Mons and Lyon, 1674), Rouen, 1698, pp. 221, 225, 227–228.

the casuists was the extent of the moral obligation of the rich to give alms to the poor. There was agreement that in the absence of extraordinary need the obligation extended only to that part of the possessions of the rich which was "superfluity," and the controversy then turned on the proper definition of superfluity.

The chief target of the Jansenists was Gabriel Vasquez, a Spanish Jesuit casuist (1549–1604). He had written:

> What persons of the world keep to raise their condition and that of their relatives is not to be called superfluous. Therefore one can scarcely find instances of superfluity among men of the world, even among kings.[69]

Pascal reported Vasquez as citing Cajetan's sanction in favor of worldly ambition in support of his opinion.[70] Pascal also cited another casuist, Diana,[71] who accepted Vasquez's opinion and characterized it as "probable," "very convenient and agreeable to the rich and their confessors," and as leading to the following practical conclusion: "with regard to the question, whether the rich are obliged to give alms out of their superfluity, though the affirmation were true, it would seldom, or almost never, happen to be obligatory in practice." Pascal commented that "according to this definition, none can have superfluity, provided they have ambition; and thus, so far as the greater part of the world is concerned, alms-giving is annihilated."[72]

Defenders of Vasquez replied that this was a distortion of his position, since, among other things, Pascal had failed to mention Vasquez's qualification that ambition for a higher status was a justification for withholding alms only when this higher status could be licitly acquired. In his edition of Pascal's *Lettres*, Nicole inserted an allegedly anonymous letter replying to Vasquez's defenders to the effect that even when the means used to rise in the world are lawful, the desire to rise is usually unlawful, because it is motivated by ambition.

> Ambition consists in the desire for elevation for elevation's sake;
> ... as avarice consists in loving riches for their own sake. If you

---

69. As cited by Jean Laporte, *La Morale selon Arnauld*, I, 65, from the original text. A kindred proposition was condemned by Innocent XI in 1679: see Denzinger, *The Sources of Catholic Dogma (Enchiridion Symbolorum)*, St. Louis, Mo., 1957, p. 325 (No. 1162).

70. See Ch. II, p. 65 above, for the position taken by Cajetan.

71. Diana was not a Jesuit.

72. Blaise Pascal, *Pensées, The Provincial Letters*, Modern Library edition, New York, 1941, Letters VI and XII, pp. 389–390, 484–490.

join to it unlawful means, you render it more criminal; but in substituting legitimate means, you do not render it innocent.[73]

Nicole here is unqualifiedly rigorous. Writing outside of the polemics with the casuists, however, Nicole deals with the extent of the obligation of almsgiving in a decidedly non-rigorous manner, though going neither explicitly nor probably even by implication as far as Vasquez or Diana.[74] It is a lack of self-discipline, he says, to dispose lightly and without sober consideration of a part of one's possessions when one has only what is necessary. Even when superfluity is involved, it is always a major indiscretion to dispose of one's goods by caprice. One can buy heaven by the disciplined use of one's means: it is therefore to misuse one's wealth to employ it to satisfy the impetuous movements of one's fancy. By "disposing of one's wealth" it seems clear that he means almsgiving and other modes of giving, and he offers no definitions of "superfluity" and "necessary." It is beyond question that his intention was to warn against heroic charity involving a lowering of one's economic status. In the absence of evidence that one has a special call from God, he regards such behavior as constituting a manifestation of very great temerity and overconfidence in one's ability to withstand the temptations attached to lack of temporal goods. Instead of being entitled to praise, such conduct calls for an appeal to God for pardon.

Laporte, a great authority on the Jansenists and admirer of them, concedes that "practically this Jansenist morality so severe in theory was scarcely less accommodating than the relaxed morality of the casuists." He maintains, however, that there nevertheless remained a capital difference between the two. The Jansenists were severe before the act, tolerant only after the act. "The casuists bent the theory to bring it down to the level of practice; the Jansenists excused the practice, while strictly maintaining the theory."[75] This is not quite as I see it. Even in theory, Jansenist rigor was largely confined to their subjective doctrine for the élite, and even here the rigor was not always unqualified, as I think I have shown for Nicole at least. In any case, the contrast between Jansenists and casuists was not as great as Jansenist polemics tried to make it appear. In both Jansenism and "laxist" casuistry there were important elements of accommodation to temporal considerations. Both played an important role in the centuries-long process of the secularization of social ethics.

73. *Les Provinciales, ou lettres écrites par Louis de Montalte*, 1700, II, 213 ff.
74. "Ne pas disposer légèrement de son bien," *Essais de morale*, VI, 218–223.
75. Jean M.F. Laporte, *La Doctrine de Port-Royal*, Vol. II, Part II, *Exposition de la doctrine (d'après Arnauld)*, sub-part I, Paris, 1951, p. 69.

Wilhelm Weber has recently raised the question of whether the Spanish Jesuit casuists—and Luis Molina in particular—as the most "liberal" of the late Scholastics in the field of economic ethics, can be regarded as preparing the way for modern "capitalism," defined as a code of economic behavior. He warns against going too far in this direction since the economic relations of their time had a degree of personal intimacy not matched by the "anonymity" of modern economic relations, and since the "market freedom" which the late Spanish Scholastics favored had different implications in the stable and organically structured society of their time than it has for modern economic society, with its market instabilities and democratic political organization.[76]

Weber clearly has in mind the objections of modern Catholic moral theology to "economic liberalism." But the casuists could have prepared the path for economic liberalism even if, upon later reconsideration and in the light of changed circumstances, Catholic moral theology was once more to become hostile to it. It seems to me, however, that with a few possible exceptions, most notably on the part of Molina, what support the casuists gave to economic freedom was based not on a reasoned belief in the serviceability of such freedom to the community, but on the narrower theological ground that theologians should not impose burdensome restraints on individual freedom of action except when these were clearly required by dogmatic considerations. Similarly, they should exercise restraint in declaring as sinful behavior what might be a matter of theological indifference. Some economic "freedoms" which casuists consequently supported were anti-capitalist in their nature, such as the license that some of them gave to servants to take surreptitiously whatever supplements were needed to make their wages adequate, or the various justifications they suggested for evading burdensome contractual obligations or customs duties. In some respects the code of the "free" market-place was a more rigorous, less elastic one than the code of individual behavior to which the casuists gave at least a measure of approval by withholding censure of it as "sinful" and by not calling for penitence and restitution. The relevance of the "laxism" of the casuists to the rise of modern economic liberalism may well have been substantial; but it was fortuitous and incidental to their central objective of finding valid means of lessening the burden of Catholic moral doctrine on the individual conscience.

76. Wilhelm Weber, *Wirtschaftsethik am Vorabend des Liberalismus*, Münster Westf., 1959, pp. 205–207.

Chapter Four

Protestantism and the rise of capitalism

The Weber Thesis

In two essays published in 1905 Max Weber presented an interpretation of the historical relations of Protestantism and capitalism which has dictated the setting in which practically all the discussion of this topic has been carried on since. Weber's thesis was enthusiastically adopted by many writers, was accepted with qualifications and reservations of various degrees of significance by others, and was stripped of its own qualifications and carried to more extreme lengths by still others. A few have rejected it out of hand, while a sizable group, though often absorbing more of it than they were conscious, have severely criticized it for alleged methodological shortcomings, defective scholarship, misuse and distortion of evidence, systematic biases of various sorts, and a miscellany of other misdemeanors.

Weber distinguished between the "spirit" (*Geist*) of capitalism, or the ruling motivation and objectives of its leaders, the businessmen, on the one hand, and capitalism itself, a particular mode of organization of economic process, on the other. It is the former which is his primary concern. His central thesis is that at least one major kind of modern capitalism—the methodical and rational organization of labor to produce gain for the entrepreneurs—which flourished especially in countries where "ascetic" forms of Protestantism were important, required for its generation a "spirit" of capitalism so irrational and unnatural that it could not have arisen without the support and sanction of certain religious doctrines peculiar to the "ascetic" species of Protestantism. Of these Calvinism was the most important, especially its doctrines of predestination and the calling, and its acceptance of success in business as a mark of salvation. This "Protestant ethic" resulted, at least for the lesser ranks of the entrepreneurial class, in dedicated and unlimited pursuit of wealth through unremitting industry, rigid limitation of expenditures on personal consumption or charity, concentration of time and attention on the pursuit of one's business affairs, avoidance of distraction through intimate friendship with others, systematic and pitiless exploitation of labor, and strict observance of honesty in one's relations with others within the limits set by "formal legality." The sole concern of this ethic was the service of the glory of a God moved by inscrutable objectives; any social consequences would be a fortuitous by-product. Love of one's neighbor for his own sake, joy in one's work, joy in the comforts and pleasures which material resources could provide for oneself, were all condemned by this ethic. A religious basis was necessary for the *generation* of a pattern of behavior which was by humanistic standards both glaringly irrational and unattractive. This religious basis was provided by the acceptance of achievement of this pattern of behavior as a mark of election and salvation. Why an irrational and unnatural pattern of life could have survival value once its religious base had evaporated, Weber does not seem to regard as a problem. Nor does he try to explain by what process the pattern could be exported when separated from its religious base. Weber's presumption is that once the pattern had become established it could persist, could be inherited, apparently for any number of generations, and could thus determine a country's style of economic life even though the religious beliefs which had originated it had evaporated or been vigorously rejected.

The Weber thesis or some later variant of it has received ready acceptance by many historians, theologians, sociologists, and other scholars; by leftists of many varieties who embraced it as an *exposé* of the unattractive origins of modern capitalism; by unbelievers whose suspicions of an alliance between religion and "mammonism" it seemed to confirm; by some Roman Catholics, Lutherans, and Anglicans as an additional stick with which to beat other Christian denominations; and in pre-World-War Germany, following a lead given by Max Weber himself, as an ingredient in a chauvinist denigration of the Anglo-Saxon world as a whole. Most theologians in the "orthodox" Calvinist tradition have denied any applicability of the thesis to Calvin or the early Calvinists, but some have been willing to go along with it in regard to later "degenerate" forms of Calvinism. Some Continental Calvinists reject the thesis as far as any Calvinist writings or practices with which they are familiar are concerned, but have been persuaded or half-persuaded by Weber's display of an apparent mastery of English and American "Puritan" literature of the existence in England of a "Puritan" ethic such as he describes, while disclaiming knowledge of any Continental analogue. Finally, the Weber thesis has received in wide circles the welcome always accorded to a plausible explanation of a historical period which fits things into a relatively simple and coherent pattern, while in more restricted circles it has been hailed for its methodological brilliance.

Social history as such lies outside the limits of this study, and in any case outside the range of my competence. The contributions of

Weber and his followers are relevant to this study only so far as they involve intellectual history, more specifically the reporting and interpretation of the doctrines of theologians with respect to economic issues and behavior. My concern here is not whether Protestantism did in fact have the economic consequences which Weber attributed to it, but solely with the issue whether Protestant doctrine, as expounded by theologians, was as he described it. Moreover, I have been unable to make up my mind whether Weber attributes to Calvinist and other theologians themselves the peculiar propositions to which he refers in his earlier writings on the theme as the "*doctrine* (*Lehre*) of Calvinism" (and later simply as "Calvinism"), or whether he only maintains that these constituted lay Calvinism as misunderstood, distorted, and corrupted by the rank and file. If Weber ever made a survey of lay Calvinist beliefs, the nature of his survey is not clear. When he cites theologians, he generally claims, or implies, or insinuates that their texts contain the irrational, unnatural, and revolting doctrines which his thesis requires.

I have given above a compressed summary of Weber's thesis. Although I can give chapter and verse in his writings for every proposition I have attributed to him, it is not a balanced account of his over-all position. Weber presented his thesis in a number of different formulations stretching over a period of fifteen years. From the start, he accompanied his positive propositions with "qualifications." I will now, therefore, attempt to give a comprehensive account of the qualifications which Weber expressly attached to his major propositions.[1]

---

1. A complete bibliography of Max Weber's publications in their original German version is given in Marianne Weber, *Max Weber; ein Lebensbild*, Tübingen, 1926, pp. 713–719. The items I will have occasion to refer to are as follows:

"Die protestantische Ethik und der 'Geist' des Kapitalismus," *Archiv für Sozialwissenschaft*, XX (1905), 1–54; XXI (1905), 1–110;

The above, reprinted in revised and expanded form in Max Weber, *Gesammelte Aufsätze zur Religionssoziologie*, 1st ed., 1920; edited and translated by Talcott Parsons, *The Protestant Ethic and the Spirit of Capitalism*, London, 1930;

"Kritische Bemerkungen zu den vorstehenden 'Kritischen Beiträgen' [von Karl Fischer]," *Archiv für Sozialwissenschaft*, XXV (1907), 243–249.

"Bemerkungen zu der vorstehenden Replik [Fischers]," *ibid.*, XXVI (1908), 275–283;

"Antikritisches zum 'Geist' des Kapitalismus," *ibid.*, XXX (1910), 176–202;

"Antikritisches Schlusswort zum 'Geist des Kapitalismus,' " *ibid.*, XXXI (1910), 554–599;

"The Protestant Sects and the Spirit of Capitalism," in H. H. Gerth and C. Wright Mills, *From Max Weber: Essays in Sociology*, New York [1946], 3rd printing, 1953, pp. 302–322; this is a translation of the German version published in 1920, which is a revised and greatly enlarged version of the first edition published in 1906;

Wirtschaft und Gesellschaft, in *Grundriss der Sozialökonomik*, III. Abteilung, Tübingen, 1922 (posthumous; probably written 1911-1913);

(i) Weber claims applicability for his thesis only to "ascetic" types of Protestantism. The most inclusive list he gives of "ascetic" types includes Calvinists, Reformed (*Reformierte*), Zwinglians, Baptists, Mennonites, Quakers, "less intensively ascetic" Lutheran pietists, and Methodists.[2] His most explicit exclusions are the main body of Lutherans and the Anglicans, although they often reenter the discussion when he is using his thesis to explain differences between "Protestants" and Roman Catholics. The status of Arminians in his thesis is ambiguous. At one point he expressly excludes the leading and most distinguished Dutch businessmen, either because they were Arminians, or because they were sceptical or indifferent to religion. At another point he excludes the Arminians in general on the grounds that they were not separately organized as a sect.[3] Nevertheless, the Wesleyan Methodists, the General Baptists, and the Quakers, who were all non-predestinarians, are not excluded.[4] Weber uses the term "Puritan" at times, but does not define it; he seems to regard it as synonymous with or as encompassed by "ascetic." Since he applies the term "ascetic" to a wider group of persons than "predestinarian" (though predestinarianism is a key element in his thesis), Weber should have explained—though I cannot find evidence that he did —the process whereby an "ascetic" or Puritan ethic of the irrational kind needed for his thesis could emerge from a non-predestinarian theology. The case of Richard Baxter, on whose ethical doctrines Weber relies heavily for support, is particularly relevant here, since Baxter was decidedly Arminian in his doctrines. To simplify exposition, I will assume throughout, except where this involves an obvious disregard of a particular text of Weber's, that up to the end of the seventeenth century, all Protestants except Lutherans and Anglicans were "Puritan," "ascetic," and predestinarian.

(ii) Weber's main emphasis is on "Calvinism," but only post-1600 Calvinism, which he refers to at times as a degraded or corrupted Calvinism.[5] He expressly exempts Calvin and his "personal" doctrine from his thesis,[6] but does not make clear whether all the

---

General Economic History, F. H. Knight, tr. [1927], reprint, Glencoe, Ill., 1950, Ch. XXX; these were lectures given in 1919–1920, and edited from students' notes.

2. *Wirtschaft und Gesellschaft*, 1922, p. 274.

3. *Ibid.*, p. 274, and *The Protestant Ethic*, pp. 200 n. 23, 217 n.1.

4. Weber says that the Methodists and the Baptists "added nothing new" to the Protestant ethic (*The Protestant Ethic*, pp. 252 n.167, 254 n.170). The more relevant issue, it seems to me, is whether they subtracted anything from the Calvinist ethic as Weber expounds it.

5. "Kritische Bemerkungen," *Archiv*, XXV (1907), 246; "Antikritisches Schlusswort," *ibid.*, XXXI (1910), 578–583; *The Protestant Ethic*, pp. 220 n.7, 228 n.41, 259.

6. "Antikritisches zum 'Geist' des Kapitalismus," *Archiv*, XXX (1910), 181; *Wirtschaft und Gesellschaft*, p. 809; *The Protestant Ethic*, pp. 110 ff., 220 n.7.

theologians who followed Calvin faithfully are also excluded.

(iii) On the question of the causal influence of "ascetic" Protestantism on the "spirit" of capitalism, Weber freely acknowledged that the religious factor had to operate alongside other factors and might at times be overcome by stronger countervailing factors, such as the nonexistence of the natural economic conditions requisite for the rise of a capitalist society.[7] As a rule he maintained that Calvinism or allied religious doctrine was a necessary though not a sufficient cause for the emergence of the "spirit" of capitalism. He does at times concede, however, that Calvinism had or might have had only adequacy (*Adäquanz*) for or congruence (*Kongruenz*) with the spirit of capitalism—by which I take him to mean that though Calvinism was well-adapted to and promotive of the spirit of capitalism, it might not have been necessary for its emergence.[8] In any case, he acknowledged that the spirit of capitalism was not present in all Calvinist communities, and expressly claimed the applicability of his thesis (as far as *Calvinist* communities were concerned?) only to England, southern France, Holland, New England, the Scotch-Irish, the German diaspora (i.e., the Calvinist refugees in Germany), Friesland, and a large number of German (non-Lutheran) communities.[9] The silent omission of Geneva and Scotland was not, I think, inadvertent.[10]

(iv) Weber explained that he did not draw on the manuals on dogma or theoretical treatises on ethics for evidence of the influence of Protestantism on economic attitudes and behavior,[11] but relied instead on the literature of practical instruction on concrete ethical questions, especially Richard Baxter, and, for the pietists, Spener.[12] This literature is now commonly referred to as the literature of Protestant casuistics. It differs, however, in one important respect from Catholic casuistics in its emphasis on what should be done rather than what it is permissible to do.* But apart from his use of Baxter's *Christian Directory* Weber makes no references to the outstanding English casuistic literature. There is no reference in his writings, for instance, to the four important English casuists, William Perkins, Wil-

7. "Kritische Bemerkungen," *Archiv*, XXV (1907), 246; "Bemerkungen," *ibid.*, XXVI (1908), 277; "Antikritisches Schlusswort," *ibid.*, XXXI (1910), 556–557.

8. "Kritische Bemerkungen," *Archiv*, XXV (1907), 246; "Bemerkungen," *ibid.*, XXVI (1908), 280 n.5; "Antikritisches zum 'Geist' des Kapitalismus," *ibid.*, XXX (1910), 200; "Antikritisches Schlusswort," *ibid.*, XXXI (1910), 556–557, 581.

9. "Bemerkungen," *Archiv*, XXVI (1908), 277; cf. *Wirtschaft und Gesellschaft*, p. 275.

10. See below, pp. 186–89.

11. "Antikritisches Schlusswort," *Archiv*, XXXI (1910), 591–592.

12. *Ibid.*

* Editors' note: For Viner's views on this subject see the Appendix: Protestant Casuistics, below.

liam Ames, Jeremy Taylor, and Robert Sanderson. His references to English Calvinist writings are—again, with the exception of Baxter —often related to treatises on dogma; and neither Weber, nor as far as I know, any of his followers, have made systematic use of the formal "creeds" and the synodal records, which are in abundant supply and would presumably be a highly relevant source of evidence. As far as I can tell these offer meager support for Weber's thesis.

Except for correspondence and autobiographies, Weber explains that the casuistic treatises are the most valuable sources for tracing the influence of religion on practice, especially with respect to what species of conduct are assigned religious "premiums," and what results subjective adoption of a faith might have on conduct. It was only the Protestant sects which "put a halo" around the economic "individualist" impulses of the modern capitalist ethos.[13] However, I cannot find any reference in Weber to Calvinist correspondence and autobiographies, and neither my examination of a small sample of the available literature nor the writings of Weber's followers offer any persuasive indication that this literature would give significant support to Weber's thesis. Weber, like his followers, generalizes freely about the actual economic behavior of Calvinists or "Puritans" in the seventeenth century; but he seems to rely on common knowledge and gives no detailed historical evidence.

In common with some of his most important followers Weber relies heavily on the results which particular beliefs "might have had" on practice. This device entails the use of what has been called "the conjectural preterite"; i.e., what a writer might "logically" have gone on to say if he had extended his remarks or, as applied to behavior, what a person might have done if he had acted out the "logical" conclusion of his beliefs. It is a species of argument from ignorance which is extremely difficult to answer except by drawing attention to its inherent subjectivity or by asking why the historian should have found it necessary to have recourse to such methods.

At times Weber explains the differences in "living-styles" or patterns of economic behavior of Protestants and Roman Catholics by the differences in their systems of church discipline. Since the discipline of the "ascetic" Protestant sects operated largely by means of lay scrutiny and admonition, it was more effective than Catholic discipline, which mainly operated through the confessional (and provided an ample supply of absolving penalties for past deficiencies of conduct), in impressing upon members of the church the approved pat-

13. "The Protestant Sects," in Gerth and Mills, *From Max Weber*, pp. 321–322, 459 n.35.

tern of behavior.[14] Apparently, Weber thought that Calvinist discipline operated differently or perhaps had different content, depending on whether the Calvinists were the ruling church with official power or were a minority sect. At other times, however, he did not emphasize rule and discipline, but doctrine, and conceded that in Calvinist theocratic states (Geneva? Scotland?) discipline operated in a reverse pattern from that called for by his thesis. In Calvinist states ecclesiastical discipline could and sometimes did operate to "retard that liberation of individual powers which was conditioned by the rational ascetic pursuit of salvation. . . ." In instances of this kind, therefore, instead of stressing church discipline Weber "preferred rather to take [= infer?] the results which subjective adoption of an ascetic faith *might have had* on the conduct of the individual."[15] This provides a probable though partial explanation for Weber's exclusion of Geneva and Scotland from his list of Calvinist communities to which his thesis was applicable.

(v) Weber's thesis claims that ascetic Protestantism generated or fostered, not "capitalism" in the sense of a system or method of economic organization of society, but the "spirit" of capitalism, the particular complex of subjective attitudes and ends of its leaders. He granted, moreover, that there were many kinds of capitalism, each with its own appropriate "spirit," and that it was only the "Puritan" form, the kind involving the bourgeois organization of wage-labor, to which he attributed a special affiliation with ascetic Protestantism. Even in countries where this form was important, other forms of capitalism would exist alongside it: speculative, adventurous, concerned with colonial enterprises, or administered by economic "supermen" who were very rich and not ascetic in their mode of life. To these his thesis did not apply. Also, even in countries where the ascetic Protestant spirit of capitalism was dominant, it was characteristic only or chiefly of the middle and lower-middle class urban bourgeois, the moderate-scale entrepreneurs.[16] For the employees, ascetic Protestantism had a special doctrine, postulating the desirability of low wages as conducive to high productivity and stressing obedient and diligent service to their masters as their path to salvation.[17] What Weber nowhere makes clear is how a spirit of capitalism which

14. *Ibid.*, p. 321; *The Protestant Ethic*, pp. 116, 233–234 n.68; *General Economic History*, pp. 365–368.

15. *The Protestant Ethic*, p. 152; italics not in the original.

16. *The Protestant Ethic*, pp. 174, 271 n.58, 279–280 n.93. "Antikritisches zum 'Geist' des Kapitalismus," *Archiv*, XXX (1910), 188; "Antikritisches Schlusswort," *ibid.*, XXXI (1910), 556.

17. *General Economic History*, p. 368.

belonged exclusively to a tiny group could nevertheless affect the living-style of entire countries—such as England, on the one hand, and Germany and Catholic countries, on the other—to such an extent that it was possible confidently to ascribe to this spirit the differences in national characteristics.

(vi) Weber was the inventor of the "ideal type" as a tool for the representation of social patterns of behavior. The method has been highly praised by scholars of high stature. I find it easier, however, to grasp in what respects an ideal type deliberately departs from historical "fact" or "reality" than to understand by what mental alchemy its product becomes a useful, communicable, and verifiable simplification of actual historical situations. Weber uses the device in his study of the relations of Protestantism to capitalism: in his words, he had used "the artificial simplicity of ideal types, as they could at best but seldom be found in history," and had found it absolutely necessary to do so "in order to bring out the characteristic differences, . . . thus in a certain sense doing violence to historical reality."[18] Since Weber's use of the "ideal type" is inextricably mingled in his writings with more pedestrian methods of reporting and interpreting historical data, it is perhaps regrettable that he did not invent a new mode of punctuation or typography so that his readers could readily determine to which category any passage in his exposition belonged. In any case, anyone seeking the "true" historical account of the relations of Protestantism to capitalism in Weber's works has in effect been warned that he does so at his own risk. I believe that this warning applies even to Weber's bibliographical and textual references.

(vii) Finally, it should be recognized that Weber himself described his writings on the relations of Protestantism to capitalism as preliminary reports on a program of research which was far from complete. He conceded that some issues were in urgent need of further exploration; and he commented that while hitherto he had laid himself open to the charge of exaggerating the influence of ideology on social history, the end result of his investigation might be to provoke the opposite charge of having capitulated to historical materialism.[19] His final

18. *The Protestant Ethic*, pp. 98, 233 n.68. See also "Antikritisches Schlusswort," *Archiv*, XXXI (1910), 580. Weber comments at one point, "Of course we must not forget that Puritanism included a world of contradictions" (*The Protestant Ethic*, p. 169). I think that his study of the relationship of Protestantism to capitalism would have been a much more valuable contribution to history and a much less vulnerable one if he had devoted more of his energy to a systematic statement, early in his exposition of his thesis, of such of these "contradictions" as were in conflict with his thesis.

19. "Kritisches Bemerkungen," *Archiv*, XXV (1907), 243–249; "Bemerkungen,"

opinion on the subject, however, amounted to a positive rejection of the possibility of a reversal of his thesis; it was not conceivable, in his view, that the bare existence of capitalism could suffice to generate a unified ethic, let alone a communal religious ethic.[20]

Some have claimed on Weber's behalf that it is incumbent on those who reject his explanation of how modern capitalism emerged from the doctrines of ascetic Protestantism to present a more plausible explanation. But my own view is that there is no obligation to believe in the possibility of "explanation" as Weber conceived it, or to believe that an ascetic Protestant doctrine such as he describes was prevalent, or to accept that bourgeois capitalist communities existed with the patterns of life and the set of values which Weber ascribed to them.

Explanations Prior to Weber of
Protestant Economic Superiority

From the seventeenth century on, there was widespread agreement, apparently unanimous on the Protestant side and rarely seriously disputed on the Catholic side, that Protestant countries and groups were generally more active economically, were more prosperous, and enjoyed more rapid economic progress than Catholic countries or groups. The validity of this opinion is not significant for my purpose, but I know of no solid grounds for questioning its correctness, and I will assume it to be true. What matters here are the explanations offered for this economic superiority. These explanations were varied and covered a wide range of possible factors. Until the seamier aspects of the industrial revolution had become manifest, the desirability of the current forms of economic progress was not seriously questioned on religious or ethical grounds by either Protestant or Catholic writers. Some English writers, however, did express concern about the consequences of the enclosure movement in ag-

---

ibid., XXVI (1908), 280–281 n.5; "Antikritisches zum 'Geist' des Kapitalismus," *ibid.*, XXX (1910), 196 n.28.

20. *Wirtschaft und Gesellschaft*, p. 274. A more important question would be whether the inherent pressures of a capitalist social system could be a decisive factor in the community's selection of the dominant religious-ethical system from the available set, even to the extent of refashioning the chosen system somewhat to its own taste. It is at least a plausible hypothesis that every traditional religion has either "accommodated" to the requirements of economic forces *or* by failing to accommodate has limited the contribution of its followers to economic development and their participation in its fruits or else has lost its followers to other faiths or to irreligion. Weber ignored or denied out of hand or conceded only in a backhanded way the evidence in support of this alternative hypothesis, which the earlier literature and the writings of his critics had made available for objective appraisal.

riculture, and both Protestant and Catholic writers expressed disapproval, based on traditional agrarian and aristocratic biases, of the relative growth of urban populations and phenomena.

In seventeenth-century England the defense of religious toleration, which usually meant Anglican toleration of non-conformists, was sometimes based on economic arguments. Those who opposed toleration often denied the economic validity of these arguments, though another response was to assert the superiority of religious over economic considerations, regardless of the validity of the latter. Charles Leslie is reported to have said that "toleration is a sacrificing of God to Mammon." In 1670 Bishop Herbert Thorndike met the claim that toleration was helpful to trade by responding as follows:

> But the question is of religion, not of trade nor riches. If it could be said that their [i.e., the Dutch] religion is improved with their trade, the example were considerable. But they that would restore and improve the religion that flourished in England thirty years ago [i.e., prior to the Puritan Revolution] must not take up with the base alloy [i.e., of religious and economic considerations] of that, which is seen in the United Provinces. Nor is this a reproach to them, but a truth of God's word; that religion and trade cannot be both at the height.[21]

Quite early in the nineteenth century the social consequences of contemporary development were criticized by Anglicans, Catholics, and socialists. The more marked industrial expansion in Protestant countries no longer provided an obvious and unchallenged ground for Protestant boasting or Catholic apology. This has been especially true since Max Weber wrote. As one writer, Jacquin, described the earlier situation:

> The problem of the relations of Catholicism and of Protestantism, with the development of capitalism is quite an old one. . . . It was exploited for apologetic purposes by the controversialists of the nineteenth century. Friends and enemies of capitalism dedicated themselves to the study of the problem in order to claim for the religion which they professed the merit of having either promoted or hindered the rise of capitalism, according to their preferences.[22]

21. Bishop Herbert Thorndike, *A Discourse of the Forbearance or the Penalties which a due Reformation Requires*, [1670], *The Theological Works*, Oxford, 1854, V, 480–481.

22. R. Jacquin, *Revue d'Economie Politique*, XLV (1940), 118 n.

Jacquin exaggerates the extent to which Catholic writers denied the economic superiority of the Protestant countries; as we shall see, a number of Catholic writers conceded that there was some truth to the charge, and some of these advocated that appropriate action be taken in Catholic countries to change the situation. Closer to the truth is the statement by another Catholic writer:

> As everybody knows, until quite recently it used to be a favourite Protestant objection against the Catholic church that the countries under her influence had the poorest trade returns. But, of course, *laissez-faire* and capitalism were in honour then, whereas now their glory has departed.[23]

Thus Max Weber had many predecessors when he argued that there was a close historical association, an "elective affinity," between Protestantism and the rise of "capitalism." This he acknowledged freely, and indeed found in it support for the validity of his thesis. Nevertheless, the same cannot be said of his central thesis, namely, that certain specific theological elements in Protestant doctrine, and especially the doctrines of election and the calling, made Protestantism a generating factor for modern capitalism. I have not been able to find any clear-cut anticipation of Weber on these matters, though many earlier explanations of the association of Protestantism with capitalism were consistent with Weber's view.

Weber's originality would, I think, become apparent if a thoroughgoing survey of earlier explanations of the differences between countries or groups in economic patterns of life and in degrees of prosperity had been made. As a partial substitute, I present the results, in summarized fashion, of my own reading, primarily directed to other problems.[24]

The prosperity of Holland in the seventeenth century aroused the interest of writers in other countries, and various explanations were

---

23. James Brodrick, S.J., *The Economic Morals of the Jesuits*, London, 1934, pp. 152–153.

24. I list here some early writings on this topic, mostly of Catholic authorship, which from their titles or other information I presume to be important, but which I was unable to consult: Adam Müller, *Warum ist der Wohlstand der protestantischen Länder sogar viel grösser als der katholischen*, 1772; Bernard Becker, *Ein Wort über die Fabrikindustrie, mit besonderer Hinsicht auf den Canton Glarus*, Basel, 1858. (See W. E. Rappard, *La Révolution industrielle et les origines de la protection légale du travail en Suisse*, Berne, 1914, p. 33 n.); Abbé F. Martin, *De l'avenir du protestantisme et du catholicisme*, Paris, 1869; Weyrich, "Infériorité économique des nations catholiques," *Revue Catholique de Louvain*, May–June 1899; Père A. Flamérion, *De la Prospérité comparée des nations catholiques et des nations protestantes . . . .*, Paris, 1899; Eugène Folletête, "De la prétendue infériorité des nations catholiques," *Revue de Fribourg*, 1904.

offered. Sir William Temple singled out for emphasis the industry and thrift of the Dutch, but attributed most "national customs" to "unseen, or unobserved, natural causes or necessities." The only characteristics of this kind which he identified in the Dutch case were poverty in natural resources and density of population.[25] He makes no mention of a religious factor.[26]

Some time before 1618, Sir Walter Raleigh singled out Holland, together with the Hanse towns and Denmark, as countries which surpassed England in commerce. He does not mention that all these countries were Protestant, and in his attempt to explain Dutch commercial success he refers only to low customs, freedom of foreigners to trade, and superior technique in shipping and fisheries. No reference is made to religion.[27]

Sir Josiah Child attributed the superiority of the Dutch in trade to a wide range of customs, institutions, and patterns of economic behavior and laws. His only reference to a religious factor is his inclusion of "toleration of different Opinions in matters of religion" as contributing to Dutch prosperity by attracting to Holland industrious and rich dissenters from other countries. He stresses the "parcimonious and thrifty Living" of the Dutch, but considered this to be a matter of laws, custom, and education. With respect to laws, he refers especially to limitations which keep the rate of interest low. "The Dutch and Italians are both frugal nations, though their climates and governments differ as much as any, because the laws of both nations incline them to thriftiness."[28]

A 1681 tract, often, though apparently wrongly, attributed to Sir Josiah Child, states that trade thrives only in Protestant countries, but not in all Protestant countries "for reasons that I could offer, but that they are not necessary here," thus leaving us to guess what his explanation would be.[29]

25. Sir William Temple, *Observations upon the United Provinces of the Netherlands* [1673], G. N. Clark ed., Cambridge, Eng., 1932, pp. ix (Introduction), 129–135, 140.

26. Cf., however, R. Jacquin, *Revue d'Economie Politique*, LIV (1940), 120: "William Temple (one of the first to establish a relationship between the economic life of Protestant countries and religion. . .)."

27. *Observations touching Trade and Commerce with the Hollander, and other Nations*, n.d. (Raleigh died in 1618), *The Works of Sir Walter Raleigh*, Oxford, 1829, VIII, 351–376.

28. Sir Josiah Child, *A New Discourse of Trade*, 4th ed., n.d., pp. 4, 6, 61 [1st ed., 1668; 1st complete ed., 1689]. Editors' note: Child himself must be consulted on the apparent paradox of the coincidence of high thrift and low rates of interest.

29. Philopatrus, *A Treatise wherein is demonstrated that the East Indies Trade is the most national of all Foreign Trades*, London, 1681, p. 27. For reasons why it is improbable that Child was the author, see William Letwin, *Sir Josiah Child, Merchant Economist*, Baker Library, Boston, Mass., 1959, pp. 33–35.

Sir Peter Pett, in a book alleging that the prospective shrinkage in the numbers of Roman Catholics and dissenters would remove all serious risk to the security and stability of England, offered an explanation of what keeps the dissenters in London unified in a tight religious community. The London dissenters were for the most part "ordinary retail-traders." Their trade was decaying as a result of the shift of trade from where they lived to the West of London; hence they clung together for mutual support and consolation. If they were to become prosperous, they would cease to keep themselves separate from the rest of the community. Pett argued that "necessity, the known mother of industry, must necessarily cure them of their poverty and temptation to heterodoxy, thereby." In a long passage —composed in uncertain proportions of quotation, paraphrase from a tract, and personal opinion—Pett analyzes the inverse of Weber's thesis, namely, the effects of economic status, interests, and attitudes on the choice and perhaps on the nature of religious affiliation:

> . . . the greater part of persons engaged in trade and traffic . . . hate ceremonies in general, and what does unnecessarily take up time, and . . . persons who nauseate ceremonies in civil things, will loath them likewise in religious, as a man who has antipathy against muscadine in his parlor cannot love it at the Sacrament.
> . . . So natural is it for men to paint God in colors suitable to their own fancies, that I do not wonder at trading persons who hate ceremonies, that they thus think God in respect of this hatred altogether such as themselves.
> . . . tis natural to men, who live by trade and whose being rich or beggars depends much on the honesty of their servants, to be enamoured on that preaching that is most passionate and loud against what looks like luxury, and is apt to occasion unnecessary expenses to them.[30]

The expensiveness of the Catholic religion was a matter of widespread comment before the Reformation and on into the nineteenth century. Both before and after the Reformation, there were repeated complaints by Catholic as well as non-Catholic writers about the large landholdings of the Church, its alleged hoarding of money, the large number of priests, monks, and nuns, the cost of its great cathedrals and other buildings, and remittances to Rome. Other complaints centered on the large number of holidays and pilgrimages which took

30. Sir Peter Pett, *The Happy Future State of England*, London, 1688; a second edition under a different title, *A Discourse of the Growth of England*, London, 1689, pp. 79, 81, 82.

men away from their work, and on the celibacy of the "religious," which checked the growth of population or otherwise worked against prosperity. This is of interest here because it was to become a major factor in explanations of the more marked economic progress of Protestant countries. As Christopher Hill has said: "The fact that Protestantism was a cheaper religion than Catholicism became a seventeenth-century commonplace."[31] It remained a commonplace in the eighteenth and nineteenth centuries. Although much of the evidence is presented with bias, and no one as far as I know has been able to provide a reliable quantitative measure of the importance of this factor, in their cumulative effect the recorded facts are impressive, and I know of no serious attempt to controvert the proposition of the higher cost of the Catholic than the Protestant religion. There is little of special interest for my purposes in the abundant literature on this theme.[32] It is interesting to note, however, that Weber makes no reference to this theme in his explanation of either the relative economic backwardness of Catholic countries or groups or the unattractiveness of "ascetic" forms of Protestantism to lower-middle-class urban populations.

The notes for a lecture prepared in about 1776 by a dissenting minister in Cambridge, England, Robert Robinson, reflect in compact form a somewhat naive recognition both of the attractiveness to dissenters of the inexpensiveness of their religion, and their view of the impact of their religion on their economic pattern of life:

A View of Modern Nonc[onformity]
Property.

The property of the dissenters is very considerable—public property [extensive] . . . Private property large—for their religion keeps them from many expensive vices—Nonc[onformity] keeps

31. Christopher Hill, "Puritans and the Poor," *Past & Present*, Nov. 1952, pp. 42–43.

32. As representative of the literature using the relative expensiveness of the Catholic as compared to the Protestant churches, ecclesiastical regimes, and disciplines, in order to explain, in part or in whole, the economic superiority of Protestant over Catholic countries or communities, I cite: [Sir Walter Harris], *Remarks on the Affairs and Trade of England and Ireland*, London, 1691, pp. 43–44; [de Soulique], *The Desolation of France Demonstrated*, [London, 1697], reprint under the title, *The Political Mischiefs of Popery*, London, 1818; John Law, *Première mémoire sur les banques*, [1715], reprinted in Eugene Daire, ed., *Economistes financiers du XVIIIe siècle*, Paris, 1843, pp. 553–554; *A Short Specimen of a New Political Arithmetic*, London, 1734, p. 116; Joseph Lowe, *The Present State of England in Regard to Agriculture, Trade, and Finance*, 2nd ed., New York, 1885, pp. 219–228. Many subsequent references to writers who cite other reasons for the economic superiority of Protestant countries or groups also cite the relative expensiveness of Catholicism.

them from many heavy episcopal exactions—clerical feasts—subscriptions—missions—&c. Religion also makes them frugal—industrious—and commercial—so that their property is more than equal to their wants.[33]

What has been labelled the "penalization" factor was given considerable weight by some early writers in their explanation of Protestant economic superiority. As stated by Arnold Toynbee, though with reference to "race" rather than "religious group," the "penalization" thesis runs as follows:

> . . . the dominant race is apt to reserve certain statuses and certain avocations as its own exclusive preserves, and to impose upon the penalized race the necessity of cultivating other fields of social activity if it is to find a living at all. The "reserved" occupations usually include all those which have high social prestige—the priesthood, the business of government, the ownership of land, the bearing of arms, and the civilian "liberal professions"—as well as the fundamental economic activity of Society, which has usually been agriculture in the social economies of societies in process of civilization down to recent times. By a process of exhaustion the penalized race is apt to find itself virtually confined to the field of trade and handicraft; and, just because the field is narrow, the penalized race is stimulated to make this field all its own and to conjure out of it, by a *tour de force* which fills the dominant race with astonishment and resentment, a harvest of wealth and power which this Naboth's vineyard would hardly have yielded to hands not debarred from other handiwork.[34]

For present purposes it is convenient to extend the concept of "penalization." The consequences of flight or forced emigration need to be taken into account, both for those of the penalized group who remained at home and for the refugee groups in the countries to which they emigrated. The émigrés could come from countries with more advanced cultures and economic technology; they could, therefore, be transmitters of new methods and products to the countries to which they migrated.[35] Even if they came from less advanced coun-

33. "A Plan of Lectures on the Principles of Nonconformity," in *Miscellaneous Works of Robert Robinson*, Harlow, 1807, II, 248–249.

34. Arnold Toynbee, *A Study of History*, London, 1934, II, 217, as cited by Warren C. Scoville, "The Huguenots in the French Economy, 1650–1750," *Quarterly Journal of Economics*, LXVII (1953), 439.

35. Max Weber makes this point, and it is developed, on the basis of Swiss ex-

tries, they could nevertheless bring with them knowledge of methods and products which were unknown in the countries to which they emigrated. The mere fact of transfer from one social background to another could remove the blinkers of the old environment without imposing on them the established codes and inhibitions of the new environment. The acquaintance with two cultures could broaden their imaginations, and the need to establish themselves in their new homes could make them more enterprising as innovators. Their contacts with relatives and friends in their native countries and with émigrés to third countries could facilitate the establishment of profitable affiliations transcending national boundaries, especially in the fields of foreign commerce and international finance. In addition to serving as the carriers of advanced technology from their native countries to their new homes, refugees might act as transmitters of new ideas and practices to their country of origin. On the other hand, refugees escaping from the penalization of their native countries might find themselves subject to a different but important penalization in the countries of refuge. Their alien status, their distinctive religious affiliations, their separation from the bulk of the population by language barriers and differences of customs and modes of life, could place them in a penalized situation comparable to that of penalized native groups, even if they had the same legal status as natives. Penalization, of course, could not act as a stimulus if it went so far as to shut off all opportunity to engage in gainful occupation.

Charles Davenant shared Sir Peter Pett's concern with the threat posed by Protestant dissent for the stability of the existing political regime and the status of the Church of England. He attributed much the same kind of psychological influence to the penalization of the sectarians as Pett attributed to their poverty:

> In all ages, and all places, hereticks and sectaries have rather been increased than diminished by persecution. It brings them to unite in a firmer band with one another; it makes them fortify themselves with industry and council, and purify their religious discipline, which is always popular. . .
>
> [Persecution terminated], they begin to mind their worldly concerns, which when the flock do, the pastor can no longer guide them as he pleases. . . .
>
> As in our Church, so in their congregations, there are both good and bad: Without doubt many of them are men of exem-

perience as a country of refuge, by W. E. Rappard, *La Révolution industrielle . . . en Suisse*, pp. 34–35 and *passim*.

plary lives, sincere piety, and meek zeal, and these will rather be confirmed in their devotion than shaken in it by any troubles they meet with in this world. Of these such as are poor, follow their handy-crafts and manufactures, think of nothing else, and because of their sobriety, thrive faster than other men. On the other hand, such as have wealth addict themselves to trade, inasmuch as their education has not fitted them for the court, the bar, or armies; to all these it will be no hurt to be shut out of employments, that are more a burthen than a profit.

Davenant goes on to argue that such of their leaders as seek power will welcome persecution, in the light of the following considerations:

Let us by thrift [they will say], and a perpetual bending of our thoughts to business, grow rich apace; for wealth begets respect, and much property cannot be long without some power. . . .

Are they not grown weaker by the toleration already granted? Has it not deadned their zeal? Has it not impaired the authority of their preachers? Do they not perceive their flocks beginning to throw off marks of distinction, in talk, dress, and way of living?[36]

Max Weber relies more heavily on Sir William Petty for support than on any writer who preceded Petty.[37] Apart from a reference to the Irish Catholics which I reserve for later comment,[38] I have found only one passage in Petty's writings which explains the economic behavior and attitudes of particular groups in terms of their religious views, thereby lending support to Weber's thesis, namely:

Dissenters of this kind [i.e., the Dutch at the time of their revolt from Spain], are for the most part, thinking, sober and patient Men, and such as believe that Labour and Industry is their Duty towards God. (How erroneous soever their Opinions be). . . . These People believing the Justice of God, and seeing the most Licentious persons, to enjoy most of the World, and its best things, will never venture to be of the same Religion and Profes-

36. Charles Davenant, *Essays upon Peace at Home and War Abroad* [1704], in *The Political and Commercial Works*, Sir Charles Whitworth, ed., London, 1771, IV, 404–405, 411–412, 414, 415. I interpret the word "popular" in the first quotation to mean accommodation to lower-class attitudes. It is to be noted that Davenant, like Pett before him, is attributing religious attitudes to economic and social status and conditions rather than the other way round, as in Weber's thesis.

37. Weber's references to Petty are in *The Protestant Ethic*, pp. 43, 179, 189 n.11, 279 n.93, 282 n.109; "Antikritischer zum 'Geist' des Kapitalismus," *Archiv* XXX (1910), 183, 184–185, 188, 189; "Antikritisches Schlusswort," *Archiv* XXXI (1910), 571.

38. See below, p. 174.

sion with Voluptuaries, and Men of extreme Wealth and Power, who they think have their Portion in this World.[39]

Weber relies heavily upon the continuation of this passage—where Petty further emphasizes the special addiction of religious heretics to trade—for confirmation of his thesis. At one point he remarks, with specific reference to the passage, that he could be charged with plagiarizing one of the central themes of Petty's thesis.[40] But it is to heterodoxy as such, and not to any special form of it, that Petty here attributes a special addiction to trade. He finds this addiction to trade in the Banians of India, the Jews and Christians in Turkey, the Jews and non-Papist Christians in Venice, and the Catholics in Ireland. It is true that in this passage Petty includes as heretic or heterodox the populations of England, Scotland, the Protestant portions of Germany, and the Scandinavian countries—which amounts to a substantial identification of heterodoxy with Protestantism. But the fact remains that he also includes the Catholics in Ireland and other non-Protestants. Moreover, he explicitly infers from the facts presented "that trade is not fixed to any species of religion as such, but rather as before hath been said to the heterodox part of the whole."[41]

The nearest I can come to a self-consistent interpretation of Petty's views on the relation of religion to economic behavior is that in general he held that Protestantism is more favorable to trade than Catholicism; that adherence to almost any religion is helpful to trade by promoting the economic virtues; but that adherence to a heterodox religion, of whatever kind, is a mark of special devoutness and therefore specially helpful to trade. There is perhaps some support here for the Weber thesis, but not, I think, very much.[42]

Petty does not stress the penalization factor, but he does state that Dutch habits of industry and of "study [of] the art of number, weight, and measure" were a necessary or almost inevitable consequence of their experiences under the Spanish regime as "a poor and oppressed people, living in a country naturally cold and unpleasant, and . . . persecuted for their heterodoxy in religion."[43]

39. Sir William Petty, *Political Arithmetick* [written in the 1670's, first published ed., 1690], *The Economic Writings of Sir William Petty*, C. H. Hull, ed., Cambridge, Eng., 1899, I, 262.

40. "Antikritisches zum 'Geist' des Kapitalismus," *Archiv*, XXX (1910), 185.

41. Petty, *Political Arithmetick*, *Works*, I, 263.

42. In Petty's explanation of Dutch prosperity, "heterodoxy" is only one of a number of factors, the others being toleration of all religions, the system of land registry, the banks, use of foreigners instead of natives to man military forces, and specialization in trade and manufactures as against the less profitable cattle-raising and tillage (*ibid.*, I, 261–267).

43. *Ibid.*, I, 261.

Warren Scoville, in the course of a perceptive discussion of the penalization thesis, reports the interpretation by a Frenchman, Beaumelle, around 1750, of the economic success of the Huguenots in France.[44] Beaumelle attributed the economic success of the Huguenots to many factors, and I will have occasion to refer to him later. One of these factors was "penalization":

> Excluded by the laws from all civic offices, and by their opinions from all ecclesiastical dignities they [the Huguenots] are in the happy circumstance of lacking the power to impoverish themselves by luxury and idleness. Obliged to engage in agriculture or in commerce, they have been abundantly recompensed for this constraint. . . . More active than other citizens because they could become their equals only by activity, they have been aided by the principles of their religion. . . . Their industry has been furthered by the knowledge which they have of foreign industry. Most of them have seen the Protestant countries, and because of that have unconsciously widened the range of their intelligence, and have given it an elasticity necessary for industry [industrie, i.e., manufactures?]. Almost all make one time in their life the pilgrimage to Geneva as the Mohammedans do to Mecca. . . . The rigor of the laws against them forces them to keep constant guard over their behavior.

Except for the reference to the "[aid] by the principles of their religion," the entire citation from Beaumelle falls neatly within the limits of the concept of "penalization" as I have extended it.

A French Protestant, C. Weiss, in an 1851 work attributed the economic success of the seventeenth-century Huguenots to the reinforcing operation of their religion, their penalized situation in France, and other factors:

> Lost, so to speak, in the midst of a people who observed them with mistrust, constantly exposed to calumny, subject to severe laws which imperiously required of them perpetual self-discipline, they commanded public esteem by the austerity of their behavior and their irreproachable integrity.[45]

44. W. Scoville, "The Huguenots in the French Economy," *Quarterly Journal of Economics*, LXVII (1953), 443–444. Professor Scoville has kindly given me a copy of his extract from Beaumelle's handwritten memorandum, which is in the Bibliothèque Nationale. In his article, Scoville says: "Although Beaumelle did not explicitly characterize the Huguenots as a 'penalized minority,' it is quite clear that his interpretation of their behavior is not at variance with the one I have suggested," namely, the view that "penalization" was a significant factor (p. 444).

45. C. Weiss, "Mémoire sur les Protestants de France au 17e siècle," *Séances et Travaux de l'Académie des Sciences Morales et Politiques*, XX (1815), 105.

Eberhard Gothein in 1892 remarked that "when one follows the trail of capitalist development anywhere in Europe, always the same circumstance makes itself manifest, the Calvinist Diaspora is the nursery of the capitalist economy. The Spaniards expressed it with bitter resignation: 'Heresy promotes the trading spirit.' "[46] Max Weber cites this passage as an anticipation of his thesis,[47] but it seems to fit the "penalization" thesis better. What Gothein is stressing, as the word "diaspora" and the context shows, is that Calvinist immigrants brought advanced industrial methods to various parts of Europe. Weber was not unaware of this, as he shows in immediately following his reference to Gothein with an acceptance of penalization as a contributing factor. Moreover, although in the equivalent paragraph of his original essay of 1905 Weber had said that *wherever* Calvinism appeared it had shown the combination of piety and "an extraordinary capitalistic business sense," and although this statement appears unaltered in the final version of the essay, in 1907 he referred to it as a slip. When writing his 1905 essay, he had in mind Gothein's statement about diaspora Calvinism. It was obvious, he stated, that the relation between ascetic Protestantism and the capitalistic spirit was not so uniform (*gesetzlich*).[48]

Weber acknowledges clearly enough that the penalization factor can contribute to the development of the spirit of capitalism. "National or religious minorities which are in a position of subordination to a group of rulers are likely, through their voluntary or involuntary exclusion from positions of political influence, to be driven with peculiar force into economic activity." Even in the case of the Calvinist diaspora, "one might consider the decisive factor to be the superiority of the French and Dutch economic cultures from which these communities sprang, or perhaps the immense influence of exile in the breakdown of traditional relationships." "Bankers of foreign extraction have existed at all times and in all countries as the rep-

46. Eberhard Gothein, *Wirtschaftsgeschichte des Schwarzwaldes*, Strassburg, 1892, p. 674. Soon after the appearance of Weber's first essays, Gothein accepted Weber's thesis and stated it in Weberian terminology; see "Staat und Gesellschaft des Zeitalters der Gegen-reformation," in *Die Kultur der Gegenwart*, Paul Hinneburg, ed., Teil II, Abteilung V, I, Berlin, 1908, pp. 170–171.

47. *The Protestant Ethic*, p. 43, and "Antikritisches Schlusswort," *Archiv*, XXXI (1910), 559, 560, 581.

48. "Kritische Bemerkungen," *Archiv*, XXV (1907), 245 n.5. Weber's willingness to make this qualification, I believe, is to be explained partly by his repeated acknowledgment that a certain minimum of favorable economic opportunities is necessary before Calvinism can produce the spirit of capitalism, and partly by a wish to retain consistent ground for excluding "theocratic" Calvinist communities, notably Geneva and Scotland, from his general thesis. See above p. 157, and below, pp. 186–89.

resentatives of commercial experience and connections."[49] But Weber regards facts such as these as being without interest as far as his thesis is concerned. He consistently refuses to attach much significance to them; he even refuses at times to admit that they had any influence whatsoever on the development of the "spirit" of capitalism. In any case, they were never, according to Weber, the "decisive" factor. Catholic and Lutheran minorities have never manifested the capitalist spirit; ascetic sects have manifested it both when they were the ruling sects and when they lived on equal terms with other sects. Tolerance and intolerance have had nothing to do, historically, with the spirit of capitalism.[50]

From the seventeenth to the nineteenth century, Ireland would seem to present an extraordinarily promising field for testing the historical validity of the "penalization" theory. For it was in Ireland that one of the most complex systems of penalization operated, with "penal" laws and institutions impinging in different ways on different religious groups, and with different degrees of comprehensiveness and severity on the same group, depending on whether they resided in southern Ireland or Ulster. English laws limited the range of industry and foreign trade which any resident of Ireland could engage in, with the highest posts in government and the established (Episcopalian) Church of Ireland largely being reserved for Englishmen. These legal and administrative discriminations were resented by all Irishmen, regardless of their religion.[51] Irish laws imposed sacramental tests which confined certain offices and professions to Episcopalians, thereby penalizing both dissenters and Roman Catholics. Other Irish laws excluded Catholics from or severely restricted their entrance into public office and most of the professions and placed severe restrictions on their succession to landed property. In southern Ireland the landlords—almost exclusively "Anglo-Irish", i.e., native Episcopalians of English ancestry, whereas their tenants were almost exclusively native Catholics—levied rack-rents which left tenants and farm laborers with a bare sufficiency and little to gain from increased effort. In Ulster a system of customary land-tenure operated ("Ulster tenure") which assured tenants of fair compensation for improve-

49. *The Protestant Ethic*, pp. 39, 43, 190 n.13.

50. *The Protestant Ethic*, pp. 43, 190 n.13; "Antikritisches zum 'Geist' des Kapitalismus," *Archiv*, XXX (1910), 183–184; "Antikritisches Schlusswort," *Archiv*, XXXI (1910), 565–569.

51. See, e.g., William Molyneux, *The Case of Ireland's being bound by Acts of Parliament in England, stated*, [1st ed., 1698], London, 1720; Francis G. James, *North Country Bishop: A Biography of William Nicolson*, New Haven, 1956, pp. 245–246.

ments. This led to longer tenures as well as giving some political rights to dissenters, the result being that the Scotch-Irish Presbyterians who constituted the bulk of Ulster's population, enjoyed a relatively unpenalized status in spite of the fact that Episcopalians were a privileged class.[52]

Protestant observers of the extreme poverty of the mass of Catholic Ireland could choose between three different explanations: that the Irish "natives" were "naturally lazy"; that their Catholic faith smothered economic ambition, willingness to work hard, and thrift; that the penal laws and the rack-rent system of the Anglo-Irish landlords closed all avenues to betterment to most of the Irish poor, except through overseas emigration.[53]

The attribution to the Irish poor of a natural or congenital laziness and thriftlessness must have been very common, since many were moved to deny the charge. More responsible persons perhaps either regarded the charge as a libel or felt that discretion called for silence. In any case, I have found few positive statements that the Irish were "naturally lazy." I present two instances:

> The kingdom [of Ireland] is very fertile and plentiful of all provisions, but by reason the people are naturally lazy, the kingdom is not husbanded and cultivated as it ought to be.[54]

> . . . Our poor [i.e., the native Irish poor] are, generally speaking, reduced to want by nothing, but their own laziness, extravagance, and dishonesty.[55]

Some distinguished Anglo-Irish Episcopalians held that the charge of laziness levied against the Irish masses was a libel. I quote two examples:

> I know that laziness is commonly objected to the Irish and this is made the ground of their poverty. . . . the common Irish are laborious people, and if we set aside the holidays their religion enjoins, they work as hard and as long as any in Ireland. I con-

---

52. On the status of dissenters in Ireland, see J. C. Beckett, *Protestant Dissent in Ireland, 1687–1780*, London, 1948, pp. 17–18.

53. Caroline Robbins, *The Eighteenth-Century Commonwealthman*, Cambridge, Mass., 1959, Ch. 5. "The Case of Ireland", pp. 134–176, presents a good deal of material relevant to the discussion of the status of the Irish masses in the eighteenth century. For the seventeenth century, see George O'Brien, *The Economic History of Ireland in the Seventeenth Century*, Dublin, 1919, pp. 14, 125–126, 214 ff., etc.

54. William Cavendish, *A Catalogue of Letters; Ireland*, p. 229.

55. Philip Skelton, *The Case of Protestant Refugees from France, Considered*, in *The Complete Works*, London, 1824, III, 385. Skelton (1707–1785) was a Church of Ireland minister.

fess not with the same success, for they have neither the assistance to labor nor the encouragement workmen have in England, their poverty will not furnish them with convenient tools. . . ; there are many accidental differences that increase their labor on them. . . [here follow such examples as the lack of enclosures on the land they lease, which prevents efficient agriculture]; he has no market for his manufactures; if he builds a good house, or incloses his grounds, to be sure he must raise his rent [i.e., pay a higher rent] or turn out [i.e., be turned out] at the end of a short lease. These and many other considerations make the Irishman's case very pitiful, and ought, as seems to me, to move compassion rather than anger or a severe condemnation. . . . [The author then considers the possibility of extracting more taxes out of them.] They have already given their bread, their flesh, their butter, their shoes, their stockings, their beds, their house furniture and houses to pay their landlords and taxes. I cannot see how any more can be got from them except we take away their potatoes and buttermilk, or flay them and sell their skins.[56]

[The English ought to be] ashamed of the reproaches they cast on the ignorance, the dulness, and the want of courage, in the Irish natives; those defects . . . arising only from the poverty and slavery they suffer from their inhuman neighbours. . . . But the millions of oppressions they lie under . . . have been enough to damp the best spirits under the sun.[57]

Bishop Berkeley, who had no doubt that the Irish Catholic masses were lazy and shiftless, rejected as a "groundless suspicion" the claim that it was Catholic doctrine which was responsible and cited in rebuttal the industry of the French, the Flemish, and "even" the Italians, as well as the efforts of the then reigning pope to promote trade and manufactures in his territories. He did summon the Catholic clergy, however, to try to evoke better economic behavior from their

---

56. Archbishop William King, "A Memorandum on Taxation in Ireland," 1716 (ms.), in Historical Manuscript Commission, *Second Report*, 1874, Appendix, pp. 256–257. Sir William Temple, *Observations upon the United Kingdom*, 1673, on the contrary, explained the laziness attributed to the Irish by the ease with which they could produce enough to feed themselves, so that necessity did not force them to acquire the custom of hard work (*The Works*, I, 165).

57. Jonathan Swift, in a letter of August 2, 1732, *The Correspondence of Jonathan Swift, D.D.*, F. E. Ball, ed., 1910–1914, IV, 328. Although the charge which Swift is specifically refuting here is not that of laziness, it concerns closely related defects of character. For the effects of penalization on the Irish, see also Edmund Burke, in A. P. I. and A. W. Samuels, *The Early Life, Correspondence and Writings of the Rt. Hon. Edmund Burke*, Cambridge, Eng., 1923, pp. 377–378, and a letter in *Works*, Bohn ed., III, 314–317.

parishioners, and did so in terms which strongly implied that the lower ranks of the Catholic clergy regarded their religion, though mistakenly, as hostile to concern for economic prosperity. "It stands upon you," he told them, "to act with vigor in this cause, and shake off the shackles of sloth from your countrymen, the rather, because there be some who surmise that yourselves have put them on. Right or wrong, men will be apt to judge of your doctrines by their fruits." He advised them to consult their superiors on the duty of diligence in one's calling. "They shall tell you the doctrine here delivered is a sound Catholic doctrine, not limited to Protestants, but extending to all, and admitted by all, whether Protestants or Roman Catholics, Christians or Mahometans, Jews or Gentiles."[58]

In the Irish discussion which I have surveyed thus far, penalization was invoked as a reason for the economic backwardness and poverty of the penalized group, instead of being considered as a stimulus to economic activity. But as I have pointed out, this constitutes a qualification, not a refutation, of the theory, since if carried beyond some degree of severity and range of application, penalization will stifle rather than stimulate economic activity on the part of the penalized group. One phase of the Irish record, however, lends positive support to the penalization thesis, namely, the role of the urban Irish Catholics in commerce, finance, and industry.

Sir William Petty, after laying down the proposition that trade everywhere is most vigorously carried out "by the heterodox. . . , and such as possess opinions different from what are publicly established," applies this principle specifically to Ireland, among other countries, saying: "nor is it to be denied but that in Ireland, where the said Roman religion is not authorized, there the professors thereof have a great part of the trade."[59] According to Petty, trade, finance, and industry were largely in Catholic hands.

In what I believe to be Weber's only reference to Catholic Ireland, he rejects Petty's interpretation and conclusions:

> Petty's reference to the case of Ireland is very simply explained by the fact that the Protestants were only involved in the capacity of absentee landlords. If he had meant to maintain more he

58. Bishop George Berkeley, *A Word to the Wise: or an Exhortation to the Catholic Clergy of Ireland*, [1752?], *The Works*, G. N. Wright, ed., London 1843, II, 230–232. An Irish Catholic priest, M. O'Riordan, in *Catholicity and Progress in Ireland*, London, 1905, pp. 163–164, criticized Berkeley sharply for unfairness in attaching so little weight to the penalizing measures and institutions which had weakened the incentive of the Irish Catholic rural masses.

59. Sir William Petty, *Political Arithmetick*, in *Economic Writings*, I, 263–264.

would have been wrong, as the situation of the Scotch-Irish shows. The typical relationship between Protestantism and capitalism existed in Ireland as well as elsewhere.[60]

There seem, however, to have been at least a million Irish Protestants outside of Ulster, predominantly belonging to the established church, and not more than a very small fraction of these could have been "absentee landlords" or dependents thereof. In fact, there is considerable evidence to support Petty's statement concerning Catholic dominance in trade, finance, and industry, at least with respect to southern Ireland.[61]

Weber also claimed that there were no recorded instances of Catholic refugee groups attaining marked success as businessmen in their new homes, though there is some evidence to the contrary as regards upper-class Irish Catholic émigrés.[62]

During the nineteenth century many writers maintained that there was a connection between the greater economic and social progress of Protestant countries and the greater degree of intellectual freedom which the Protestant enjoyed as opposed to the Catholic. Protestantism, they claimed, by removing any authoritative intermediaries between the Bible and the individual conscience had fostered habits of free inquiry and rational scrutiny on religious and moral issues. By a natural process, such habits were extended to political and other as-

60. *The Protestant Ethic*, p. 189 n.12. Weber offers in support only a general reference to C. A. Hanna, *The Scotch-Irish*, New York, 1902, in which I can find no particularly relevant material.

61. See the statements of John Dalrymple, *Considerations upon the Policy of Entails in Great Britain*, Edinburgh, 1764, p. 25; J. C. Beckett, *Protestant Dissent in Ireland*, 1948, p. 144; Vincent T. Harlow, *The Founding of the Second British Empire, 1763–1793*, London, 1952, I, 632; and above all, the material presented by M. O'Riordan, *Catholicity and Progress in Ireland*, pp. 180–184, and by Maureen Wall, "The Rise of a Catholic Middle Class in Eighteenth-Century Ireland," *Irish Historical Studies*, XI (1958), 91–115. See also Maureen Wall, "The Catholic Merchants, Manufacturers and Traders of Dublin, 1778–1782", in *Reportorium Novum, Dublin Diocesan Historical Record*, II (1959–1960), 298–323, where a list is given of over 1200 names of Catholics in Dublin who were engaged in commerce and manufactures, broadly interpreted. Isabel Grubb, *Quakers in Ireland, 1654–1900*, London, 1927, pp. 17–18, minimizes the role of Irish Catholics in trade, while perhaps exaggerating that of the Quakers. I cannot see where she presents any evidence that the Catholics were unimportant in trade beyond her citation of Arthur Young's statement that the Quakers "are the only wealthy traders in the island," in *Tour in Ireland (1776–1779)*, ed. A. W. Hutton, London, 1892, II, 247–248.

62. See J. Mathorez, *Les Etrangers en France sous l'ancien régime*, Paris, 1919–1921, I, 99: "In the eighteenth century the Irish who crossed the Channel and settled in France did not all enter the army; many of them held high commercial status." See also Leonard Krieger, *The German Idea of Freedom*, Boston, 1957, p. 38: "Scotch Catholics and Calvinists who fled to Germany during the 16th and 17th centuries . . . became prominent merchants along the Baltic littoral . . . ."

pects of everyday life. The Protestant approach to the Bible placed a high premium on literacy and led to greater efforts in the field of general education. The rejection of tradition as authoritative in the field of religion was applied to other fields as well; it promoted a receptivity to new ideas and ways of doing things in business and industry and contributed to the development of a more rational social ethic. All of this, these writers claimed, favored the more efficient and more diligent pursuit of economic affairs.

This brings us closer to the Weber thesis concerning the fashioning of a bourgeois social ethic by Protestant religious belief than we have been previously in most of our survey. I would nevertheless insist on one important difference between this line of reasoning and the Weber thesis. The literature prior to Weber which follows this line, as far as I have been able to discover, does not contain a single explicit statement to the effect that it was the special doctrines of predestination, election, the calling, and business success as a mark of salvation, that were responsible, directly or indirectly, for the generation of that set of economic attitudes and patterns of behavior which constituted the "spirit" of capitalism and which crucially modified the development of modern capitalism.

I will select for special comment a few items from the relevant literature which contribute fresh and interesting ideas to the general argument that Protestantism, through its emphasis on freedom of individual conscience in interpreting the message of the Gospel, not only placed great emphasis on education but fostered the development of habits of free examination—all of which was conducive to the growth of civil freedom and economic and cultural progress.[63]

Israel Worsley, an English "Presbyterian," writing in 1816, credited English dissent with the progress of manufactures which had brought about the growth and prosperity of England:

And if it can be made to appear, that these manufactures were originally introduced into our island by Presbyterians, that the

63. Representative of this type of argument are Charles Grant, "Observations on the State of Society Among the Asiatic Subjects of Great Britain", [1797], reprinted in Great Britain, *Parliamentary Papers*, X (1813), 31; Charles F. D. de Villers, *Essai sur l'esprit et l'influence de la réformation de Luther*, Paris, 1804 (several times reprinted and also published in English translation); Napoléon Roussel, *Catholic Nations and Protestant Nations Compared in Their Threefold Relation to Wealth, Knowledge and Morality* (tr. from the French ed. of 1854), London, 1855; C. Weiss, "Mémoire," pp. 105–106. Roussel presents badly coordinated but impressively wide evidence of economic superiority of Protestant over Catholic regions, even within the same latitude and when inhabited by persons of the same racial origins. Weiss makes a point which fits in well with Weber's thesis when he says that there has been historically a special affinity between the factory method of organizing industry ("les manufactures réunies") and Calvinism.

direction of all our principal manufactories had been almost exclusively in their hands, and that the chief of the capital vested in them has been the property of dissenters, it must follow as an undeniable consequence, that the present high state of prosperity, on account of which we are the envy of the world, has arisen from the free and bold exercise of religious liberty, which unshackled the minds of our ancestors, threw off the fetters in which their thoughts had long been bound, and, leading them through a straight a clear and an easy road up to the throne of God presented them with a distinct view of whatever earth can offer, and made it an easy thing for them to direct their energies to the comparatively smaller concerns of an earthly maintenance. The mind that is bound by a religious creed of man's composing, and dares not look out of it, thinks feebly upon other subjects. . . .

But, when the mind unbends to the dictates of religious truth, and is free to submit to its instructions, all its powers receive a spring which aids in the research of knowledge of every kind; and it becomes a matter of habit to a mind so circumstanced to think freely and to act independently on all questions, whether they be religious, political, oeconomical, or other.[64]

This is a clear anticipation of Weber's thesis that Protestant nonconformity operated to release energies for the pursuit of economic ends. Worsley, however, provides no support for Weber's central point that by giving special religious sanctions or "premiums" to gainful economic activity, Calvinist or "ascetic Protestant" doctrine acted as a special stimulus to economic activity. By Worsley's time what was left of English "Presbyterianism" had rejected Calvinist doctrine and, like Worsley himself, was largely unitarian in its beliefs. Worsley's book makes clear that he attributes English prosperity to the freedom it had gained not only from Catholic but also from Calvinist dogma and mental discipline. The sort of "Presbyterianism" to which he ascribes importance in the development of English industrial prosperity was not that of the pre-Restoration period but the later English "Presbyterianism" which was in revolt against Calvinist doctrine.

---

64. Israel Worsley, *Observations on the State and Changes in the Presbyterian Societies of England during the last half century; also, on the Manufactures of Great Britain; which have been for the most part established and supported by the Protestant Dissenters: tending to illustrate the Importance of religious Liberty and free Inquiry to the Welfare and Prosperity of a People; preceded by a Sermon. . . ,* London, 1816, pp. 70–72.

In a book published in 1843, Robert Vaughan, an English Congregational minister, presented an elaborate version of the thesis that Protestantism, by its teaching of individual freedom of judgment on religious matters, prepared men "to look with a new intelligence on many other matters," and thus brought about a "mental and spiritual revolution" which extended to political and economic matters, and made "the strength of Protestantism . . . a strength on the side of industry, of human improvement, and of the civilization which leads to the formation of great cities." The urban note is one special feature of his thesis and in a discreet way is utilized to throw a more favorable light on English dissent, a "purer" form of Christianity, than on the Church of England with its residues of an older feudalistic and agrarian culture.[65] Moreover, Vaughan is so favorably impressed by the culture which urban commerce and manufacturing generates that although throughout his discussion of the relation of religion and "industry"[66] he insists on their mutual interaction, he seems to place greater weight on the contribution which the city pattern of life makes to the purification of religion than on the contribution which religion makes to the urban pattern of life. In fact, the book as a whole is a eulogy of the city. "It is in the nature of religion," he says, to seize upon and consecrate the self-discipline and patterns of thought and behavior generated by successful commerce, now manifested most clearly in Protestant urban communities:

> [Commerce] is constantly teaching men that thought and labour, during the years immediately before them, present the only path to repose and enjoyment during the years in the distance. Men are thus taught, that in relation to the affairs of the world, no less than to the affairs of religion, the man who would be successful "must take up his cross and deny himself." In the case of no people, perhaps, is this doctrine more strikingly illustrated than in the history of the Anglo-Americans.[67]
> . . . industry, in place of being merely a social virtue, inculcated on the principles of human wisdom or expediency, is made to be indispensable, in the great majority of mankind, to religious

65. Robert Vaughan, D.D., *The Age of Great Cities; or, Modern Society Viewed in Its Relation to Intelligence, Morals, and Religion*, London, 1843. See especially Ch. 3, pp. 72–78: "On the Principle of the Protestant Reformation, and on Its Relation to the Progress of Society."

66. "It is industry—all that we intend by the terms, application, self-culture, energy—which, more than any other cause, gives some men their superiority to others, and, upon the same principle, some nations their superiority to other nations." *Ibid.*, pp. 357–358.

67. *Ibid.*, p. 312.

consistency, and is enforced, accordingly, by the highest possible sanctions.

In consonance with these views, it is found, that in these later ages the commercial ingenuity and enterprise of the world have their place, for the most part, among Christian nations; and, since the Reformation, among those states of Christendom professing the faith of the gospel in its purer form. . . . In all these instances there has probably been a large amount of action and reaction between religion and social character:—but the adaptation of Christianity to the higher forms of national greatness, and its tendencies to raise nations to such greatness, are not the less certain or manifest on that account.[68]

The self-denial which religion and commerce both require and both inculcate is not, however, in either case a perpetual abstention from enjoyment of temporal goods:

The body is from God in common with the soul, . . . and it is as truly the duty of men to use the temporal good which the Divine hand has bestowed upon them as to abstain from the abuse of it.

. . . if religion is ever to be diffused in a form adapted to elevate society at large, it must be religion divested, after this manner, of the gloom and asceticism which the monks of the middle ages borrowed from the disciples of the old oriental philosophy. We may rest assured, that in no connexion will follies of this nature obtain so little patronage, as among the crowds who busy themselves with manufactures and commerce.[69]

The cooperation, however, between religion and "industry" ensures that the enjoyment of temporal goods does not take forms that would act as a barrier to economic progress:

It is scarcely necessary to add that the industry of religious men—separated as such persons commonly are from the fashionable and frivolous amusements which absorb so much of the time and spirits of such as do not participate in their graver feeling—is in part a natural result of the habits peculiar to them. Shut out by their principles and preferences from the avenues to forbidden pleasure or unjust gain, they pursue their lawful objects with more steadiness, in consequence of pursuing them with an undivided mind.[70]

68. *Ibid.*, pp. 359–360.
69. *Ibid.*, pp. 314–315.
70. *Ibid.*, p. 360.

Vaughan's doctrine has some elements in common with Weber's thesis. It is an explicitly "bourgeois" doctrine, linking non-conformist Protestant religion with bourgeois standards in a harmonious partnership; it is a doctrine of sobriety, self-discipline, and unashamed pursuit of wealth. But it expressly rejects either secular or religious asceticism, and there is no indication that it endorses or in any way derives from the doctrines of predestination and the calling upon which Weber places exclusive emphasis. Vaughan, moreover, comes close to explaining the businessman's pattern of behavior by the inherent requirements and stimuli of business itself, and he almost suggests that the businessman's ethical notions have more influence on his religious beliefs than the latter have on his behavior. Such suggestions had been made by others prior to Vaughan, as I believe I have shown, but Vaughan did precede Karl Marx in this respect and was the first writer, to my knowledge, to present such notions with any degree of emphasis and elaboration.

H. J. L. Baudrillart, in a discussion of the economic superiority of Protestant peoples written in 1853, was apparently the first writer to introduce the "paradox" of the Reformed faith. Instead of having, as the mysticism of the faith might have led one to expect, an enervating effect on industry, which flourishes on liberty and terrestrial hopes, it had the opposite effect:

Protestantism has created industrial peoples. It has not spread anywhere without bringing along with it a parallel development of industry and of commerce. Required seemingly to be purely mystic, it showed itself to be, even to excess, utilitarian. One may appeal to the climate of the Reform countries, more favorable than that of the south to the development of labor; one may say that industry should have profited from all that the Reform withdrew from art and from the satisfactions of sense and of imagination which art provides; but the essential reason is that the Reformed religion made an appeal, an energetic appeal and present every minute, to the spirit of reflection which develops the consciousness of human personality and which cannot disassociate itself, no matter what one does, from the spirit of liberty and of responsibility. To read, to interpret as a matter of obligation, to consult one's conscience, to examine one's thought, to place confidence in it, to do nothing without having judged, reasoned, calculated—what an apprenticeship for the qualities specially required in industry! The purely theological system may have been dominant for the doctors of the Reform. But in general practice, among the masses, what was to prevail was not the *doctrine*, which is repugnant to human nature no less than to emancipated reason, but the *principle* of liberty, of progress, so in harmony with our most hidden instincts, with our most legitimate and most invincible aspirations.[71]

Baudrillart's stress on the role of the Reformation in liberating the individual judgment from ecclesiastical restraints anticipates one element in Weber's thesis, but in rejecting as ineffective the theological doctrine of the Reformers, he rejects the central and original element in Weber's thesis.

Emile de Laveleye, a Belgian "liberal Catholic" economist, in a wide-ranging survey found Protestant countries to be superior in political freedom, general education, moral standards (with emphasis on sex morality), and economic well-being. He blamed the Catholic Church for this backwardness, and depicted it as preferring absolutist and despotic government to representative government, both within the Church itself and in the political world; as lacking in zeal for general education; and as constantly working to suppress liberal ideas of all kinds. In Protestant countries there was no war between religion and liberal ideas; liberalism had found its inspiration in moral leaders like Luther, Calvin, and John Knox. In Catholic countries, on the other hand, liberalism took its inspiration from the Pagan Renaissance and was both irreligious and licentious in its moral ideas. But the economic world needed political freedom, general education, and a rigorous morality to flourish. Thus Ultramontane Catholicism was responsible for the economic backwardness of Catholic countries.[72]

Herman Schell, a Catholic professor of theology at the University of Würzburg, writing in 1897 in response to a Prussian official report of 1896 showing a disproportionately low number of Catholics in the higher secondary schools and learned professions, attributed these facts largely to the mistaken educational principles followed by Catholic churchmen and educators, especially in the Catholic theological seminaries.[73] His central criticism was that the intellectual lead-

---

71. H. J. L. Baudrillart, *J. Bodin et son temps*, Paris, 1853, p. 43. George O'Brien, *An Essay on the Economic Effects of the Reformation*, London, 1923, pp. 131–132, gives, I think, too free a translation of this paragraph and thus alters its significance. He cites E. Vermeil, *Etudes sur la réforme*, which I have not been able to consult, as presenting a similar view.

72. Emile de Laveleye, *Protestantism and Catholicism, in Their Bearing upon the Liberty and Prosperity of Nations* (tr. from the French), London, 1875. Laveleye conceded that England was also backward in education and explained it by the fact that of all forms of Protestantism, Anglicanism was closest to Roman Catholicism.

73. Herman Schell, *Der Katholicismus als Princip des Fortschritts* [1st ed. 1897], 7th ed., Würzburg, 1899. Franz X. Kiefl, *Herman Schell*, Mainz, 1907, p. 126, says

ers of the Church put much more emphasis on the conflict between the "worldly" and divine than on the capacity of the "worldly" to be a carrier and mediator of the divine. He criticized what he regarded as excessive "Roman" and Jesuit influences over German Catholic thought and educational institutions and the neglect in Catholic education of concern for such values as the State, secular science, cultural progress, and the development of economic and industrial skills. In support of his plea for lessening the degree of ecclesiastical control over Catholic education, including education for the priesthood, he claimed that Revelation supported a "universal priesthood," such that all directions and forms of human work would be consecrated to God. His objective was apparently to bring about a greater participation of German Catholic clerics and educational institutions in the cultural and scientific activities of the German people as a whole. One implication of his argument was that Catholic educators, by modelling their teaching on tradition and the belief in the sufficiency of the oracular powers of the Church even in the realm of science and technology, was contributing to the cultural and economic backwardness of the Catholic sections of the German population.

I have found, I repeat, no writer, Catholic or non-Catholic, who seriously disputed the claim that Protestant countries were generally more prosperous than Catholic ones. Some Catholics did deny, however, that *all* Protestant countries were more prosperous or more industrious than *any* Catholic country,[74] and some Catholic writers insisted that non-religious factors were responsible for, or at least were important contributing factors to, the economic superiority of Protestant countries. Cardinal Baudrillart, for instance, claimed that religion was only one among an indefinite number of other factors which needed to be taken into account, emphasizing coal resources and climate especially. He charged de Laveleye with unfairness in comparing Protestant valley cantons in Switzerland with Alpine Catholic ones, and pointed to the contrast between North and South Italy, and to the flourishing industry in Belgium and the Catholic

---

that this book created a sensation in Catholic circles. Some of Schell's writings were put on the *Index*, and I presume that, like Laveleye before him, he was a "liberal Catholic."

74. See, e.g., Heinrich Pesch, "Ursachen des wirtschaftlichen Niederganges katholischer Völker," *Stimmen zur Maria Laach*, XLVIII (1895), 361–371. A. Onclair, *Les Causes et les remèdes du socialisme*, Paris, 1896, pp. 263–265, rejected as libel the charge that by condemning luxury, Catholicism had removed a stimulus to industrial progress. He also denied as calumny the charge that Catholic laborers were inferior to Protestant laborers in exactness and regularity and cited testimony to the contrary with respect to the factory workers in the Prussian Rhineland. By its moral teaching, moreover, Catholicism prevented the oppression of the workers and thus forestalled a socialist reaction.

Swiss canton of Fribourg, as evidence that religion was not the sole factor and that prosperity was not exclusively Protestant. "God," he wrote, "would have put the true faith to too severe a test if he had permitted all the prizes of the temporal order to go to the side of error. But that has not been the case, even in the purely economic order."[75]

Catholic writers in the nineteenth century repeatedly took the line that the economic superiority of Protestant countries, and especially England, was associated with an extremely uneven distribution of wealth and with "pauperism" and the degradation of the masses.[76] Occasionally, at least, Protestantism was charged with some of the responsibility for this state of affairs.[77] It was also held that by encouraging an exaggerated individualism, Protestantism had opened the way to the emergence of class conflict and, by way of reaction, the socialist movement.[78]

Catholic writers replied to claims of Protestant superiority in economic matters by stating that other things were relevant in comparing the merits of different societies; that Catholic countries were superior not only in the quality of their religious beliefs and practices but in the moral and other aspects of their civilization as well. Any economic inferiority was not the result of religion or of the priority given to salvation over material achievement.[79] As an Irish priest put the issue:

75. Alfred Baudrillart, *L'Eglise catholique, la Renaissance, le protestantisme*, Paris, 1908, pp. 406, 429–436, quotation on p. 435. Weber's first essays had already appeared (1904–1905) by the time Baudrillart wrote, but they do not seem to have attracted attention in France until considerably later.

76. Robert Michels, *Die Verelendungstheorie*, Leipzig, 1928, pp. 65–83, gives an extensive survey of the Continental literature commenting on English "pauperism," but does not refer to any religious interpretation of it.

77. See Joachim Ventura de Raulica (a Vatican official), *Die christliche Politik* (tr. from a French ed.) Mainz, 1857, pp. 224–225. Also some of the French writers cited later. In his *History of the Protestant "Reformation," in England and Ireland*, London, 1824, Letter XVI, William Cobbett, though a professed Anglican, claimed that there was greater prosperity in England, especially for the lower classes, before the Reformation and that English pauperism was a product of the Reformation. He was often cited by Catholic writers later in the century, and in 1896 Cardinal F. A. Gasquet published an edition with a highly laudatory introduction.

78. See, e.g., A. Onclair, *Les Causes et les remèdes du socialisme*; Abbé J. J. Gaume, *L'Europe en 1848, ou Considérations sur l'organisation du travail, le communisme et le chrétianisme*, Paris, 1848, pp. 15–16, 22; and Abbé Albert Delaporte, *Le Problème économique et la doctrine catholique*, Paris, 1867, p. 156: "It suffices for the Catholic countries to keep the first rank among countries honestly enriched, and this rank will perhaps not be seriously denied to them."

79. See, e.g., Jaime Luciano Balmes, *Protestantism and Catholicity Compared in Their Effects on the Civilization of Europe*, 2nd ed. (tr. from the French version), Baltimore, 1851; Auguste Nicolas, *Du Protestantisme et de toutes les hérésies dans leur rapport avec le socialisme*, Paris, 1852.

. . . I am not, as a Catholic, at all concerned to prove that Catholicism is better or even equal to non-Catholicism of any kind in the matter of trade, commerce, manufactures, or making money. Those matters, of course, form part of human duty; but to take them as implying a philosophy of human life is as foolish as to take a fraction of a man's body for the whole.[80]

In the French-speaking countries, it was the treatment of the issue by a Belgian Catholic economist, Villeneuve-Bargemont, in a work first published in 1835 to 1839, which most influenced later Catholic discussion. What was good in modern society had originated in pre-Reformation Christianity and the Renaissance. Had it not been for the Reformation there would have been greater economic and social progress. The Reformation had removed the salutary brake which Catholicism had imposed on the sensuality and irrationality of men. The current social evils in Catholic countries were the result of imitation and diffusion of practices originating in Protestant countries. The superiority of several Protestant countries in industry, commerce, and shipping stemmed from factors antedating the Reformation, among them geographical situation, climate, and infertility of the soil, which made greater effort necessary to overcome the natural handicaps. Associated with this economic superiority, moreover, were serious social evils. Protestantism had weakened the attachment of peoples to agriculture; it had thus led to the abandonment of natural for artificial riches and prepared the way for the spirit of "industrialism"—a novel term then—which had resulted in the enslavement of the working classes. Protestantism had deprived the poor and infirm of their natural protector, the Church, and had substituted a false and arid philanthropy for Christian charity. In suppressing the celibacy of the priesthood and in proclaiming as the greatest of goods an abundant population it had fostered an excessive growth in population which Catholicism, with great social foresight, had striven to restrain and moderate. While Catholicism had constantly advanced, with a firm but prudent step, toward the freeing of peoples and the gradual emancipation of slaves and serfs by means of a wide diffusion of ownership of land, Protestantism had fostered the emergence of industrial entrepreneurs and speculators, who sought profit by keeping wages low, by imposing excessive labor, and by the monopolistic concentration of capital, thereby gradually subjecting the working classes anew to the feudal servitude from which Catholicism had rescued them, while

80. M. O'Riordan, *Catholicity and Progress in Ireland*, 4th ed., London, 1906, p. 169.

denying them the earlier protection of the Church and the tremendous resources of its charitable and religious institutions.[81]

The conclusion I draw from this survey of the pre-Weber literature comparing Protestant and Catholic economies is that none of the writers that I have read explicitly attributed the differences to those elements in Protestant theology which Weber emphasized, the doctrines of predestination and calling, with acceptance of success in one's calling as the sign of salvation. Many of them presented explanations which in varying degrees were in conflict with the Weber thesis. They generally emphasized the plurality of causal factors, and assigned weight to factors which Weber either ignored or minimized. There was almost universal agreement before Weber, however, that there was a close historical association between Protestantism and the development of capitalism in its modern forms. In this respect Weber was not an innovator. His originality was confined to his account of the nature of the particular "spirit" of capitalism associated with Protestantism, of the causal process whereby Protestant theology had brought this "spirit" into existence, and of the role this "spirit" had played in giving modern capitalism its specific character.

A few years before the appearance of Weber's first essays on the relationship of Protestantism to capitalism, one of Weber's students, Martin Offenbacher, published a study based on German—chiefly Baden—official statistics of the comparative educational and occupational status of Protestants and Catholics.[82] Offenbacher concluded from his analysis of the data that Catholics were in every respect inferior to Protestants in their educational and economic status. He conceded that the greater expensiveness of the Catholic religious institutions was a factor, but on the basis of Prussian statistics of Church revenues claimed that it could be only a minor one.[83] His own explanation of the economic superiority of the Protestants was that their religious training made Catholics less disposed to economic

81. Viscount Alban de Villeneuve-Bargemont, *Histoire de l'économie politique*, Paris, 1841 (a revision of a course of lectures published in a Belgian Catholic periodical, 1835–1837), I, 316–317. All of Ch. 9 in I, 288–319, "Influence of the Religious Reform of Luther on Political Economy," is relevant. In an earlier work, *Economie politique chrétienne, ou recherches sur la nature et les causes du paupérisme*, Paris, 1834, II, 1–12, Villeneuve-Bargemont presented an elaborate statistical comparison purporting to show that "indigents" were more numerous in proportion to total population in Protestant countries, which is notable at least for its early and skillful use of tabular and "tinted map" devices in presenting statistical data. For an appreciation of Villeneuve-Bargemont's work as a "social Catholic" economist, see Sister Mary Ignatius Ring, *Villeneuve-Bargemont, Precursor of Modern Social Catholicism, 1784–1850*, Milwaukee, 1935.
82. Martin Offenbacher, *Konfession und soziale Schichtung*, Tübingen, 1900.
83. *Ibid.*, p. 22.

striving and more inclined to seek security of income and status in preference to a more risky and exciting mode of life, even though the latter might bring the chance of honor and riches.[84]

In a study of the causes responsible for the progress of science, Alphonse de Candolle, himself a distinguished Genevese scientist, included a section on the influence of religion on science. In the course of this study Candolle presented a statistical comparison of the proportions of Protestants and Catholics in the foreign membership of the three great European societies, the Royal Society and the Academies of Paris and Berlin, during the eighteenth and nineteenth centuries. He compared these proportions with the proportions of Protestants and Catholics in Europe as a whole and in the particular countries represented in the foreign membership of these societies and found a tremendous disproportion of Protestant membership.[85] De Candolle attributed very little of this indicated difference in scientific achievement to differences in dogma, which in large part were not concerned with matters which affected ordinary life. Rather, he believed that differences in the methods of teaching dogma were important, Catholicism being more authoritarian and admitting less free examination:

> A population educated during several generations on the basis of authority would be naturally timid in intellectual matters. On the contrary, a population accustomed from childhood to scrutinize the things which they had been told were the most important would have no fear of examining purely scientific questions and would grapple more effectively with them in order to resolve them.[86]

De Candolle's claims for a distinctly greater measure of free inquiry under Protestantism apply only to the period beginning with the early decades of the eighteenth century. He cites Geneva as an example. From 1525 to 1725 an authoritarian Calvinism, imposed by the clergy, prevailed there. During this period Geneva did not produce a single distinguished scientist. In the period 1720 to 1730 the authority of Calvinist doctrine was weakened and education and manners were

---

84. *Ibid.*, p. 68. For Weber's use of Offenbacher's findings see *The Protestant Ethic*, pp. 35–41, 188–190 nn.4–14. On Offenbacher's statistical findings as defective in method and inconclusive, see Kurt Samuelsson, *Ekonomi och Religion*, Stockholm, 1957, now available in an English translation [*Religion and Economic Action*, New York, 1961].

85. Alphonse de Candolle, *Histoire des sciences et des savants depuis deux siècles*, 2nd ed., Geneva, 1885, pp. 328 ff.

86. *Ibid.*, p. 332.

liberalized. From 1739 on, when a Genevese was first elected to an important foreign scientific society, Geneva never ceased to produce mathematicians, physicists, and natural scientists in a remarkable number relative to its tiny population.[87]

The pre-Weberian comments I have found with respect to the influence of Calvinism on Scottish economic conditions and motivation are, with one exception—a letter of John Keats, the poet—in sharp contradiction with Weber's main thesis and his rare explicit references to Scottish experience. But they do support Weber's concession that where Calvinism was a state religion it could operate as a restraint rather than as a stimulus to economic progress:

> . . . the ecclesiastical supervision of the life of the individual, which, as it was practised in the Calvinistic State Churches almost amounted to an inquisition, might even retard that liberation of individual powers which was conditioned by the rational ascetic pursuit of salvation, and in some cases actually did so.[88]

Until well into the eighteenth century, Scotland was a desperately poor country. Scottish and English commentators repeatedly remarked on the lack of economic initiative or ambition and on the sluggishness and lack of enterprise and economic discipline of the population in general. What is of special interest here is that several writers, both Scottish and non-Scottish, attributed Scotland's economic backwardness in large part to the deadening effect of Calvinist doctrine and discipline, as forcibly applied to them by Church and State.

The most important exponent of this view was Henry T. Buckle, himself a Scotsman, but a rather violent critic of Calvinism, at least in its Scottish manifestations.[89] Buckle writes from an "Enlightenment" point of view, in which cultural and economic development is treated as the rational goal for a society, even to the extent of frankly eulogizing "the love of money": "it is certain that, after the love of knowledge, there is no one passion which has done so much good to man-

---

87. *Ibid.*, pp. 335–336. The bearing of this fact on the attempts which have been made to show a disproportionate contribution to science in seventeenth-century England by Calvinists or "Puritans" deserves consideration.

88. *The Protestant Ethic*, p. 152. Weber probably regarded this as applicable to Scotland.

89. *Introduction to the History of Civilization in England*, 1st ed., 2 vols., London [1857, 1861]. Because of the valuable editorial notes, I have used the J. M. Robertson edition published by George Routledge & Sons, Ltd., London, 1904. The relevant material is in Ch. 18, "Condition of Scotland During the Seventeenth and Eighteenth Centuries," pp. 696–740, and Ch. 19, "An Examination of the Scotch Intellect during the Seventeenth Century," pp. 741–791.

kind as the love of money.''[90] He summarizes the economic teaching of Scottish Calvinists in the seventeenth century as follows:

> To wish for more than was necessary to keep oneself alive was a sin as well as a folly and was a violation of the subjection we owe to God. That it was contrary to His desire was moreover evident from the fact that He bestowed wealth liberally upon misers and covetous men; a remarkable circumstance, which, in the opinion of Scotch divines, proved that He was no lover of riches, otherwise He would not give them to such base and sordid persons.
>
> To be poor, dirty, and hungry, to pass through life in misery, and to leave it with fear, to be plagued with boils, and sores, and diseases of every kind, to be always sighing and groaning, . . . in a word, to suffer constant affliction, and to be tormented in all possible ways; to undergo these things was deemed a proof of goodness, just as the contrary was a proof of evil.[91]

Nevertheless, Max Weber cites Buckle as one of his predecessors in finding an affinity between Calvinism and capitalism,[92] and he refers expressly to Scotland only to cite a letter of John Keats to his brother, written from Ireland in 1818 after a visit to Scotland, which contains the following passage:

> . . . I can perceive a great difference in the nations, from the chambermaid at this *nate toone* [Port Patrick, in Ireland] . . . . She is fair, kind, and ready to laugh, because she is out of the horrible dominion of the Scotch Kirk. A Scotch girl stands in terrible awe of the Elders. . . . These Kirk-men have done Scotland good (Query?). They have made men, women; old men, young men; old women, young women; boys, girls; and all infants careful—so that they are formed into regular Phalanges of savers and gainers. Such a thrifty army cannot fail to enrich their Country, and give it a greater appearance of Comfort than that of this poor [Irish] neighbourhood. These Kirk-men have done Scotland harm; they have banished puns, and laughing, and kissing.
> . . .

90. *Ibid.*, p. 788.
91. *Ibid.*, pp. 784–785. See also, p. 784: "It was wrong for a man to wish to advance himself in life, or in any way to better his condition."
92. *The Protestant Ethic*, p. 44.

I have not sufficient reasoning faculty to settle the doctrine of thrift, as it is consistent with the dignity of human society—with the happiness of cottagers.[93]

There is no lack of contemporary comment on the economic backwardness of Scotland during the period of dominance of orthodox Calvinism, but I have been unable to find any writer before Buckle who attributed it to the influence of Calvinist teaching. During the Restoration period, however, Roger L'Estrange, a violent Anglican and Royalist critic of the Presbyterians, urged English businessmen to look to the record of the Scottish Presbyterians in interfering injuriously with commerce and industry for religious reasons.[94] James Anthony Froude, in 1865, accepted Buckle's account of the Scottish Calvinist attitude towards economic activity, but defended this attitude on moral grounds: the Scottish Calvinists had superior values to those of Buckle.[95] Sir Henry Craik in 1901 attributed the cultural and economic progress of Scotland in the late eighteenth century in part to the rise of the "moderate" (i.e., Arminian and liberal) movement and the decline of the influence of the orthodox or "High Flyer" Calvinists.[96] In 1902, W. L. Mathieson characterized the Calvinist religious spirit as "the most serious of all obstacles to industrial progress" in Scotland.[97]

93. M. B. Forman, ed., *The Letters of John Keats*, London, 1931, I, 186–187; Max Weber, "Antikritisches Schlusswort", *Archiv* XXXI, 594; *The Protestant Ethic*, pp. 44, 270 n.58.

94. [Roger L'Estrange], *Tyranny and Popery Lording It over the Consciences, Lives, Liberties, and Estates both of King and People*, London, 1678, p. 85; Roger L'Estrange, *Toleration Discuss'd*, 3rd ed., London, 1681, pp. 160–161.

95. James Anthony Froude, *The Influence of the Reformation on the Scottish Character*, [1865], a lecture reprinted in *Short Studies on Great Subjects*, New York, 1879, pp. 128–154, at p. 151.

96. Sir Henry Craik, *A Century of Scottish History*, Edinburgh, 1901, I, 69–70, 379–381; II, 386.

97. W. L. Mathieson, *Politics and Religion: A Study in Scottish History from the Reformation to the Revolution*, Glasgow, 1902, I, 202–203.

Protestant casuistics

Protestant casuistics never flourished on a scale comparable to Catholic casuistics, but the chief explanation for this, I believe, lies in differences between them in ecclesiastical structure and discipline rather than in differences in basic theological or ethical principles. In the eighteenth century, translations of Catholic manuals in modern languages do not seem to have been uncommon. (Examples are J. Pontas, *Dictionnaire des cas de conscience*, 1734; A. A. de B. de Lamet et Fromageau, *Dictionnaire des cas de conscience*, 1744.) The Catholic manuals were generally published only in Latin; they were addressed primarily to confessors; they were concerned with the administration of penance and absolution, and therefore with *minima* of obligation, having behind them the support of an authoritative church and tradition. Such manuals continue to be published and serve their traditional functions to the present day. Protestant casuistics, on the other hand, was, by the nature of Protestant ecclesiastical machinery, largely without an authoritative basis, the nearest thing to it, perhaps, being the decisions of Calvinist (or Presbyterian) synods. There was no institutional process whereby uniformity of decisions through time and place could be reached or enforced. It was addressed to the general body of believers and not exclusively to a professional priesthood, as in the Catholic Church. It was concerned with what to believe as well as what to do, and with persuasion to a more righteous life, that is, it had primarily a homiletic purpose and therefore carefully abstained from systematic exploration of the lower limits of permissible behavior. It had as a whole a more rigoristic tone than the Catholic manuals and was uniformly probabilistic when not perfectionist, as compared to the strong probabilist tone of much of the Catholic casuistics. But this was fairly obviously the consequence of its different function rather than of a basic difference in principle. It was, in fact, largely an imitation of Catholic casuistics, and this was often frankly conceded by the Protestant casuists. Credit was often freely given to the Catholic casuistical literature for the guidance and analytical procedures which it provided as the pioneer and leader in this field. In the same way, Anglican and non-conformist casuists treated with respect and borrowed freely from each other's manuals. A careful comparison between the three major bodies of casuistical literature would, perhaps, reveal some systematic differences of tone and substance with respect to significant ethical issues, but my superficial and limited examination of this literature impresses me with its essential unity as exposition of a common moral tradition, the question of usury being the only specific topic with respect to which it could plausibly be argued that there was a basic clash of doctrine. The fact that Catholic casuistics still survives and functions, whereas Protestant casuistics was practically dead everywhere in the Protestant world before the end of the seventeenth century,[1] is, I think, to be explained mainly by the fact that it never had so clear-cut a function to perform as did Catholic casuistics. The absence in Protestantism of an established doctrinal authority prevented the Protestant manuals from acquiring anything like an official status, and the general latitudinarian tendencies and the acceptance of "Enlightenment" views on ethical issues operated to shift the role of moral instruction from the clerics as clerics to clerical and lay exponents of a secular thesis.[2]

1. This is not to be taken as literally true. An English non-conformist treatise on theological and ethical problems constructed on the model of older casuist literature was issued in 1775 and republished as late as 1808. I have examined the 1807 edition: S. Pike and S. Hayward, *Religious Cases of Conscience Answered in an Evangelical Manner*, London, 1807. It deals mainly with questions of faith and grace and with ethical questions as related to obtaining and retaining assurance of salvation, without entering into any concrete issues of economic behavior. It ends, however, with two brief "Characters," "The Character of an Honest Man" and "The Character of the Faithful Man," of which the former explicitly and the latter implicitly lay down some general guides for behavior in the world, including its economic sector.

2. Protestant casuistics is treated in: J. J. Cyprien Majal, *Etude comparée des deux morales luthérienne et reformée*, Paris, 1901, pp. 140–158; H. Hensley Henson, *Studies in English Religion in the Seventeenth Century*, London, 1903; Walter E. Houghton, Jr., *The Formation of Thomas Fuller's Holy and Profane States*, Cambridge, Mass., 1938, pp. 69 ff.; Kenneth E. Kirk, *Conscience and Its Problems*, [1st ed., 1927] new ed., London, 1948; Thomas Wood, *English Casuistical Divinity During the Seventeenth Century*, London, 1952; George L. Mosse, "The Importance of Jacques Saurin in the History of Casuistry, and the Enlightenment," *Church History*, XXV (1956), 195–209.

Index to the documentation

Compiled by John A. Vickers

Adler, Georg, *Geschichte des Sozialismus und Kommunismus*, 39 n.87

Agrippa, Henry Cornelius, *Sur l'incertitude aussi bien que la vanité des sciences et des arts*, 121 n.12

Allard, Paul, *Les Esclaves chrétiens*, 29 n.56

Allix, E., and Génestal, R., "Les opérations financières de l'Abbaye de Troarn du XI au XIV siècles," 98 n.131

Amberg, Rudolph, *Die Steuer in der Rechtsphilosophie der Scholastiker*, 106 n.147

Ambrose, St., *De Nabuthae*, 22 n.30; *De Officiis Ministrorum*, 70 n.65

Aquinas. *See* Thomas Aquinas

Aristotle, *Nicomachean Ethics*, 51 n.9; 63 n.40; 101 n.134; *Politics*, 90 nn.106, 108; 101 n.134

Arnauld, Antoine, *Œuvres*, 120 n.12; 135 nn.38, 45; 143 n.59

Arnobius of Sicca, *The Case Against the Pagans*, 31 n.63

Ashley, W. J., *Economic History of England*, 80 n.87; 81 n.88; *An Introduction to English Economic History and Theory*, 66 n.52; 81 n.89

Asterius, St., *Sermons*, 22 n.31

Aubenas, Roger, "L'Ordinatio pro Anima en Languedoc au XVe–XVIe siècles," 47 n.1

Aubenas, Roger, and Richard, Robert, *L'Eglise et la Renaissance*, 47 n.5

Aubert, Jean-Marie, *Le Droit romain dans l'œuvre de Saint Thomas*, 83 n.93

Augustine, St., *Ad fratres Eremo*, 36 n.76; *City of God*, 9 n.5; 11 n.9; 27 n.52; 55 n.20; *Commentary on Sermon on the Mount*, 24 n.39; *Contra Faustum*, 42 n.92; *De Dilectione Parentum et Dedicinis*, 74 n.77; *De Haeresibus*, 42 n.92; 43 n.95; *Expositions on the Book of Psalms*, 27 n.52; 28 n.53; 35 n.75; *Letters*, 15 n.14; 42 nn.92, 93, 94; 44 n.98

Aulus Gellius, *Les Nuits attiques*, 58 n.28

Bacon, Roger, *Compendium studii philosophiae*, 61 n.35

Bailey, D. S., *The Man-Woman Relation in Christian Thought*, 33 n.69

Baldwin, John W., "Medieval Theories of the Just Price," 81 n.89

Balmes, Jaime Luciano, *Protestantism and Catholicity Compared*, 183 n.79

Barbeyrac, Jean, *Traité de la morale des Pères*, 11 n.8

Bariani, Nicolas, *De Montes Impietatis*, 98 n.130

Barker, Ernest, *Social and Political Thought in Byzantium*, 107 n.148

Baron, Hans, "Franciscan Poverty and Civic Wealth as Factors in Rise of Humanistic Thought," 125 n.16

Basil, St., the Great, *Hexaemeron*, 32 n.65; 37 n.81; letter 150, 21 n.28; *On the Spirit*, 28 n.55; *Sermons*, 21 n.27; 22 nn.30, 31, 32

Bataillon, M., "J. L. Vives, réformateur de la bienfaisance," 79 n.85

Baudrillart, Alfred, *L'Eglise catholique, la Renaissance, le protestantisme*, 183 n.75

Baudrillart, H. J. L., *Histoire du luxe privé et public*, 138 n.45; *J. Bodin et son temps*, 181 n.71

Bauer, Clemens, "Conrad Peutingers Gutachten zur Monopolfrage," 126 n.20; "Conrad Peutinger und der Durchbruch des neuen ökonomischen Denkens in der Wende zur Neuzeit," 126 n.20

Bechtel, Heinrich, *Wirtschaftsstil des deutschen Spätmittelalters*, 127 n.21

193

Beck, Andrew, "The Common Good in Law and Legislation," 54 n.18
Becker, Bernard, *Ein Wort über die Fabrikindustrie*, 161 n.24
Beckett, J. C., *Protestant Dissent in Ireland, 1687–1780*, 172 n.52; 175 n.61
Beer, Max, *The General History of Socialism*, 39 n.87; *Social Struggles in the Middle Ages*, 107 n.149; 109 n.153
Benedict XIV, Pope, *Vix Pervenit*, 97 n.129
Bénichou, Paul, *Morales au Grand Siècle*, 132 n.31; 137 n.43
Bentham, Jeremy, *The Rationale of Reward*, 140 n.52
Berkeley, George, Bishop, *A Word to the Wise*, 174 n.58
Bernardino of Siena, St., *Le prediche volgari*, 65 n.45
Berthe, Augustin, *Saint Alphonse de Liguori*, 142 nn.56, 57
Besse, J., "Hospitaliers," 80 n.87
Betzendörfer, W., *Die Lehre von der zweifachen Wahrheit bei Pomponatius*, 117 n.5
Bigelmair, Andréas, "Zur Frage des Sozialismus und Kommunismus in Christentum," 17 n.17
Bingham, Joseph, *Origines Ecclesiasticae*, 40 n.88
Biot, Edouard, *De l'abolition de l'esclavage ancien*, 29 n.56
Blanchet, Léon, *Campanella*, 128 n.23
Blie, de, "La théologie morale dans la compagnie de Jésus," 142 n.56
Boas, George, *Essays on Primitivism . . . in the Middle Ages*, 16 n.16
Bonar, James, "The Austrian Economists and Their View of Value," 55 n.19
Bonenfant, P., "Les origines et le caractère de la réforme de la bienfaisance publique aux Pays-Bas sous le règne de Charles Quint," 79 n.85
Borst, Arno, *Die Katharer*, 107 n.148
Botero, Giovanni, *Greatness of Cities*, 61 n.36
Boutruche, R., "Aux origines d'une crise nobiliaire," 47 n.1
Boutteville, M.-L., *La Morale de l'Eglise et la morale naturelle*, 47 n.2; 120 n.9
Branchu. *See* Le Branchu
Brants, Victor, *L'Economie politique au moyen-âge*, 62 n.37; 66 n.52; 81 n.89; 85 n.101; "L'économie politique et sociale dans les écrits de L. Lessius," 66 n.50; 81 n.89; *L'Economie sociale au moyen-âge*, 66 n.52; "Un fragment inédit de L. Lessius, *De Eleemosyna*," 66 n.50
Brémond, Henri, *Histoire littéraire du sentiment religieux en France*, 138 n.44
Brentano, Lujo, *Die Anfänge der modernen Kapitalismus*, 66 n.51; "Die wirtschaftlichen Lehren des christlichen Altertums," 9 n.1; 29 n.56; "Zur Genealogie der Angriffe auf das Privateigentum," 73 n.74
Brey, Hedwig, *Hochscholastik und Geist des Kapitalismus*, 96 n.126
Bridrey, Emile, *La Théorie de la monnaie au XIVe siècle, Nicole Oresme*, 101 nn.135, 136
Brock, Peter, *The Political and Social Doctrines of the Unity of Czech Brethren in the Fifteenth and Early Sixteenth Centuries*, 107 n.148
Brodrick, J., *The Economic Morals of the Jesuits*, 133 n.35; 161 n.23
Broglie, Guy de, in *Recherches de Science Religieuse*, 57 n.25
Brou, Alexandre, *Les Jésuites de la légende*, 133 n.35
Brownlow, W. R., *Lectures on Slavery and Serfdom in Europe*, 29 n.58; 30 n.59
Bruck, Eberhard F., *Kirchenväter und soziales Erbrecht*, 15 n.12
Buckland, W. W., and McNair, Arnold, *Roman Law and Common Law*, 83 n.93
Buckle, Henry T., *Introduction to History of Civilization in England*, 187 n.89; 188 nn.90, 91
Bulteau, L., *Le Faux Depôt*, 147 n.68
Burgh, W. G. de, *From Morality to Religion*, 59 n.31
Burke, Edmund, *Works*, 173 n.57
Burr, Nelson R., ed., *Critical Bibliography of American Religion*, 1 n.2
Bury, R. G., *Sextus Empiricus, Against the Ethicists*, 115 n.1

Cabet, Etienne, *Le Vrai Christianisme suivant Jésus-Christ*, 17 n.17
Cadoux, C. J., *The Early Church and the World*, 9 n.1; 29 n.56; 30 n.60; "Should We All Be Perfect?," 15 n.12
Caesarius, St. (attributed), *De Dilectione Parentum et Dedicinis*, 74 n.77
Cajetan, Thomas de Vio, *Comment. ad S. Thom.*, 65 n.47
Campanella, Tommaso, *Œuvres choisies*, 110 n.158
Candolle, Alphonse de, *Histoire des sciences et des savants depuis deux siècles*, 186 nn.85, 86; 187 n.87
Cannan, Edwin, et al., "Who said 'Barren Metal'?" 91 n.109
Canons and Decrees of the Council of Trent, 56 n.21
Carlyle, R. W. and A. J., *A History of Mediaeval Political Theory in the West*, 9 n.1; 26 n.50; 29 n.56
Carré, Meyrick H., *Realists and Nominalists*, 67 n.53
Caspari, C. P., *Briefe, Abhandlungen und Predigten*, 41 n.90
Castelli, Enrico, *Les Présupposés d'une théologie de l'histoire*, 125 n.17
Cate, J. L., "The English Mission of Eustace of Flay," 46 n.1
Cavendish, William, *Catalogue of Letters: Ireland*, 172 n.54
Ceillier, Remy, *Apologie de la morale des Pères de l'église*, 11 n.8
Chastel, Etienne, *Etudes historiques sur l'influence de la charité*, 19 n.21; 34 n.74
Chenu, M.-D., "La théologie comme science au XIIIe siècle," 120 n.11
[Chevé, Charles F.], *Histoire de la communauté des biens*, 17 n.17
Child, Sir Josiah, *A New Discourse of Trade*, 162 n.28
Chinard, Gilbert, *En lisant Pascal*, 134 n.37
Chroust, A. H., "Hugo Grotius and the Scholastic Natural Law Tradition," 119 n.8
Chrysostom, St. John, *Homilies on the Acts*, 25 n.46; 26 n.47; *Homilies on the Gospel of St. Matthew*, 25 n.45; *sermon on Alms*, 23 n.38
Cicotti, Ettore, *Il tramonto della sciavitù nel mondo antico*, 27 n.51; 29 n.56
Clark, J, M., "Aims of Economic Life as Seen by Economists," 55 n.19
Clarke, M. L., *The Roman Mind*, 36 n.78
Clement of Alexandria, St., *Christ the Educator (Paedagogus)*, 25 nn.43, 44; 30 n.60; 41 n.91; "Rich Man's Salvation," 41 n.91
Cobbett, William, *History of the Protestant "Reformation" in England and Ireland*, 183 n.77
Cohn, Norman, *The Pursuit of the Millennium*, 39 n.86
Colet, John, "Exposition of . . . Epistle to the Romans," 69 n.62
Collingwood, R. G., *An Essay on Philosophical Method*, 59 n.31
Colwell, E. C., "Popular Reactions Against Christianity in the Roman Empire," 26 n.49
Cortelyou, William T., *Banking Profit*, 91 n.112
Coulton, G. G., *Five Centuries of Religion*, 35 n.75
Courtonne, Yves, *Saint Basile, homélies sur la richesse*, 21 n.28
Craik, Sir Henry, *A Century of Scottish History*, 189 n.96
Crousaz-Crétet, *La Morale et les moralistes sous l'ancien régime*, 140 n.50
Curcio, Carlo, *La politica italiana del 400*, 125 n.16
Cyprian, St., *The Genuine Works*, 22 n.33

Dalrymple, John, *Considerations upon the Policy of Entails in Great Britain*, 175 n.61
[Daniel, Gabriel], *Résponse aux Lettres provinciales*, 66 n.49; 96 n.128
Davenant, Charles, *Essays upon Peace at Home and War Abroad*, 167 n.36
Davis, H., et al., "Birth Control: The Perverted Faculty Argument," 91 n.113
Delaporte, Albert, *Le Problème économique et la doctrine catholique*, 183 n.78
Delhaye, Ph., "La théologie morale d'hier et d'aujourd'hui," 112 n.159; 141 n.55
Dempf, Alois, *Sacrum Imperium*, 119 n.8
Denis, J., *Histoire des théories et des idées morales*, 37 n.79

Denzinger, Henry J. D., *The Sources of Catholic Dogma (Enchiridion Symbolorum)*, 63 n.41; 108 n.151; 148 n.69
Desjacques, F., "Les Saints Pères et les origines du droit de propriété," 70 n.65
Deville, Abbé, *Le Droit canon et le droit naturel*, 96 n.124
De Zulueta, F., *The Roman Law of Sale*, 83 n.93
Didache, The, 23 n.36
[Didier, Matthieu Petit], *Apologie des Lettres Provinciales*, 133 n.35
Diesner, Hans-Joachim, *Studien zur Gesellschaftslehre und sozialen Haltung Augustins*, 45 n.102
Döllinger, Ignaz von, and Reusch, Heinrich, *Geschichte der Moralstreitigkeiten in der römisch-katholischen Kirche seit dem sechzehnten Jahrhundert*, 133 n.35
Domat, Jean, *Harangue prononcée aux assises de 1679*, 139 n.47; *Traité des loix*, 139 n.48
Dopsch, Alfons, *Herrschaft und Bauer in der deutschen Kaiserzeit*, 127 n.21
Douglas, Andrew H., *The Philosophy and Psychology of Pietro Pomponazzi*, 128 n.23
Doyle, Phyllis, *A History of Political Thought*, 117 n.4
Droulers, Charles, *La Cité de Pascal*, 134 nn.37, 43
Ducatillon, Father, "Doctrine communiste et doctrine catholique," 108 n.152
Duhamel, P. Albert, "Medievalism of More's Utopia," 109 n.155
Dulameau, Jean, *Vie économique et sociale de Rome dans la seconde moitié du XVIe siècle*, 78 n.83
Dumas, Auguste, "Intérêt et usure," 99 n.132
Duncan, O. D. *See* Spengler and Duncan
Dutilleul, J., "Esclavage," 29 n.56
Duvergier de Hauranne, Jean, "Pensées sur le sacerdoce," 134 n.38

Edler, Florence, "Eclaircissements à propos des considérations de R. Davidsohn sur la productivité de l'argent au moyen-âge," 93 n.115
Egenter, Richard, "Gemeinnutz vor Eigennutz," 53 n.17
Ehrle, Franz, *Beiträge zur Geschichte und Reform der Armenpflege*, 24 n.41; 77 n.80; 80 n.86
Endemann, Wilhelm, *Die nationalökonomische Grundsätze der kanonische Lehre*, 66 n.52; 81 n.89; *Studien in der romanischen-kanonistischen Wirtschafts- und Rechtslehre*, 66 n.52; 81 n.89; 103 n.140
Engel-Jánosi, Friedrich, "Soziale Probleme der Renaissance," 65 n.48; 125 n.16
Erasmus, Desiderius, *The Education of a Christian Prince*, 128 n.24; *Handbüchlein des christlichen Streiters*, 70 n.63
Eschmann, Th., "Bonum commune melius est quam bonum unius," 51 n.11; 53 n.15; "A Thomistic Glossary on the Principle of the Preeminence of a Common Good," 50 n.8; 51 n.10
Evans, Austin P., "Social Aspects of Medieval Heresy," 107 n.148

Fanfani, Amintore, *Catholicism, Protestantism and Capitalism*, 64 n.45; 65 n.48; *Le origini dello spirito capitalistico in Italia*, 64 n.45; 125 n.16; *Storio del lavoro in Italia dalla fine del secolo XV agli inizi del XVIII*, 125 n.16
Febvre, Lucien, "L'Application du Concile de Trente et l'excommunication pour dettes en Franche-Comté," 48 n.5; *Le Problème de l'incroyance au XVIe siècle*, 47 n.1
Ferguson, W. K., *The Renaissance in Historical Thought*, 123 n.15; 127 n.21
Fischer, Emil A., *Giovanni Botero*, 112 n.160
Flamérion, A., *De la prospérité comparée des nations catholiques et des nations protestantes*, 161 n.24
Folletête, Eugène, "De la prétendue inferiorité des nations catholiques," 161 n.24
Fontaine, Nicolas, *Mémoires pour servir à l'histoire de Port-Royal*, 134 n.38
Fox, James J., "Slavery," 26 n.48
Francis de Mayronis, *Sent.*, 96 n.126
French, F. C., "The Doctrine of the Twofold Truth," 117 n.5

Frend, W. H. C., *The Donatist Church*, 44 nn.99, 100, 101
Froude, James Anthony, *The Influence of the Reformation on the Scottish Character*, 189 n.95
Funck-Brentano, Th., "Le droit naturel au XVIIe siècle," 138 n.46
Funk, F. X., "Neben Reichtum und Handel in christlichen Altertum," 9 n.1; 29 n.56

Gardiner, Stephen, reply to John Rastell, 70 n.64
Garin, E., *L'Umanesimo italiano*, 125 n.16
Garnier, Henri, *De l'idée du juste prix*, 81 n.89
Garriguet, L., *Manuel de sociologie et d'économie sociale*, 73 n.74
Gaume, Jean Joseph, *L'Europe en 1848*, 183 n.78; *La Révolution*, 129 n.27; *Le Ver rongeur*, 129 n.27
Génestal, Robert, *Rôle des monastères comme établissements de credit—XI à XIII siècle*, 98 n.131. *See also* Allix, E.
Gerson, John, *De Contractibus*, 96 n.125
Giet, Stanislas, *Les Idées et l'action sociales de Saint Basile*, 21 n.28
Gilles of Lessines, *De usuris*, 91 n.111
Gilson, Etienne, *L'Esprit de la philosophie médiévale*, 11 n.8; 120 n.11; *Les Métamorphoses de la cité de Dieu*, 61 n.35
Godard, Léon, *Les Principes de '89 et la doctrine catholique*, 105 n.145
Goldmann, Lucien, "Remarques sur le jansénisme," 134 n.36
Goris, J. A., *Etude sur les colonies marchandes méridionales . . . à Anvers*, 47 n.4
Gothein, Eberhard, "Staat und Gesellschaft des Zeitalters der Gegen-reformation," 170 n.46; *Wirtschaftsgeschichte des Schwarzwaldes*, 170 n.46
Gother, John, *Good Advice to the Public*, 78 n.80
Gottlob, U., "Päpstliche Darlehenschulden des 13. Jahrhunderts," 98 n.131
Gotwald, W. K., *Ecclesiastical Censure at the End of the Fifteenth Century*, 48 n.5
Gousset, Th., *Justification de la théologie morale du B. Alfonse Marie de Ligorio*, 142 n.56
Grant, Charles, "Observations on the State of Society Among the Asiatic Subjects of Great Britain," 176 n.63
Grotius, Hugo, *War and Peace*, 37 n.80
Grubb, Isabel, *Quakers in Ireland, 1654–1900*, 175 n.61
Gudde, Erwin Gustav, *Social Conflicts in Medieval German Poetry*, 127 n.21
Guido Vernanus, *De Reprobatione Dantes Monarchiae*, 52 n.14
Guignebert, Charles, *Tertullien*, 9 n.1; 23 n.37; 29 n.56; 31 n.62
Guillaume, Alexandre, *Jeûne et charité dans l'église latine*, 21 n.26

Haessle, Johannes, *Das Arbeitsethos der Kirche nach Thomas von Aquin und Leo XIII*, 61 n.34
Hagen, K., *Deutschlands literarische und religiöse Verhältnisse im Reformationszeitalter*, 127 n.21
Hagenauer, Selma, *Das justum pretium bei Thomas von Aquino*, 81 n.89
Hamm, Franz, *Geschichte der Steuermoral in der Kirche*, 106 n.147
Hanna, C. A., *The Scotch-Irish*, 175 n.60
Harlow, Vincent T., *The Founding of the Second British Empire, 1763–1793*, 175 n.61
Harrington, James, *Some Reflexions upon a Treatise Called Pietas Romana et Parisiensis*, 77 n.80
Harris, Sir Walter, *Remarks on the Affairs and Trade of England and Ireland*, 164 n.32
Hayward, S. *See* Pike and Hayward
Hefele, K. J. von, *Histoire des conciles d'après les documents originaux*, 43 n.96; 48 n.5
Helvétius, Claude Adrien, "Intérêt," 140 n.51
Hennepin, Louis, *La Morale pratique du jansénisme*, 131 n.29
Henry of Ghent, *Quodlibet*, 59 n.29
Henry of Langenstein, *Tractatus bipartitus*, 62 n.37

Henson, H. Hensley, *Studies in English Religion in Seventeenth Century*, 192 n.2

Hill, Christopher, "Puritans and the Poor," 164 n.31

Höffner, Joseph, "Statik und Dynamik in der scholastischen Wirtschaftsethik," 85 n.100; *Wirtschaftsethik und Monopole*, 85 n.100

Hohoff, W., review of Schilling, *Reichtum und Eigentum*, 17 n.17

Holborn, Hajo, *Ulrich von Hutten and the German Reformation*, 129 n.25

Holtzmann, H., *Die ersten Christen und die soziale Frage*, 17 n.17

Holzapfel, P. H., *Die Anfänge der Montes Pietatis*, 98 n.130

Honigsheim, Paul, "Die soziologische Bedeutung der nominalistischen Philosophie," 67 n.53; *Die Staats- und Soziallehren der französischen Jansenisten im 17. Jahrhundert*, 134 n.37

Houghton, Walter E. Jr., *The Formation of Thomas Fuller's Holy and Profane States*, 192 n.2

Hugueny, "Imperfection," 115 n.1

Husslein, Joseph, *Social Wellsprings*, 30 n.59

Ilgner, Carl, *Die volkswirtschaftlichen Anschauungen Antonius von Florenz*, 38 n.84

Jacquin, R., in *Revue d'Economie Politique*, 160 n.22; 162 n.26

James, Francis G., *North Country Bishop . . . William Nicolson*, 171 n.51

Jansen, F. X., *Baius et le baianisme*, 131 n.30

Jerome, St., *Against Jovinianus*, 33 n.71; *Letters*, 14 n.11; 15 n.13; 24 n.40; 33 n.70; 34 n.72; 36 n.76; *The Perpetual Virginity of Blessed Mary*, 34 n.73

Joinville, Jean Sire de, *The History of St. Louis*, 47 n.3

Jonkers, E. J., "De l'influence du christianisme sur la législation relative à l'esclavage," 29 n.56

Jordan, W. K., *Philanthropy in England, 1480–1660*, 77 n.80

Jourdain, Charles, "Mémoire sur les commencements de l'économie politique dans les écoles du moyen âge," 66 n.52; 81 n.89; 96 n.125

Jowett, Benjamin, *The Dialogues of Plato*, 90 n.108

Justin Martyr, *Writings, The First Apology*, 9 n.2

Kautz, Julius, *Die Entwickelung der National-Oekonomik und ihrer Literatur*, 29 n.57; *Die geschichtliche Entwickelung der National-Oekonomik*, 9 n.1; 29 n.56

Keats, John, *Letters*, 189 n.93

Kiefl, Franz X., *Herman Schell*, 181 n.73

King, William, Archbishop, "A Memorandum on Taxation in Ireland," 173 n.56

Kirk, Kenneth E., *Conscience and Its Problems*, 84 n.98; 192 n.2; *The Vision of God*, 15 n.12

Kleist, James A., ed., *The Didache*, 23 n.36

Kluckhohn, August, "Zur Geschichte der Handelsgesellschaften und -monopole im Zeitalter der Reformation," 129 n.26

König, Erich, *Peutingerstudien*, 126 n.20

Kopp, Georg, *Die Stellung des hl. Johannes Chrysostomus zum weltlichen Leben*, 23 n.35; 37 n.81

Krasinski, Cyrill K. von, "Über die Krisis des modernen Sondereigentumsbegriffes," 72 n.70

Krieger, Leonard, *The German Idea of Freedom*, 175 n.62

Kristeller, Paul O., *The Classics and Renaissance Thought*, 123 n.15; "Humanism and Scholasticism in the Italian Renaissance," 123 n.15

Lachance, Louis, *Le Concept de droit selon Aristote et St. Thomas*, 53 n.15

Lacordaire, H.-D., *Conférences de Notre-Dame de Paris*, 72 n.72

Lactantius, *The Divine Institutes*, 9 n.4; 18 nn.18, 19; 22 n.29; 28 n.54; 33 n.67; *Of the Manner in Which the Persecutors Died*, 32 n.66

Ladner, Gerhart B., *The Idea of Reform*, 45 n.102

Lagarde, Georges de, "Individualisme et corporatisme au moyen âge," 52 n.14; *La Naissance de l'esprit laïque au déclin du moyen âge*, 52 n.12; 67 n.53; 69 nn.59, 60; 107 n.148; 121 n.13

Laird, John, *The Idea of Value*, 60 n.33

Lallemand, Léon, *Histoire de la charité*, 77 n.80; 78 n.82; 98 n.130; *Histoire de la charité à Rome*, 78 n.83

Landry, Adolphe, *Essai économique sur les mutations des monnaies dans l'ancienne France*, 101 n.135; "Notes critiques sur le 'Nicole Oresme' de M. Bridrey," 101 n.135

Landry, Bernard, *Duns Scotus*, 67 n.53

Langenstein, Henry de, *De Contractibus*, 62 n.37

Laporte, Jean M. F., *La Doctrine de Port-Royal*, 132 n.33; 134 n.38; 149 n.75; *Etudes d'histoire*, 137 n.42; *La Morale d'après Arnauld*, 143 n.59; *La Morale selon Arnauld*, 148 n.69; "Pascal et la doctrine de Port Royal," 134 n.37

Larroque, Patrice, *De l'esclavage chez les nations chrétiennes*, 27 n.51; 29 n.56

Laures, John, "Ideas fiscales de cinco grandes jesuitas españoles," 106 n.147; *The Political Economy of Juan de Mariana*, 38 n.84

Laveleye, Emile de, *Protestantism and Catholicism, in Their Bearing upon the Liberty and Prosperity of Nations*, 181 n.72

Law, John, *Première mémoire sur les banques*, 164 n.32

Le Branchu, Jean-Yves, *Ecrits notables sur la monnaie, XVI siècle*, 104 n.141

Leclercq, Jacques, *La Philosophie morale de Saint Thomas*, 51 n.10

Lecoy de la Marche, A., *La Chaire française au moyen âge*, 38 n.84; 66 n.51

Lemay, Hugolin, "Etude bibliographique et historique sur la *Morale pratique* du P. Louis Hennepin," 131 n.29

L'Enfant, Jacques, *The History of the Council of Constance*, 108 n.152

Leo XIII, Pope, *The Great Encyclical Letters*, 71 nn.67, 68; *Aeterni Patris*, 120 n.11; *In Plurimis*, 30 n.59; *Quod Apostolici Muneris*, 71 n.67; *Rerum Novarum*, 71 n.68; *Sapientiae Christianae*, 56 n.23

[L'Estrange, Roger], *Toleration Discuss'd*, 189 n.94; *Tyranny and Popery Lording It over . . . King and People*, 189 n.94

Letwin, William, *Sir Josiah Child, Merchant Economist*, 162 n.29

Lewis, Ewart, "Organic Theories in Medieval Political Thought," 51 n.11

Libanius, *Orationes*, 37 n.80

Ligtenberg, Christine, *De Armezog te Leiden tot het Einde van de 16e Eeuw*, 80 n.87

Liguori, Alfonso de, *Œuvres complètes*, 142 n.56

Locke, John, *Two Treatises of Civil Government*, 72 n.69

Lottin, Odon, "La théorie des vertus cardinales de 1230 à 1260," 117 n.4

Lotz, Walther, *Die drei Flugschriften über den Munzstreit der sächsischen Albertiner und Ernestiner um 1530*, 104 n.141

Loubers, Henry, *J. Domat philosophe et magistrat*, 138 n.46

Lovejoy, Arthur O., "The Communism of St. Ambrose," 20 n.25

Lowe, Joseph, *The Present State of England in Regard to Agriculture, Trade, and Finance*, 164 n.32

Lucas, Herbert, *Fra Girolamo Savonarola*, 15 n.15

Lugo, John de, *De Justitia*, 73 n.73

Macdonald, W. J., *The Social Value of Property*, 73 n.74

Machlup, Fritz, "What Was Left on Viner's Desk," 1 n.1

McKeon, Richard, "The Development of the Concept of Property in Political Philosophy," 118 n.7

McLaughlin, T. P., "The Teaching of the Canonists on Usury," 96 n.127

McNabb, Vincent, *The Catholic Church and Philosophy*, 49 n.6

McNair, Arnold. *See* Buckland and McNair

Maistre, Joseph de, *Du pape*, 105 n.146

Maitland, F. W. *See* Pollock and Maitland

Majal, J. J. Cyprien, *Etude comparée des deux morales luthérienne et réformée*, 192 n.2

Mandeville, Bernard, *The Fable of the Bees*, 136 n.41; *Letter to Dion*, 136 n.41

Map, Walter, *De Nugis Curialium*, 108 n.150

Margaret Mary, Sister, "Slavery in the Writings of St. Augustine," 27 n.52

Maritain, Jacques, "Humanisme de Saint Thomas Aquin," 53 n.15; "The Person and the Common Good," 54 n.18; *Religion et culture*, 122 n.14

Martin, F., *De l'avenir du protestantisme et du catholicisme*, 161 n.24

Martin, Oliver, "L'Assemblée de Vincennes de 1329," 46 n.1

Martineau, James, *Types of Ethical Theory*, 59 n.31

Mathieson, W. L., *Politics and Religion*, 189 n.97

Mathorez, J., *Les Etrangers en France sous l'ancien régime*, 175 n.62

Matter, Jacques, *Histoire des doctrines morales et politiques*, 128 n.23

Maurer, Wilhelm, *Das Verhältnis des Staates zu Kirche nach humanistischen Anschauung vornehmlich bei Erasmus*, 128 n.24

Mausbach, Joseph, *Catholic Moral Teaching and Its Antagonists*, 141 n.54

Mayronis. *See* Francis de Mayronis

Maywald, Max, *Die Lehre von der zweifachen Wahrheit*, 117 n.5

Meunier, V., *Essai sur la vie et les ouvrages de N. d'Oresme*, 103 n.139

Meyer, Albert de, *Les Premiers Controverses jansénistes en France*, 133 n.35

Meylan, Edward F., "The Stoic Doctrine of Indifferent Things and the Conception of Christian Liberty in Calvin's *Institutio*," 115 n.1

Michel, P. H., *La Pensée de L.B. Alberti*, 125 n.16

Michel, Suzanne, *La Notion thomiste du bien commun*, 57 n.25

Michels, Robert, *Die Verelendungstheorie*, 183 n.76

Miller, Constantin, *Studien zur Geschichte der Geldlehre*, 101 nn.134, 135

Miron, C. H., *The Problem of Altruism in the Philosophy of St. Thomas*, 53 n.15

Molen. *See* Van der Molen

Molina, Luis, *De Justitia et Jure*, 65 n.47

Molyneux, William, *The Case of Ireland's being bound by Acts of Parliament in England, stated*, 171 n.51

Morale des jésuites, La, 131 n.29

Morale pratique des jésuites, La, 131 n.29

More, Sir Thomas, *Apology*, 109 n.156; *Dialogue of Comfort*, 109 n.156; *Supplication of Soules*, 109 n.156; *Utopia*, 109 n.156; 110 n.157

Mosse, George L., "The Importance of Jacques Saurin in The History of Casuistry," 192 n.2

Mossman, X., "De l'épargne au moyen âge," 98 n.131

Müller, Adam, *Warum ist der Wohlstand der protestantischen Länder sogar viel grösser als der katholischen*, 161 n.24

Müller-Armack, Alfred, *Genealogie der Wirtschaftsstile*, 104 n.142; 109 n.154

Mullinger, J. B., "Slavery," 29 n.56

Mund, Vernon A., *Open Markets*, 85 n.100

Nell-Breuning, Oswald von, *Reorganization of Social Economy*, 63 n.42

Nelson, Benjamin N., *The Idea of Usury*, 86 n.101

Newman, John Henry, *Lectures on Certain Difficulties Felt by Anglicans*, 56 n.22

Nicolas, Auguste, *Du Protestantisme et de toutes les hérésies dans leur rapport avec le socialisme*, 183 n.79

Nicole, Pierre, *L'Esprit de M. Nicole*, 133 n.34; *Essais de morale*, 132 nn.31, 32; 135 n.40; 144 n.62; 147 n.67; 149 n.74; *Les Provinciales*, 144 n.61; 149 n.73

Nolf, J., *La Réforme de la bienfaisance publique à Ypres au XVIe siècle*, 78 n.84

Nolte, Peter, *Der Kaufmann in der deutschen Sprache und Literatur des Mittelalters*, 127 n.21

Noonan, John T., *The Scholastic Analysis of Usury*, 7 n.7; 86 n.101; 88 n.103; 90 n.107; 91 n.111; 95 n.123

Oberfohren, Ernst, *Die Idee der Universalökonomie*, 38 n.85

O'Brien, George, *The Economic History of Ireland in the Seventeenth Century*, 172 n.53; *An Essay on the Economic Effects of the Reformation*, 181 n.71; *An Essay on Medieval Economic Teaching*, 96 n.125

Offenbacher, Martin, *Konfession und soziale Schichtung*, 185 nn.82, 83, 84

Onclair, Auguste, *Les Causes et les remèdes du socialisme*, 182 n.74; 183 n.78; in *Revue Catholique des Institutions et du Droit*, 73 n.74

O'Rahilly, Alfred, *Aquinas versus Marx*, 50 n.7; 69 n.58; 103 n.139

Oresme, Nicholas, *De Moneta*, 101 nn.135, 136; 102 nn.137, 138

O'Riordan, M., *Catholicity and Progress in Ireland*, 174 n.58; 175 n.61; 184 n.80

Overbeck, Franz, *Studien zur Geschichte der altern Kirche*, 27 n.51; 29 n.56

Palmelle, R.-A. de la, *Résolutions des plus importantes questions de la coutume et du barreau*, 47 n.1

Parsons, Robert, *A Memorial of the Reformation in England*, 78 n.80

Pascal, Blaise, *Pensées*, 70 n.65; 120 n.12; 148 n.72; *Provincial Letters*, 138 n.45; 143 n.60; 148 n.72

Pascal, Roy, "Communism in the Middle Ages and Reformation," 40 n.89; 107 n.148

Perry, R. B., *General Theory of Value*, 60 n.32

Pesch, Heinrich, "Ursachen des wirtschaftlichen Niederganges katholischer Völker," 182 n.74

Pett, Sir Peter, *A Discourse of the Growth of England*, 163 n.30; *The Happy Future State of England*, 163 n.30

Petty, Sir William, *Political Arithmetick*, 168 nn.39, 41, 42, 43; 174 n.59

Philopatrus, *A Treatise wherein is demonstrated that the East Indies Trade is the most national of all Foreign Trades*, 162 n.29

Pike, S., and Hayward, S., *Religious Cases of Conscience Answered in an Evangelical Manner*, 192 n.1

Pius XI, Pope, *Quadragesimo Anno*, 63 n.41

Pöhlmann, Robert von, *Geschichte der sozialen Frage und des Sozialismus in der antiken Welt*, 9 n.1; 29 n.56; 41 n.90

Pollock, Sir Frederick, and Maitland, F. W., *The History of English Law Before the Time of Edward I*, 46 n.1

Pomponazzi, Pietro, *De Immortalitate Animae*, 117 n.6

Pope, Alexander, *Epistle to Burlington*, 64 n.43

Powers, George C., *Nationalism at the Council of Constance*, 108 n.152

Préclin, E., "Les conséquences sociales du jansénisme," 134 n.37

Pribram, Karl, *Die Enstehung der individualistischen Sozialphilosophie*, 67 n.53

Puech, Aimé, *St. Jean Chrysostome et les mœurs de son temps*, 25 n.45

Pufendorf, Samuel, *De Jure Naturae*, 11 n.8

R.B.V., "The Gaume Controversy on Classical Studies," 129 n.27

Raleigh, Sir Walter, *Observations touching Trade and Commerce with the Hollander*, 162 n.27

Ram, Canon Pierre F. X. de, "Opinions des théologiens de Louvain sur la répression administrative de la mendicité en 1562 et 1565," 80 n.86

Rappard, W. E., *La Revolution industrielle . . . en Suisse*, 161 n.24; 166 n.35

Ratzinger, Georg, *Geschichte der kirklichen Armenpflege*, 77 n.80

Régnier, Louis, *Histoire de l'état de France*, 126 n.19

Réguron, Paule, *Les Origines du mouvement anti-janséniste*, 134 n.38

Renaudet, A., "Erasme économiste," 128 n.24

Renouard, Yves, *Les Hommes d'affaires italiens du moyen âge*, 125 n.16

Reusch, Heinrich. *See* Döllinger and Reusch

Rice, Eugene F., Jr., *The Renaissance Idea of Wisdom*, 125 nn.16, 18

Richard, Robert. *See* Aubenas and Richard

Richey, Francis A., *Character Control of Wealth According to Saint Thomas Acquinas*, 64 nn.43, 44

Ring, Sister Mary Ignatius, *Villeneuve-Bargemont, Precursor of Modern Social Catholicism*, 185 n.81

Robbins, Caroline, *The Eighteenth-Century Commonwealthman*, 172 n.53

Robinson, Robert, "A Plan of Lectures on the Principles of Nonconformity," 165 n.33

Rocha, Manuel, *Travail et salaire à travers la scolastique*, 62 n.37; 85 n.100

Roey, E. Van, "La monnaie d'après Saint Thomas d'Aquin," 86 n.101; 93 n.115; 94 n.121

Roland-Gosselin, Bernard, *La Morale de Saint Augustin*, 41 n.92

Rommen, Heinrich, "The Church and Human Rights," 69 n.59

Roover, Raymond de, *Business, Banking and Economic Thought*, 7 n.7; "La doctrine scolastique en matière de monopole," 85 n.100; "Monopoly Theory Prior to Adam Smith: A Revision," 85 n.100; "The Story of the Alberti Company," 93 n.115

Ross, W. D., *The Right and the Good*, 59 n.31

Rougier, Louis, *Celse ou le conflit de la civilisation antique et du christianisme primitif*, 31 n.62

Roussel, Napoléon, *Catholic Nations and Protestant Nations Compared*, 176 n.63

Rüegg, August, "Des Erasmus 'Lob der Torheit' und Thomas More's 'Utopie,' " 109 n.155

Rüstow, Alexander, *Das Versagen des Wirtschaftsliberalismus*, 38 n.84

Saint-Prix, Berrat, "Recherches sur le paupérisme en France au XVIe siècle," 77 n.80; 78 n.82

Salvian, *Ad Ecclesiam*, 23 n.34; *On the Government of God*, 33 n.68

Salvioli, Giuseppe, "L'economia medievale e le dottrine economiche nella scolastica pretomista," 67 n.52; 81 n.89

Samuels, A. P. I. and A. W., *The Early Life, Correspondence and Writings of . . . Edmund Burke*, 173 n.57

Samuelsson, Kurt, *Ekonomi och Religion*, 186 n.84

Sandoz, A., "La notion du juste prix," 81 n.89

Sapori, Armando, "Il giusto prezzo nella dottrina de San Tommaso," 81 n.89; *Le Marchand italien au moyen âge*, 47 n.1

Schaub, Friedrich, "Studien zur Geschichte der Sklaverei im Frühmittelalter," 27 n.51; 29 n.56

Schell, Herman, *Der Katholicismus als Princip des Fortschritts*, 181 n.73

Schick, Léon, *Un Grand Homme d'affaires au début du XVIe siècle, Jacob Fugger*, 126 n.20

Schilling, Otto, *Die christlichen Soziallehren*, 38 n.83; *Reichtum und Eigentum*, 9 n.1; 24 n.42; 29 n.56; *Die Staats- und Soziallehre des hl. Augustinus*, 9 n.1; 29 n.56; 35 n.75; 42 n.92; *Die Staats- und Soziallehre des hl. Thomas v. Aquin*, 99 n.132

Schimberg, André, *L'Education morale dans les collèges de la compagnie de Jésus en France sous l'ancien régime*, 141 n.53

Schneider, Fedor, "Das kirkliche Zinsverbot und die kuriale Praxis im 13. Jahrhundert," 98 n.131

Schreiber, Edmund, *Die volkswirtschaftlichen Anschauungen der Scholastik seit Thomas v. Aquin*, 66 n.52; 81 n.89; 91 n.110

Schultze, Alfred, *Stadtgemeinde und Reformation*, 127 n.21

Schwab, J. B. S., *Johannes Gerson*, 108 n.152

Scoville, Warren C., "The Huguenots in the French Economy," 165 n.34; 169 n.44

Secrétan, Charles, *La Philosophie de la liberté: l'histoire*, 67 n.53

Seipel, Ignaz, *Die wirtschaftsethischen Lehren der Kirchenvater*, 9 n.1; 29 n.56

Semaines sociales de France, 38 n.85

Seneca, *Moral Essays*, 94 n.117

Sherman, Charles P., *Roman Law in the Modern World*, 87 n.102

Short Specimen of a New Political Arithmetic, A, 164 n.32

Singer, Charles, *The Earliest Chemical Industry*, 47 n.4

Skelton, Philip, *The Case of Protestant Refugees from France, Considered*, 172 n.55
Slater, Thomas, *Cases of Conscience for English-Speaking Countries*, 142 n.56; *A Short History of Moral Theology*, 142 n.56
Sommerlad, Theo, *Das Wirtschaftsprogramm der Kirche des Mittelalters*, 9 n.1; 29 n.56
Sorley, W. R., *Moral Values and the Idea of God*, 59 n.31
[Souligne, de], *The Desolation of France Demonstrated/The Political Mischiefs of Popery*, 164 n.32
Sousberghe, L. de, "Propriété de 'droit naturel,' " 72 n.70
Spengler, Joseph J., and Duncan, O. D., *Population Theory and Policy*, 34 n.74
Stapleton, Thomas, *The Life and Illustrious Martyrdom of Sir Thomas More*, 110 n.157
Stark, Werner, *The Contained Economy*, 50 n.7
Steinmann, Alphons, *Sklavenlos und alte Kirche*, 29 n.56
Steuer, Gunther, *Studien über die theoretischen Grundlagen der Zinslehre bei Thomas v. Aquin*, 95 n.123
Stewart, H. F., *Les Lettres Provinciales de Blaise Pascal*, 143 n.60
Stockwood, John, *A Very Fruitful Sermon Preached at Paules Crosse*, 77 n.80
Streider, Jakob, *Studien zur Geschichte der kapitalistischen Organisationsformen*, 47 n.4
Supino, "La scienza economica in Italia della seconda metà del secolo XVI alla prima del XVII," 127 n.22
Surtz, Edward L., *The Praise of Pleasure: Philosophy, Education and Communism in More's Utopia*, 109 n.155; 110 n.157; 128 n.24; "Thomas More and Communism," 109 n.155
Swift, Jonathan, *Correspondence*, 173 n.57

Taeuber, Walter, *Geld und Kredit im Mittelalter*, 103 n.140
Tanquerey, F. J., "Le Jansénisme et les tragédies de Racine," 132 n.31
Taparelli d'Azeglio, Luigi, *Essai théorique de droit naturel*, 72 n.71
Tawney, R. H., *Religion and the Rise of Capitalism*, 62 n.37
Taylor, Jeremy, "The Rule of Conscience," 59 n.30
Temple, Sir William, *Observations upon the United Kingdom*, 173 n.56; *Observations upon the United Provinces of the Netherlands*, 162 n.25
Tenison, Thomas, *Sermon Concerning Discretion in Giving Alms*, 77 n.80
Tertullian, *Apologeticus*, 9 n.3; 30 n.61; 31 n.64; *De Anima*, 34 n.74
Thamin, Raymond, *Un Problème moral dans l'antiquité*, 58 n.28
Theodoret de Cyr, *Discours sur la providence*, 19 nn.20, 21, 22, 23; 20 n.24; 37 n.82
Theodosian Code, 43 n.97
Théologie morale des jésuites, La, 131 n.29
Thomas Aquinas, St., *De Emptione et Venditione ad Tempus*, 93 n.116; 94 n.118; 95 n.122; *De Malo*, 95 n.123; *De Regimine Judaeorum*, 105 n.144; *De Regimine Principum*, 99 n.133; *In commentum in . . . Sententarium*, 91 n.110; *In Epistola and Rom. Expositio*, 105 n.145; *On Kingship to the King of Cyprus*, 99 n.133; *Quodlibetales*, 144 n.63; *Scriptum super Sententiis Magistri Petri Lombardi*, 84 n.99; *Summa Contra Gentiles*, 57 n.24; *Summa Theologica*, 12 n.10; 15 n.15; 43 n.95; 49 n.6; 53 nn.16, 17; 57 n.24; 58 n.27; 62 n.38; 63 n.39; 64 n.44; 68 nn.54, 55, 56, 57; 74 nn.75, 76; 75 nn.78, 79; 82 nn.91, 92; 83 nn.93, 94; 84 nn.96, 97; 88 n.103; 89 n.105; 90 n.107; 91 n.110; 92 n.114; 93 n.116; 94 nn.119, 120, 121; 95 n.122; 96 n.124; 105 n.143; 115 n.2; 120 n.11; 135 n.39; 145 n.65
Thonissen, J. J., *Le Socialisme depuis l'antiquité*, 17 n.17
Thorndike, Herbert, Bishop, *A Discourse of the Forbearance or the Penalties which a due Reformation Requires*, 160 n.21
Tiberghien, Canon, "Comment intégrer dans l'économie moderne les conceptions chrétiennes . . . ," 73 n.74
Tierney, Brian, *Medieval Poor Law*, 77 n.80; 81 n.88

Tonneau, J. J., "Morale et politique," 57 n.25
Toynbee, Arnold, *A Study of History*, 165 n.34
Tractatus de Divitiis, 41 n.90
Trevor-Roper, H. R., *Historical Essays*, 78 n.80
Trinkhaus, Charles E., *Adversity's Noblemen*, 123 n.15
Troeltsch, Enrst, *The Social Teaching of the Christian Churches*, 10 nn.6, 7
Turgeon, Charles, "L'Economie chrétienne du moyen âge," 67 n.52; 81 n.89

Uhlhorn, Gerhard, *Christian Charity in the Ancient Church*, 77 n.80
Ullman, C., *Reformers Before the Reformation*, 108 n.152
Ullman, Walter, *The Growth of Papal Government in the Middle Ages*, 120 n.10; *The Medieval Idea of Law as Represented by Lucas de Penna*, 69 n.61
United Nations, *The Determinants and Consequences of Population Trends*, 34 n.74

Van der Molen, G. H., *Alberico Gentili and the Development of International Law*, 118 n.7
Vaughan, Bernard, *Socialism from the Christian Standpoint*, 10 n.6
Vaughan, Robert, *The Age of Great Cities*, 178 nn.65, 66, 67; 179 nn.68, 69, 70
Ventura de Raulica, Joachim, *Die christliche Politik*, 183 n.77
Verlinden, Charles, *L'Esclavage dans l'Europe médiévale*, 27 n.51; 29 n.56
Vermeil, E., *Etude sur la réforme*, 181 n.71
Verpaalen, A. P., "Der Begriff des Gemeinwohls bei Thomas von Aquin," 52 n.13; 57 n.26
Vialatoux, Joseph, *Questions disputées, morale et politique*, 57 n.25
Villeneuve-Bargemont, Alban de, Viscount, *Economie politique chrétienne*, 185 n.81; *Histoire de l'économie politique*, 185 n.81
Villers, Charles F. D. de, *Essai sur l'esprit et l'influence de la réformation de Luther*, 176 n.63
Villey, Pierre, *Montaigne devant la postérité*, 135 n.39
Viner, Jacob, "Bentham and J. S. Mill," 55 n.19; *The Long View and the Short*, 6 n.6; 55 n.19; 136 n.41; "Man's Economic Status," 4 n.4; *The Role of Providence in the Social Order*, 5 n.5; 34 n.*; 114 n.*; "Satire and Economics in the Augustan Age," 4 n.4
Vinogradoff, Paul, *Roman Law in Medieval Europe*, 93 n.115
Vives, Juan-Luis, "Concerning the Relief of the Poor," 79 n.85
Vollmann, Franz, *Uber das Verhältnis der späteren Stoa zur Sklaverei im römischen Reiche*, 29 n.56

Wall, Maureen, "The Catholic Merchants, Manufacturers and Traders of Dublin, 1778–1782," 175 n.61; "The Rise of a Catholic Middle Class in Eighteenth-Century Ireland," 175 n.61
Wallon, Henri A., *Histoire de l'esclavage dans l'antiquité*, 29 n.56
Walser, Ernst, *Poggius Florentinus Leben und Werke*, 125 n.16
Wasserman, Earl R., *Pope's Epistle to Bathurst*, 64 n.43
Watt, Lewis, "The Theory Lying Behind the Historical Conception of the Just Price," 81 n.89
Weber, Marianne, *Max Weber: ein Lebensbild*, 153 n.1
Weber, Max "Antikritisches Schlusswort zum 'Geist des Kapitalismus,' " 153 n.1; 155 nn.7, 8, 11, 12; 157 n.16; 158 n.18; 167 n.37; 170 n.47; 171 n.50; 189 n.93; "Antikritisches zum 'Geist' des Kapitalismus," 153 n.1; 154 nn.5, 6; 155 n.8; 157 n.16; 159 n.19; 167 n.37; 168 n.40; 171 n.50; "Bemerkungen zu der vorstehenden Replik," 153 n.1; 155 nn.7, 8, 9; 158 n.19; "Die protestantische Ethik und der 'Geist' des Kapitalismus," 153 n.1; *General Economic History*, 154 n.1; 157 nn.14, 17; *Gesammelte Aufsätze zur Religionssoziologie (The Protestant Ethic)*, 153 n.1; 154 nn.3, 4, 5, 6; 157 nn.14, 15, 16; 158 n.18; 167 n.37; 170 n.47; 171 nn.49, 50; 175 n.60; 186 n.84; 187 n.88; 188 n.92; 189 n.93; "Kritische Bemerkungen zu den vor-

stehenden 'Kritischen Beiträgen,' " 153 n.1; 154 n.5; 155 nn.7, 8; 158 n.19; 170 n.48; "The Protestant Sects and the Spirit of Capitalism," 153 n.1; 156 n.13; 157 n.14; *Wirtschaft und Gesellschaft*, 153 n.1; 154 nn.2, 3, 5; 155 n.9; 159 n.20

Weber, Wilhelm, *Wirtschaftsethik am Vorabend des Liberalismus*, 65 n.47; 67 n.53; 71 n.66; 73 n.73; 85 n.100; 106 n.147; 150 n.76

Weigel, Helmut, "Die Entstehung der sog. Reformation Kaiser Sigmunds," 127 n.21

Weisinger, Herbert, "The Attack on the Renaissance in Theology Today," 129 n.27

Weiss, C., "Mémoire sur les Protestants de France au 17e siècle," 169 n.45; 176 n.63

Werner, Ernst, *Pauperes Christi*, 109 n.153

Werner, Heinrich, *Die Reformation des Kaisers Sigmund*, 127 n.21

Werner, Martin, *The Formation of Christian Dogma*, 39 n.86

Westermann, William L., "The Slave Systems of Greek and Roman Antiquity," 27 n.51; 29 n.56

Weyrich, René, "Infériorité économique des nations catholiques," 161 n.24

Wheeler, Marcus, "Self-Sufficiency and the Greek City," 36 n.78

Willaert, Leopold, *Bibliotheca Janseniana Belgica*, 131 n.28

Willett, Andrew, *Synopsis Papismi*, 77 n.80

Wiskemann, Heinrich, *Darstellung der in Deutschland zur Zeit der Reformation herrschenden Nationalökonomischen*, 128 n.24

Wood, Thomas, *English Casuistical Divinity During the Seventeenth Century*, 192 n.2

Worsley, Israel, *Observations on the State and Changes in the Presbyterian Societies of England*, 177 n.64

Young, Arthur, *Tour in Ireland (1776–1779)*, 175 n.61

Zeeveld, W. Gordon, *Foundations of Tudor Policy*, 155 n.1

Zimmermann, J. P., "La morale laïque au commencement du XVIIIe siècle," 140 n.50

General index

Absolution, 47
Academies, of Europe, 186
Adiaphora, 115, 116
Agrippa, Henry Cornelius, 120–21
Albert the Great, 48
Almsgiving: appeals for, 20–26; Aquinas on, 73–74; indiscriminate, 23–24, 76, 78; Jansenists on, 148–50; voluntary, 17, 20–21
Ambition, 148–149. *See also* Social status
Ambrose, St., 68, 70n
Ames, William, 156
Antioch, Syria, poverty in, 25
Antonius of Florence, 127
Apocalyptic. *See* Chiliasm
Apostolici, 40, 43n; St. Augustine on, 42–43
Aratus, 18
Aristotle, 48, 68, 82, 116; on coinage, 99; on the common good, 50–51; on magnificence, 63; on slavery, 27; on usury, 86, 89–91
Arminianism, 119, 189; Weber on, 154
Arnauld, Antoine, 138, 143
Arnobius of Sicca, 31
"Ascetic," Weber's use of, 154
Asterius, St., 22
Augsburg, 126
Augustine, St., 33, 37, 41–45, 74, 82, 131, 132; on almsgiving, 24; on private property, 43–44, 67; on profit, 145, 146; on scales of values, 55, 83; on slavery, 28; on temporal happiness, 11; on trade, 35; on wealth, 42
Avarice, social value of, 136, 138. *See also* Money, love of; Self-interest

Bacon, Roger, 61
Baius, Michel, 131
Ball, John, 107
Baptists, 154
Barcos, Martin de, 134
"Barter," Jowett's use of, 90n
Basel, Council of, 48n
Basil, St., 32; on almsgiving, 21, 22; on slavery, 28; on trade, 37
Baudrillart, H. J. L., 180–183
Baxter, Richard, 154–156

Bayle, Pierre, 121
Beaumelle, 169
Beer, Max, 108
Begging, 75, 78, 81
Belgium, 182. *See also* Bruges
Benedict XIV, Pope, 97, 98
Berkeley, George, Bishop, 173–174
Berlin, Academy of, 186
Bernardino of Siena, St., 64–65, 127
Bingham, Joseph, 40
Birth control, 91n. *See also* Population
Bodin, Jean, 38
Borrowing, legitimacy of, 94–95
Botero, Giovanni, 61, 112n
Bourdaloue, Louis, 130
Broglie, Guy de, 57
Bruges, 79, 79–80
Buckle, Henry T., 187–188
Bulteau, L., *Le Faux Dépôt*, 147
Buridan, John, 96n, 101
Busleyden, Jerome, 110n
Byzantium, communism in, 197n

Caesarius, St., 74
Cajetan, Cardinal, 65, 97, 127, 148
Calling, doctrine of, 23, 161, 180, 185
Calvin, Jean, 11, 181
Calvinism, 23, 119n, 129; and capitalism, 151–158, 170, 177; church discipline, 156–157, 187; and factory system, 176n; in Geneva, 186–187; in Scotland, 187–189
Campanella, Tommaso, 109; *Civitas Solis*, 110
Candolle, Alphonse de, 186
Canon Law, 98-99, 145
Capitalism: Spanish Jesuit casuists and, 150; Protestant and Catholic countries compared, 160–189; Weber on, 151–159, 161, 167–168, 170, 176, 185, 188
Cardinal virtues, 116–117
Casuistics: Catholic, 191–192; Jesuit, 134, 140–150; Protestant, 155–156; 191–192
Catholic Church: accommodation to feudal society, 98, 106, 109; in Germany, 181–182; international, 112n; monopoly of learning, 49, 115, 120; in

206

Spain, 113n; temporal authority, 46–47; wealth, 163. *See also* Irish Catholics

Catholicism: expensiveness of, 163–164; traditionalism of, 111

Celibacy, 44, 164

Charity (*caritas*), 132, 135–136. *See also* Almsgiving

Charles V, Emperor, 79

Charron, Pierre, 121

Chastity, 33–34

Child, Sir Josiah, 162

Chiliasm, 28, 39n; in Early Church, 12–13; among the heretics, 39, 110

Chrysostom, St. John, 23, 25–26, 37

Church discipline, Catholic and Protestant, 156–57

Cicero, 18, 24, 32, 50, 118, 130

Cistercians, 108

Civil government, 13–14, 84, 138, 139; criticism of, 32–33

Civil law, and morality, 47n, 83, 95–96, 98, 115, 116, 118, 119, 135, 137, 144–47, 162. *See also* Obedience; Roman law

Class distinctions. *See* Social stratification

Clement of Alexandria, 23, 25, 30, 41, 119

Coinage, 99–104. *See also* Money

Colet, John, 69

Commerce: the Fathers on, 34–38; heterodoxy and, 168; London dissenters and, 163; Nicole on, 145–146; toleration and, 160. *See also* Just price; Usury

Common good, doctrine of, 50–54, 58, 61, 69, 99

Communistic ideal, 14, 107n, 109; among the heretics, 39, 42, 108; in More's *Utopia*, 109; in Plato, 18, 69

Community of goods, 10, 16, 40, 67, 108

Commutative justice, 68, 82, 84, 139

Confession, 47

Constance, Council of, 108

Constantinople, poverty in, 25

"Counsel" vs. "precept." *See* Morality, dual standard

Craik, Sir Henry, 189

Credit sales, 93, 145, 146

Cupidity. *See* Avarice; Self-interest

Cyprian, St., on almsgiving, 22

Damnum emergens, 94, 95

Dante, 52

Davenant, Charles, 166–167

Debasement of coinage, 100–104

Decalogue, two tables of, 116

Deism, 121

Denmark, 162

Diana (casuist), 148, 149

Didache, 23

Diocletian, 32

Dissent: and bourgeois standards, 180; in Holland, 167–168; in London, 163; and manufacture, 176–177, 178–180; persecution , 11, 166–167

Distributive justice, 68

Domat, Jean, 131, 138–139, 143

Dominium. *See* Ownership

Donatists, 39, 41, 43–45, 67

Dual standard. *See* Morality

Duns Scotus, 67n; Scotists, 119

Dutch. *See* Holland

Duvergier de Hauranne, Jean, 137

Economic inequality, 15–21, 183. *See also* Social stratification

Economic liberalism, laxism and, 150

Economic superiority of Protestant countries, 159–189

Economic theory, Christian contribution to, 49–50

Economics: and ethics, 122; Renaissance economics, 127

Eden, Garden of, 16

Education: in England, 181n; Protestant emphasis on, 176

Election, doctrine of, 161. *See also* Predestination

Emigration and émigrés, 165–166, 170–171, 175

Enclosure movement, 159–160

England, 80–81, 181n, 183

Enlightenment, the, 140

Erasmus, Desiderius, 69–70, 128

Erastianism, 123

Esprit, Jacques, 140

Eustatheans, 43

Excommunication, 47

Fall of man, 14, 16, 18, 67, 69, 131, 138, 139. *See also* Original Sin

Fanfani, Amintore, 3n, 64–65

Foenum, 86

France, 38n, 175n; coinage, fourteenth-century, 100; prosperity of Huguenots, 169

Francis de Mayronis, 96

Franciscans, 107

Freedom, intellectual, 175–178, 180–182, 186
Frend, W. H. C., on Donatism, 44
Froude, James Anthony, 189
Fructus civiles et naturales, 92
Fuggers, 126, 129
"Fungibles" and "non-fungibles," 86–88

Gaetano. *See* Cajetan
Gallicanism, 112
Gangra, Council of, 43
Gardiner, Stephen, Bishop, 70
Gaume, Jean Joseph, 129–130
Geneva: excluded from Weber's thesis, 155, 157, 170n; intellectual freedom in, 186–187
Gentilis, Alberico, 118
Germany, 175n; Catholicism in, 181–182; pauperism in, 78–79; Renaissance in, 125–127
Gerson, John, 96, 108
Godefroid de Fontaines, 52
Golden Age, 16, 18
Goldmann, Lucien, 134
Gothein, Eberhard, 170
Government. *See* Civil government
Grabou, Mathieu, 108, 109
Grace, doctrine of, 131
Grotius, Hugo, 38, 119
Guido Vernanus, 52

Haessle, Johannes, on scale of value, 60–61
Hanse towns, 162
Helvétius, 140
Henry of Ghent, 58–59, 69
Henry of Langenstein, 62
Heretics, 14, 18, 106–109, 123; industriousness of, 167–168, 170, 174; property doctrines, 38–45; as social revolutionaries, 39, 107
Hill, Christopher, 164
Hobbes, Thomas, 135
Holland, 160, 161–162, 167–168, 170
Honnêtes hommes, 132n, 135, 137–138, 143
Hospitallers, 108
Huguenots, prosperity of, 169
Humanism. *See* Renaissance; Secularization
Humanitarian considerations, 97–98
Hutten, Ulrich von, 128–129

In Coena Domini, 105
"Individual" and "person," 54

Industrialism, 184
Industry, virtue of, 31–32, 178–179
Innocent III, Pope, 108
Insurance, 97
Interest. *See* Usury
Investment, 92–93
Irish Catholics, 167, 168, 171–175; clergy, 174; urban Catholics, 174–175
Italy, 182; Renaissance in, 123–130

Jacquin, R., 160–161
Jansenists, 11, 129; controversy with Jesuits, 130–140; social status of, 137n
Jansenius, 130, 131
Jerome, St., 24, 33–34, 62; on commercial profit, 36; on dual standard, 33
Jesuits: casuistry, 140–150; controversy with Jansenists, 130–140
Joachim of Floris, 107
Julius II, Pope, 47
Just price, 7, 81–85, 93, 111, 145
Justice: commutative, 68, 82, 84, 139; distributive, 68
Justin, St., 23

Keats, John, 187, 188
Keynes, Lord, 88
Knox, John, 181

La Rochefoucauld, 140
Labor, virtue of. *See* Industry
Lacordaire, H.-D., 72
Lactantius, 119; on almsgiving, 22; on communistic ideas, 18; on Diocletian, 32; on slavery, 28
Lagarde, Georges de, 121
Laicization, 122–123. *See also* Secularization
Laird, John, on scales of values, 60
Laity in Protestantism, 156
Laporte, Jean M. F., 149
Lateran Council, Fifth, 97, 117
Laveleye, Emile de, 181, 182
Law. *See* Civil law; Natural law; Roman law
Laxism, 65, 96–97, 106, 111, 113, 130–141, 144; and economic liberalism, 150
Lecoy de la Marche, 66
Leo XIII, Pope, 48, 70–73
Leslie, Charles, 160
Lessius, L., 66
L'Estrange, Roger, 189
Libanius, on trade, 37, 38
Liberalism, of the Fathers, 17–18

Liguori, St. Alphonse, 71
Liquidity, 89n
Loan contract, 146
Locke, John, 71, 72
London dissenters, 163
Louis the Good, 47n
Luca de Penna, 69
Lucrum cessans, 94, 95, 97
Lugo, John de, 73
Luther, Martin, 11, 75, 129, 181
Lutheranism: and capitalism, 171; pietistic, 154
Luxury, 21, 138, 139

Magnificence, 63–64, 127
Maistre, Joseph de, 105
Mandeville, Bernard de, 121
Manichaeans, 41, 42n
Map, Walter, 107–108
Maritain, Jacques, 54, 122
Marx, Karl, 180
Matthieson, W. L., 189
Mennonites, 154
Mercantilism, 112, 139, 146
Merchant classes of Italy, 124–125
Methodism, 154
Middleman, 82, 85; social usefulness of, 81
Millennium, *See* Chiliasm
Minorities, 107. *See also* Emigration; Penalization theory
Mohatra contract, 143
Molina, Luis de, 65n, 133, 150
Monastic movement, 106–108, 121
Money: Aquinas on, 88–91; Aristotle on, 89–91; a fungible, 87–88; love of, 187–188. *See also* Avarice; Coinage; Usury
Monopolies, condemnation of, 85
Montaigne, Michel de, 121
Montes pietatis, 97
Morality: authority of the Church, 46–47; development of moral teaching, 48; dual standard, 14–15, 33, 41, 42, 73, 86, 116; subjective and objective, 133–140, 149
More, Sir Thomas, *Utopia*, 109–110
Mortgages, 97
Müller-Armack, Alfred, 104
Mutuum, 86

Nationalism, 112, 179
Natural law, 7, 51, 69–71, 111, 116, 118–121, 143
Nell-Breuning, Oswald von, 63
Netherlands. *See* Holland

Nicole, Pierre, 131–140, 143–147
Nominalists: on the just price, 84; on reason and natural law, 119
Nonconformists. *See* Dissent
Noonan, John T., 88
Nuremberg, 78

Obedience to civil authority, 13–14, 138
Ockham, William of, 67n; on private property, 69
Offenbacher, Martin, 185–186
Optatus of Thamugadi, 44
Oresme, Nicholas, 101–103
Original sin, 119, 120, 131, 133. *See also* Fall
Otherworldliness of the Fathers, 9–11
Ownership (*dominium*), 87, 92–93. *See also* Private property

Partnership, investment in, 92–93
Pascal, Blaise, 70, 91, 120–121, 140, 148; *Lettres provinciales*, 131
Pascal, Roy, 40
Patriotism, 13. *See also* Nationalism
Paul II, Pope, 47n
Pawnshops, 97
Peasants' Revolt (England, 1381), 107
Pelagianism, 41, 42, 133
Penalization theory of minority groups, 165–175
Perfection, counsel of, 14–15, 41, 42, 116
Periculum sortis, 97
Perkins, William, 155
Perry, R. B., on scales of value, 59–60
Persecution, 12–13; of dissenters, 166–167; of Donatists, 43
"Perverted faculty," 91n
Pett, Sir Peter, 163, 166, 167n
Petty, Sir William, 167–168, 174–175
Peutinger, Konrad, 126, 129
Philippe le Bel, king of France, 100
Pius XI, Pope, 63, 64
Plato, 27, 116, 121; and communism, 18, 69
Poena conventionalis, 97
Pomponazzi, Pietro, 117
Poor relief, 75–81; pauperism, 183
Population, 184; the Fathers on, 33–34. *See also* Birth control; Celibacy
Poverty, voluntary, 16, 61
Precept. *See* Morality, dual standard
Predestination, 119, 131, 154, 176, 180, 185. *See also* Calvinism; Election
Premiums, religious, 156, 177

Presbyterians: English, 176–177; Scotch-Irish, 172, 175; Scottish, 189
Private property: Augustine on, 43–44; the Fathers on, 10, 16–20, 70n; Grabou on, 108; heretics on, 40–43, 108; labor theory of origin, 71–73; More on, 109–110; Scholastics on, 67–73
Probabilism, 142n
Productivity and fertility, 92
Profits. See Just price; Usury.
Prosperity, temporal, 179; the Fathers on, 30–34; Renaissance humanists on, 124–129; Scholastics on, 61–67, 111
Protestantism, 111–112, ascetic forms of, 154–156, 164, 171, 177; casuistics, 191–192; and Catholic charity, 75–77; cheapness of, 164–165, 185; criticism of, 183, 184; economic superiority of, 159–189; intellectual freedom, 175–178, 180–182, 186; in Ireland, 171–172, 174–175; laity in, 156; and poor relief, 75–80; Renaissance humanism and, 129, 130; and rise of capitalism, 151–189
Public works, 63, 64n
Puritan ethic, 152, 154. See also Protestantism, ascetic forms of
Pusillanimity, 64–65

Quakers, 154, 175n

Raleigh, Sir Walter, 162
Rastell, John, 70
Reason: appeal to, see Natural law; autonomy of, 116–121
Reformed tradition, 154, 180. See also Calvinism; Presbyterianism
Refugees. See Emigration
Remigius of Florence, 53n
Renaissance humanism, 181, 184; French Catholicism and, 129–130; in Italy, 123–130; Protestant Reformation and, 129, 130
Rentes, 97
Revelation. See Scripture
Riches: Aquinas on, 62–65; Augustine on, 42; defense of, 19, 61, 63; inherited, 22, 62; warning against, 16, 61, 62. See also Avarice; Money
Richey, Francis A., 63–64
Rigorism. See Jansenism; Morality, subjective and objective
Robinson, Robert, 164–165
Roman law, 83n, 86–88, 92, 116–118
Royal Society, 186

Salutari, Coluccio, of Florence, 125
Salvian, 33; on inherited wealth, 22–23
Sanderson, Robert, 156
Saxony, Electorate of, 103–104
Scales of value, doctrine of, 53–61, 83–84
Schell, Herman, 181–182
Schumpeter, Joseph, 88
Science, influence of religion on, 186–187
Scotists, 67n, 119
Scotland: Calvinism in, 187–189; excluded from Weber's thesis, 155, 157, 170n
Scovill, Warren, 169
Scripture and revelation, appeal to: by the Fathers, 14, 19n, 20–21, 23, 24, 33–37, 42, 43; by Jansenists, 132, 143–146; by Scholastics, 48, 64, 74n, 82, 86, 101, 111, 116, 117
Sea, commercial value of, 36–37
Secularism, 112
Secularization: concept of, 114–123; Jansenist influence on 139–140, 149
Seignorage, 100, 101
Self-denial, limitation of, 179
Self-interest (amour propre), 132, 135–136, 138–140. See also Avarice
Seneca, 50, 93–94, 130
Sin: and private property, 67, 69; venial, 132n. See also Original sin
Slavery: Catholicism and, 184; early Church and, 26–27; the Fathers and, 19, 27–29
Smith, Adam, 102n, 139
Social status, betterment of, 62, 64–66, 148. See also Standard of living
Social stratification, 138
"Socialism" of the Fathers, 16–17
Soto, Dominic, 91, 97
Sousberghe, L. de, 73
Spanish Catholicism, 113n
Spener, Philipp Jakob, 155
Standard of living, maintenance or improvement of, 24, 25, 62, 148–149. See also Social status
Stoicism, 115n, 116
Straw, Jack, 107
Superfluity and almsgiving, 148, 149
Switzerland, 165n, 182, 183. See also Geneva

Taparelli d'Azeglio, Luigi, 72
Taxation, 104–106
Taylor, Jeremy, 59, 156
Templars, 108

Temple, Sir William, 162
Temporal happiness. *See* Prosperity
Térillus, 142
Tertullian, 23, 30–32, 34
Theodoretus: on economic inequality, 18–20; on trade, 37
Theodosian Code, 43
Theophrastus, on scales of values, 58
Thomas Aquinas, St., 7, 48–50, 144; on almsgiving, 73–75; on the common good, 50–53; on the good, 11–12; on the just price, 82–84, 93; on property, 67–68; on pusillanimity, 64; on reason and faith, 120; on scales of value, 53–54, 56–58, 83–84; on taxation, 104–105; on use of riches, 62–63, 65; on usury, 88–96, 145
Thorndike, Herbert, 160
Tierney, Brian, 80
Time, sale of, 93–94
Titles to interest, 94–98
Tokos, Plato's use of, 90n
Toleration, religious, and economics, 160, 171; in Holland, 162
Trade. *See* Commerce
Tyler, Wat, 107

Ulster, 171–172
United Provinces. *See* Holland
Urban growth, 160, 178
Usurpare, 70n

Usury, 7, 32, 81, 85–99, 128, 143–147, 192
Utopias, Catholic, 109–110. *See also* More, Sir Thomas

Vasquez, Gabriel, 66, 148–149
Vaughan, Robert, 178–180
Verpaalen, A. P., 52
Villeneuve-Bargemont, Alban de, 184–185
Virtue: imperfect, 133; true, 132, 140
Vives, Juan-Luis, 79

Waldensians, 108
Wealth. *See* Riches
Weber, Max: on Protestantism and capitalism, 2, 3, 7–8, 77, 151–159, 161, 167–168, 170–171, 174–177, 180, 181, 185, 187, 188; use of ideal types, 158
Weber, Wilhelm, 73, 150
Weiss, C., 169
Welsers, 126, 129
Wesleyan Methodists, 154
Wordly goods. *See* Prosperity; Riches
Worsley, Israel, 176–177
Wycliffe, John, 107

Ypres, 78

Zwinglians, 154